er
s

Baedeker's

GREEK ISLANDS

Imprint

Cover picture: Santoríni

122 colour photographs
9 special plans, 6 town plans, 7 ground-plans, 12 drawings
8 special maps, 3 general maps, 1 fold-out map

Text contributions:
Monika I. Baumgarten (introductory chapters, part; description of islands from A to Z)
Peter M. Nahm (Practical Information)

Consultant: Axel Kramer

Editorial work:
Baedeker Stuttgart
England Language Edition: Alec Court

Design and layout: Creativ GmbH, Ulrich Kolb, Stuttgart

General direction: Dr Peter Baumgarten, Baedeker Stuttgart

Cartography:
Gert Oberländer, Munich; Mairs Geographischer Verlag GmbH & Co.,
Ostfildern-Kemnat (fold-out map)

English translation: James Hogarth

Source of illustrations:
Amberg (5), Assimakopouli (4), Baedeker-Archiv (1), Baier (13), Baumgarten (1), Bavaria
(1), Delta (3), dpa (1), Gärtner (4), Greek National Tourist Organisation (5), Günther (11),
Hannibal (7), Historia-Photo (6), Kramer (40), Iraklion Museum (2), Olympic (12), Rogge
(4), Schmidt-Diemitz (2)

To make it easier to locate the various islands and the three mainland towns listed in the
"A to Z" section of the Guide, their coordinates on the fold-out plan of the Greek islands
are shown in red at the head of each entry.

Following the tradition established by Karl Baedeker in 1844, sights of particular interest and
hotels of particular quality are distinguished by either one or two asterisks.

Only a selection of hotels can be given: no reflection is implied, therefore, on establishments
not included.

The symbol ⓘ on a town plan indicates the local tourist office from which further information
can be obtained. The post-horn symbol indicates a post office.

In a time of rapid change it is difficult to ensure that all the information given is entirely
accurate and up to date, and the possibility of error can never be completely eliminated.
Although the publishers can accept no responsibility for inaccuracies and omissions, they are
always grateful for corrections and suggestions for improvement.

Contents

Preface

This pocket guide to the Greek islands is one of the new generation of Baedeker guides.

Baedeker pocket guides, illustrated throughout in colour, are designed to meet the needs of the modern traveller. They are quick and easy to consult, with the principal places of interest described in alphabetical order, and the information is presented in a format that is both attractive and easy to follow.

The present guide is concerned with the whole of the Greek island world, in both the Aegean and the Ionian Sea, and also includes the Greek capital, Athens, and the two important mainland ports of Piraeus and Salonica, all points of access to the islands. The guide is in three parts. The first part gives a general account of the Greek islands, their climate, flora and fauna, population and religion, economy, notable personalities, history, art and architecture. A glossary of architectural and archaeological terms will be found on pages 35–40. A brief consideration of the "Odyssey", the story of an earlier island traveller, prepares the way for the second part, in which the individual islands and towns with their principal sights are described. The third part contains a variety of practical information. Both the sights and the practical information are listed in alphabetical order.

The Baedeker pocket guides are noted for their concentration on essentials and their convenience of use. They contain numerous specially drawn plans and coloured illustrations; and at the end of the book is a fold-out map making it easy to locate the various islands and towns described in the "A to Z" section of the guide with the help of the coordinates given at the head of each entry.

Facts and Figures

General

The intricate pattern of the coastline of Greece is matched to the east in the Aegean Sea and to the west in the Ionian Sea by a profusion of islands which in ancient times encouraged the development of seafaring and from an early period made the Greeks economic and cultural mediators between the three continents of the Ancient World.

The densest concentration of islands is in the Aegean, between the Greek mainland and the coasts of Turkey. Euboea, the largest of the islands in Central Greece, was, like the Northern Sporades extending to the north-east, a continuation of the Othrys mountain range, and was already seen in ancient times as a detached fragment of Boeotia. The south-eastern continuation of Euboea and Attica is the scattered group of the Cyclades, centred on Delos and occupying the southern Aegean in successive strings of islands. Kýthira, off the south-eastern tip of the Peloponnese, points the way towards Crete, the largest of the Greek islands (excluding the independent island of Cyprus), which closes off the Aegean on the south; a long narrow island extending from east to west, it is a southerly counterpart to the mountains of Anatolia. Off the south-west coast of Asia Minor, between Rhodes and Sámos, is the string of the Southern Sporades, most of them belonging to the Dodecanese ("Twelve Islands"). Widely scattered in the north-eastern Aegean are the large islands of Chíos, Lésbos, Lemnos, Samothrace and Thásos. Off the west coast of Greece are the Ionian Islands, the central group of which is closely linked, ethnically and historically, with the nearby mainland of Central Greece.

Greece and its islands extend between latitude 41° 45' N (at the meeting of the Greek, Bulgarian and Turkish frontiers north-west of Edirne; the most northerly island is Thásos) and 34° 48' N (the islet of Gávdos, south of Crete, which is the most southerly point in Europe) and between longitude 19° 22' E (the island of Othoni, north-west of Corfu) and 29° 38' E (the islet of Strongylí, south-east of Kastellórizo).

Altogether there are more than 2000 Greek islands, with a total area of 25,213 sq. km (9735 sq. miles; a fifth of the area of Greece) and a coastline of 11,000 km (6800 miles), out of a total of 15,000 km (9300 miles). 151 of the islands, with a combined area of 24,866 sq. km (9600 sq. miles), are inhabited. The largest are Crete – 8331 sq. km (3217 sq. miles) Euboea – 3654 sq. km (1411 sq. miles); Lésbos – 1630 sq. km (629 sq. miles); and Rhodes – 1398 sq. km (540 sq. miles). Administratively the islands belong to the following nomoi (administrative districts; singular nomos; chief towns in parenthesis): in the Ionian Sea Corfu (Corfu town), Lefkás (Lefkás), Kefallinía (Argostóli) and Zákynthos (Zákynthos); in the Aegean Euboea (Khalkís; including the island of Skýros), the Cyclades (Ermoúpolis, on Sýros), Chaniá (Chaniá),

◀ *Vai Bay, on the east coast of Crete*

Greece
(Hellenic Republic)

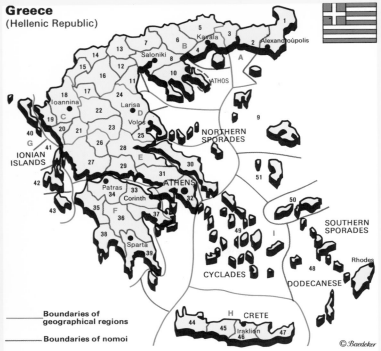

Boundaries of geographical regions

Boundaries of nomoi

© Baedeker

Regions	Nomoi (chief towns in parentheses)		
A Thrace	1 Evros (Alexandroúpolis)	18 Ioannina	35 Elis (Pýrgos)
	2 Rodopi (Komotini)	19 Thesprotia (Igoumenitsa)	36 Arcadia (Tripolis)
B Macedonia	3 Xanthi	20 Preveza	37 Argolid (Nauplia)
	4 Kavala	21 Arta	38 Messenia (Kalamata)
C Epirus	5 Drama	22 Trikala	39 Laconia (Sparta)
	6 Serrai	23 Karditsa	40 Corfu
D Thessaly	7 Kilkis	24 Larissa	41 Lefkás
	8 Salonica	25 Magnesia (Volos)	42 Kefallinía (Argostóli)
E Central Greece	9 Lésbos (Mytilíni)	26 Evritania (Karpenision)	43 Zakynthos
	10 Chalcidice (Poliyiros)	27 Aetolia/Acarnania (Agrinion)	44 Chaniá
F Peloponnese	11 Pieria (Katerini)	28 Phthiotis (Lamia)	45 Réthymnon
	12 Imathia (Veria)	29 Phocis (Amfissa)	46 Iráklion
G Ionian Islands	13 Pella (Edessa)	30 Euboea (Khalkis)	47 Lasíthi (Ayios Nikólaos))
	14 Florina	31 Boeotia (Levadia)	48 Dodecanese (Rhodes)
H Crete	15 Kastoria	32 Attica (Athens)	49 Cyclades (Ermoúpolis)
	16 Kozani	33 Corinth	50 Sámos (Vathý)
I Aegean Islands	17 Grevena	34 Achaea (Pátras)	51 Chíos

An ideal holiday: cruising from island to island

Iráklion (Iráklion), Réthymnon (Réthymnon), Lasíthi (Ayios Nikólaos; the last four on Crete), the Dodecanese (Rhodes town), Sámos (Vathý), Chíos (Chíos) and Lésbos (Mytilíni). Some islands belong to nomoi on the mainland – the Northern Sporades (except Skýros) to Magnesia (Volos), Samothrace to Evros (Alexandroúpolis), Thásos to Kavala (Kavala) and the islands in the Saronic Gulf, together with Kýthira and Antikýthira, to Piraeus (Pireás). No island is more than 40 km (25 miles) away from another island.

The highest point on the islands is Mount Ida (Ídi Óros; 2456 m (8058 ft)), in the Psiloritis range on Crete. The greatest depth of sea lies 115 km (71 miles) south-west of Cape Tainaron (the southern tip of the Peloponnese), in the Inoúsai Deep (4850 m/15,913 ft).

The salt content of the Aegean (lat. 41°–35° N) increases from north to south (33–39 per 1000), and is above the average for the Mediterranean (33 per 1000). The water temperature also increases from north to south, reaching 20–26 °C (68–79 °F) in summer and 12–15 °C (54–59 °F) in winter; on the sea bed it remains fairly constant at 13–14 °C (55–57 °F). There is little tidal movement; it is only in the Evripos, the channel between Euboea and the mainland, that the ebb and flow of the tides produce frequently changing currents.

In the Palaeozoic era the Aegean area was occupied by an ancient mountain range, mostly of crystalline and metamorphic rocks, the eroded remains of which survive in Thrace and Macedonia (the Rhodope Massif), the Cyclades (the Cycladic Massif) and the southern Peloponnese (the Pelagonian Massif); the peaks emerge from the sea in the form of islands.

Geology

11

Climate

In the Mesozoic era these ancient monuments were covered by the Tethys Sea, which left massive deposits of schists, sandstones and limestones. During the Pleistocene, after the lowering of the sea-level, they formed a land link between Greece and Asia Minor. Then in the Quaternary period three large depressions were formed in this area – the Northern Aegean Basin (up to 1950 m (6400 ft) deep), to the north of an imaginary line from the Magnesian Peninsula by way of Lemnos to the Gallipoli Peninsula (the Dardanelles, however, being a drowned river valley), the Central Aegean Basin (up to 4850 m (15,910 ft) deep) between Euboea, the Cyclades, Sámos and Chíos, and the Southern Aegean Basin (up to 4453 m (14,610 ft) deep), north of a line from Kýthira by way of Santoríni to Rhodes. These submarine depressions are separated by ridges about 500 m (1640 ft) deep, and are marked off from the south-eastern Mediterranean by a shelf some 800 m (2625 ft) deep. In the fault zones there was violent volcanic activity, decreasing in more recent times (Santoríni, Melos, Nísyros), with its accompaniment of earth tremors and thermal springs. The folding and faulting of easily eroded limestones has produced the karstic formations to be seen all over Greece and on the islands, particularly in the Ionian Sea (and even more markedly in the Adriatic).

Earthquakes

The Greek islands have suffered devastating earthquakes both in antiquity (*c.* 1400 B.C., destruction of Minoan culture) and in modern times (1856, Crete; 1926, Rhodes; 1953, Ionian Islands).

Climate

The Greek islands have a Mediterranean-type culture, with rainy winters and hot dry summers.

Temperatures increase from west to east, with annual means ranging from 17·4 °C (63·3 °F; Corfu town) to 19 °C (66·2 °F; Iráklion on Crete), while annual precipitation increases from east to west (Iráklion 539 mm (21 in), Corfu 1137 mm (45 in)). The precipitation is almost wholly in the form of rain, with snow only occasionally at heights above 1000 m (3300 ft). Very heavy showers are the rule; long periods of steady rain are exceedingly rare.

Region	Temperatures in °C (°F)							Mean annual precipitation in mm/in
	Air					Sea		
	Annual average	Jan.	July/Aug.	Annual min.	Annual max.	Jan.	July/Aug.	
Athens	17·8 (64·0)	9·3 (48·7)	27·5/27·5 (81·5/81·5)	−5·5 (22·1)	43·0 (109·4)	14·8 (58·6)	24·9/25·6 (76·8/78·1)	401/16
Salonica	16·4 (61·5)	5·0 (41·0)	26·6/26·3 (79·9/79·3)	−9·5 (14·9)	41·6 (106·9)	11·5 (52·7)	24·9/25·6 (76·1/76·6)	477/19
Corfu	17·4 (63·3)	10·0 (50·0)	26·7/26·6 (80·1/79·9)	−2·8 (27·0)	41·0 (105·8)	15·5 (59·9)	25·7/26·8 (78·3/80·2)	1137/45
Crete	19·0 (66·2)	12·3 (54·1)	25·9/25·6 (78·6/78·1)	+0·1 (32·2)	45·7 (114·3)	15·2 (59·4)	25·9/25·6 (78·6/78·1)	539/21

Average annual sunshine: 2500–3000 hours.

Tree on a wind-swept island   *Oleander in full bloom*

A typical feature of the climate in the islands is the meltémi, a sharp dry wind which blows from the north-west between May and September, rising to considerable violence in the early afternoon and falling again towards evening, which may create difficulties for shipping. In summer there are frequent thunder-showers.

Flora and Fauna

The flora of the islands is of typically Mediterranean character, with leathery leaved evergreens and succulents; the trees never exceed a very moderate height. In the fertile depressions and coastal regions, up to a height of about 800 m (2625 ft), mixed forests of oaks, planes, Aleppo pines, carob trees, etc., alternate with a longos (macchia) of holm-oaks, kermes oaks, arbutus, mastic bushes, laurel, broom, oleander and wild olives. In the wetter regions in the west the macchia is found higher up (800–2000 m (2625–6560 ft)), in the drier south-east at lesser heights, becoming increasingly sparse and merging into the type of dry macchia known as frygana, with semi-shrub-like plants, junipers, heaths and spurges, which provides meagre grazing for sheep and goats. Mixed deciduous forests are found up to about 1500 m (4900 ft), coniferous forests to about 1700 m (5600 ft); above this height, up to 2000 m (6560 ft), only the Apollo fir is found. Above the tree-line are scanty Alpine meadows – in so far as the karstic formations of the limestone hills permit the growth of any vegetation at all.

Since ancient times the natural cover of trees and macchia has

Flora

13

been largely destroyed by cultivation and animal grazing. At best it has given place to olive groves, plantations of figs and vineyards; at worst it has reverted to wasteland.

Additions to the native flora of Greece have been the agave and prickly pear from Central America and the date-palm from Africa, originally introduced as an ornamental tree but also found growing wild.

Fauna

As a result of the cutting-off of the islands from the mainland at an early stage in their geological history the fauna consists of a relatively limited range of species. Reptiles (lizards, snakes, tortoises) are fairly numerous, and countless species of birds pass over the Greek islands on their southward migration. The wild goat (*Capra aegagrus*), ancestor of the domestic goat, has survived on Crete. A popular sport among Greeks, and one sometimes offered to visitors, is the shooting of rabbits and birds (particularly quails). Sea-caves provide a refuge for monk seals, a species threatened with extinction.

The fishing grounds in the Aegean, offering a poor food-supply and constantly overfished, are relatively unproductive, and catches are barely sufficient to meet the needs of the island population. Apart from the various species found all over the Mediterranean, octopuses, shellfish, lobsters and spiny lobsters are caught off the coasts of the islands.

The sponge-fishing which was formerly practised all over the Aegean is now concentrated in the waters off the North African coast.

Population and Religion

Population

Out of the total Greek population, now approaching 10,000,000 some 1,300,000 live on the islands With an average population density of 95 people to the square kilometre (246 to the square mile) the Ionian Islands are much above the Greek average of 75 to the square kilometre (194 to the square mile), and with an average of 35 to the square kilometre (91 to the square mile) the Aegean Islands are much below it. Most of the islands show a steady decline in population, and several (e.g. Kastellórizo) are faced with complete depopulation. The poor quality of the soil and the fragmentation of holdings by inheritance have so reduced the standard of living that many young people prefer to seek a better livelihood in mainland Greece, the industrialised countries of western Europe or the United States. The consequence is a steady ageing of the island population and the neglect or abandonment of farms which the older people are no longer able to run. The population, basically rural, is almost entirely of Greek descent. Since the great population exchange of 1922–23 there are only small Turkish minorities on Rhodes and Kos and in Thrace. A few groups of Albanians, particularly on Hýdra and Spétsai, who proved sturdy Greek patriots during the War of Greek Independence, are now largely assimilated to the Greek population, and only the older members of the community still speak or understand Albanian.

An imprint was left on the Dodecanese by the long period of Turkish and later Italian rule, and on the Ionian Islands by the British Protectorate during the 19th c., which gave these islands an enduring link with Western culture.

In spite of regional differences resulting from the circumstances of history and extreme geographical fragmentation, the Greeks of the islands have preserved a profound national awareness. One great unifying force, particularly in times of trouble, has been the Greek Orthodox Church, which has maintained its full authority in both private and public life. In 1833 the Greek Church became autonomous and from 1850 recognised by the Oecumenical Patriarchate in Constantinople (Istanbul) as being autocephalous (i.e. governed by its own synod and having power to appoint its own Patriarch. Since 1865 it has been the established State Church with the Archbishop of Athens as its supreme head. Only the Dodecanese, not united with Greece until 1912–13, and the Monastic Republic of Athos are still subject to the jurisdiction of the Patriarchate of Constantinople, while Crete occupies a special position as a semi-autonomous province of the Church.

Some 95 per cent of the island population profess the Greek Orthodox faith; the rest are Muslims, Jews, Roman Catholics (a relic of the Venetian occupation of the Cyclades) and Protestants.

Religion

Economy

The islands are among the least developed parts of Greece. There is practically no industry, and commerce and craft production depend on agriculture, which is the islands' principal source of revenue. With 520,000 hectares (1,284,000 acres) of cultivable land the islands account for 13·2 per cent of the national total. While the smaller islands can do little more than supply their own needs, the larger ones export agricultural produce to mainland Greece and to other countries.

The main crops since ancient times have been olives (both for oil and for eating), wine and honey or beeswax, and in recent times also melons and early vegetables, cucumbers (Crete), tomatoes (Cyclades; mainly for the making of tomato purée), sultanas, almonds and groundnuts (Crete), table grapes and currants (Ionian Islands), cotton, tobacco, mastic (Chíos), and peaches, apricots, apples and pears (canning-factory on Crete).

Sheep and goats are still, as in the past, the main suppliers of milk and meat. The poor road system on most of the islands means that the mule is still indispensable as a draught animal and beast of burden.

Agriculture

The fisheries are unproductive as a result of inadequate regeneration of the food-supply and continual overfishing, and it is necessary to import fish to supply domestic needs. Sponge-diving, once one of the major sources of income in the eastern Aegean, is declining as a result of competition from synthetic sponges, and is now concentrated in the waters off the North African coast. The Greek sponge-fishing fleet is traditionally based in the Dodecanese, where there are small boatyards which build and repair the local caiques.

Fisheries

The working of minerals on the islands (by small and medium-sized undertakings with not more than 400 workers) is confined to small deposits of iron, manganese, nickel, chromium, zinc, lead and molybdenum (Euboea and Melos).

Minerals

Economy

World-famous marble has been worked since ancient times on Tínos, Chíos, Náxos and Páros. Pozzolana, a volcanic earth found on Santoríni and Melos, was already valued in ancient times as a water-resistant mortar used in the construction of harbour installations.

Craft production

Craft production is based on local supplies of clay (pottery, ceramics) and the rearing of sheep and goats (woollen carpets, textiles, leather goods).

Tourism

The tourist trade is a rapidly developing branch of the economy. Favoured by an excellent climate, good beaches, beautiful scenery and fascinating remains of the past, it holds great promise for the future, though in many places there is room for improvement in the standard of hotels, restaurants and transport facilities.

Notable Personalities

The Greek poet Alkaios (Alcaeus), a contemporary of the poetess Sappho and, like her, a native of Mytilene on Lésbos, ranks after Sappho as the greatest lyric poet of his day. A scion of an old aristocratic family, he was passionately involved in the struggle against the tyrants (sole rulers) of Lésbos, Myrsilos and Pittakos. In his poems, of which only fragments survive, he is concerned mainly with this political struggle, but also sings of love and of wine.
Alkaios has given his name to the alcaic stanza, used by Horace and some Italian Renaissance poets and occasionally experimented with by English poets.

Alkaios
(c. 620 B.C.)

The lyric poet Anakreon was born in the Ionian city of Teos (near present-day Izmir). About 545 B.C. he fled to Abdera to escape the advancing Persians; later he moved to the Court of Polykrates on the island of Sámos, and after Polykrates' murder in 522 B.C. went on to Athens.
Anakreon's poems, composed for a luxurious aristocratic society, celebrate pleasure, gaiety, wine and love. Only a few of his poems have survived complete, in addition to numerous fragments.

Anakreon
(c. 580–c. 495 B.C.)

The lyric poet Archilochos is one of the earliest figures in the Ancient World about whose life we have any reliable information. Born on the island of Páros, the son of a local aristocrat and a slave girl, he was excluded from his inheritance, lived an unsettled life as a soldier and an itinerant minstrel and was killed in a battle with the Naxians. His poetry, which has survived only in fragments, centres on his unhappy love for Neoboule, daughter of Lykambes, whom he was not permitted to marry because of his birth. He wrote poems of great delicacy and tenderness, but also verses of extreme eroticism and vigorous satire.

Archilochos
(c. 700–c. 645 B.C.)

George Gordon Noel Byron, born in London in 1788, unexpectedly inherited the family title and estates on the death of a great-uncle in 1798. He wrote his first poems while still at school. After taking his seat in the House of Lords he travelled extensively in Europe and Asia Minor. The publication of the first two cantos of "Childe Harold's Pilgrimage" brought him sudden fame. After a brief and unhappy marriage, outlawed by society, he left England for ever. He spent some weeks with Shelley by the Lake of Geneva, but the friendship did not last, and he went on to Italy, where he led an unsettled life but continued to write his poems. In 1824 he was attracted to Greece to take part in the Greek struggle for independence, and armed a force of some 500 men at his own expense for an attack on Lepanto. He died of malaria at Mesolongi in April 1824.

Lord Byron
(1788–1824)

The Greek physician Diokles was born in Kárystos on the island of Euboea. An adherent of the Sicilian school of medicine, he lived in Athens and was second only to Hippokrates in fame. He wrote works – preserved only in fragments – on human anatomy and women's diseases, the symptoms of disease and herbal medicine.

Diokles
(4th c. B.C.)

Notable Personalities

Archilochos

Ugo Foscolo

El Greco

Ugo Foscolo
(1778–1827)

The Italian poet and literary historian Ugo (Niccoló) Foscolo was born on Zante (Zákynthos), the son of a Venetian father and a Greek mother. A philhellene, an Italian patriot and a cosmopolitan, he led an unsettled life. His work was wholly devoted to the Risorgimento, the political rebirth of Italy, showing a remarkable fusion of political zeal and Romantic feeling. He was unsparing in his attacks on Napoleon, who had at first been hailed in Italy as a liberator, and on the Austrians, and in consequence was compelled in 1808 to give up his Chair as Professor of Eloquence at Pavia and in 1815 to leave Italy. He died in exile at Turnham Green, near London, leaving 12 volumes of odes, sonnets, hymns, tragedies and novels.

El Greco
(c. 1541–1614)

El Greco (Spanish, "The Greek") was born Domenikos Theotokópoulos at Fodele, near Iráklion (Crete). As a boy he learned the craft of icon-painting; then as a young man he went to Venice, where he was trained in Titian's studio, and later to Rome. From 1577 he lived and worked in Toledo, where he sought commissions from King Philip II and from the Church. Although mainly devoting himself to religious themes, he also painted some striking portraits and landscapes. He represents the high point of Mannerism. Characteristic features of his work are the elongated and contorted figures, the unnaturally pale colouring and the unreal light effects, which create an impression of spiritualisation and the transcendental. It has been suggested that El Greco's distorted proportions were the result of an eye defect, but against this explanation is the fact that the later pictures of Tintoretto show the same characteristic. El Greco died in Toledo in April 1614.

Epicurus
(341–271 B.C.)

The philosopher Epicurus (Epikouros) was born on the island of Samos in 341 B.C. and taught in Mytilene (Lésbos) and Lampsakos (on the east side of the Dardanelles) before going to Athens, where he established his own school in a garden (the "Garden of Epicurus") in 306 B.C. His doctrine, which has come down to us in three letters and numerous fragments, is concerned with man's life in this world, defining philosophy as the attempt to achieve happiness by discussion and reasoning. He divided it into three parts – the theory of knowledge (the basis of which is sense-perception), physics (based on Democritus' doctrine on the movement of atoms) and ethics (with virtue and a peaceful state of mind as the basic principles). Epicurus died in Athens in 271 B.C.

Epicureanism, as further developed by Zeno and Demetrios, became a popular philosophy in late antiquity, but increasingly degenerated into a superficial hedonism. In Roman times the term "epicurean" had already acquired the connotation of an unscrupulous quest for pleasure.

The mathematician Hippokrates of Chíos taught in Athens in the second half of the 5th c. B.C. He created the first comprehensive system of geometry and discovered the "lunulae Hippocratis" (the "little moons" of Hippokrates) on a right-angled triangle, showing that the sum of the crescent-shaped areas bounded by the semicircles on the three sides of the triangle equals the area of the triangle.

Hippokrates of Chíos
(c. 450 B.C.)

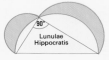

Hippokrates, the most celebrated physician of ancient times, was born on Kos, the son of a respected doctor, and died, after a long and eventful life, at Larissa in Thessaly. He is honoured as the founder of scientific medicine, which seeks to establish the principles of health and disease by critical observation and analytical reasoning. To Hippokrates disease was an imbalance of the vital forces resulting from external influences. He attached great importance to the natural healing processes, regarding these processes and prophylactic measures as preferable to therapeutic treatment. His numerous writings covered a wide range of basic medical problems. The Hippocratic oath which is still binding on all medical practitioners was probably not formulated by Hippokrates himself.

Hippokrates of Kos
(c. 460–c. 370 B.C.)

The town of Smyrna (now Izmir) in Asia Minor claimed, probably with justice, to be the birthplace of Homer (Homeros), the legendary author of the "Iliad" and the "Odyssey", the earliest epic poet of the Western World. According to tradition he was a blind rhapsode (reciter of epic poems) who travelled round the courts of Ionian princes. The guilds of rhapsodes which developed about 700 B.C. in Ionian territory, particularly on the island of Chíos, honoured Homer as their founder and teacher and called themselves Homerids. Nevertheless there was always controversy about the existence of Homer as a historical figure; in particular it was doubted whether any one man was capable of composing two such mighty works. In 1795 the German scholar Friedrich August Wolf raised what became known as the "Homeric question", suggesting that the "Iliad" and the "Odyssey" were collections of separate songs by different poets. On this theory the name of Homer became a collective designation for Early Greek epic poetry.

Homer
(c. 8th c. B.C.)

The prevailing view now, however, is that there was a historical Homer, who lived and composed his poems on the west coast of Asia Minor, and that he had many links with the island of Chíos. In writing his great works he probably based himself on earlier and shorter epic poems. The "Iliad" is thought to have preceded the "Odyssey"; but both works underwent much alteration and expansion after Homer's time.

Homer is also credited with the authorship of a number of hymns and epigrams and two comic epics, "Margites" and the "Batrachomyomachia" ("War of the Frogs and Mice").

Notable Personalities

**Ioannes Antonios,
Count Kapodistrias
(1776–1831)**

The statesman Ioannis Antonios, Count Kapodistrias, born on Corfu, entered the diplomatic service of Tsarist Russia at the beginning of the 19th c. and played a prominent part at the Congress of Vienna (1815). Having incurred Tsar Alexander I's displeasure by supporting the Greek struggle for independence, he retired from the Russian service and in 1822 settled in Switzerland, where he continued to promote the Greek cause. In April 1827 he was elected President of the newly established independent State of Greece, an office he held until his murder at Nauplia in October 1831 by Konstantinos and Yeoryios Mavromikhalis, who accused him of acting unconstitutionally and autocratically.

**Nikos Kazantzakis
(1883–1957)**

The writer Nikos Kazantzakis was born in Iráklion (Crete) in February 1883, and from his earliest youth was interested in the intellectual movements of the day. After taking a law degree in Athens in 1906 he went to Paris, where he studied philosophy (one of his teachers being Henri Bergson) and political science. Returning to Greece, he became a senior civil servant and in 1945–46 a Minister.

He travelled widely in Britain, Spain, Russia, Japan and China, recording his impressions in a number of notable travel books. He also wrote lyric and epic poetry, short stories, novels and tragedies on ancient Greek, Early Christian and Byzantine themes as well as works of philosophy. His writing is notable for its vigorous narrative power, fresh language, lyrical abundance and philosophical profundity. In his novel "Zorba the Greek" (1946), which achieved world-wide fame as a film, he revealed in two of the principal characters the two souls of his Cretan personality. He was also active as a translator (Homer, Dante, Goethe, Shakespeare, Darwin, Nietzsche, Rimbaud, Lorca, etc.).

After the Second World War Kazantzakis lived mainly in the south of France. He died in Freiburg (south-west Germany) and is buried in his native Iráklion.

**Menedemos
(3rd c. B.C.)**

The philosopher Menedemos, a disciple of Phaidon of Elis, followed the doctrines of the Eleatic school in founding in his native city of Erétria on the island of Euboea the Erétrian school of philosophy, which continued in existence until 260 B.C. and was influenced by the teachings of Sokrates. Menedemos also enjoyed a great reputation as a statesman in Erétria. He died in exile in Macedonia at some time after 278 B.C.

**Ioannis Metaxas
(1871–1941)**

The Greek general and statesman Ioannis Metaxas was born on the island of Ithaca. In 1915 he became Chief of Staff of the Greek forces but, having opposed the then Prime Minister, Venizelos, was interned by the French from 1917 to 1920. In 1923 he led an unsuccessful military putsch, and later played a major part in bringing about the return of King George II to the Greek throne (1935). After the *coup d'état* of August 1936 he became Prime Minister and Foreign Minister, showing himself authoritarian and strongly anti-Communist. After his rejection of the Italian ultimatum of 28 October 1940 Greek forces succeeded in beating off the Italian attack from Albania. Metaxas died in Athens in January 1941.

The Metaxas Line, a strongly fortified defensive line in eastern Macedonia directed against Bulgaria, was overrun by German forces in April 1941.

Hippokrates of Kos

Pythagoras

E. K. Venizélos

Little authenic information has come down to us about the Greek philosopher Pythagoras. He himself left no writings, and his pupils were sworn to secrecy and a life of monastic asceticism. He was born on Samos about 570 B.C., left the island about 530, apparently to escape from the arbitrary rule of Polykrates, and founded at Kroton in southern Italy a community of Pythagoreans based on ethical, political, philosophical and religious principles. Even during his lifetime he was revered by his disciples as a man of perfect wisdom. After repeated attack and persecution, however, he left Kroton and died at Metapontion in southern Italy, probably between 500 and 480 B.C.

The Pythagoreans saw number as the basis of all things, a principle of universal harmony and thus applicable also to music. The doctrine of the transmigration of souls is believed to have been developed by Pythagoras himself. The geometrical theorem which bears his name, however – the proposition that the square on the hypotenuse of a right-angled triangle is equal to the sum of the squares on the other two sides – seems likely to have been known before his time.

Pythagoras
(c. 570–c. 500/480 B.C.)

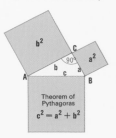

Theorem of Pythagoras
$$c^2 = a^2 + b^2$$

The Greek poetess Sappho, born on the island of Lésbos about 600 B.C., was the greatest lyric poet of classical antiquity. Plato called her the tenth Muse, and Horace named the sapphic stanza after her. She was the head of a community in Mytilene, the capital of Lésbos, in which she instructed young girls until their marriage in the art of poetry and in ritual dances in honour of Aphrodite, goddess of love. There was no question, however, of what later became known as Lesbian love. After the expulsion of aristocrats from Lésbos Sappho spent some time in Sicily. She is said to have thrown herself to her death from the Leucadian Rock when her love for the handsome Phaon was unrequited.

Sappho's rich output of lyric poetry is unfortunately known to us only in fragments. It consists mainly of hymns to the gods and marriage and love-songs in simple, vivid language.

Sappho
(7th–6th c. B.C.)

The lyric poets of the Archaic period Simonides (b. c. 556 B.C.) and his nephew Bakchylides (b. c. 505 B.C.) were born in Ioulis on the island of Keos (Kéa). Simonides is credited with the

Simonides and Bakchylides
(6th–5th c. B.C.)

21

Notable Personalities

invention of a mnemonic (memory-aiding) technique. A sophisticated Ionian, he frequented the princely courts of the Greek World, taking part in poetic contests and writing witty and sensitive epigrams and eulogies for the great ones of his time. His work is preserved only in fragments, and many of the epigrams attributed to him were certainly not his work. He died in 468 B.C. at Akragas (now Agrigento) in Sicily.

Like Simonides, Bakchylides gained early fame in poetic contests, in which he is said to have competed against Pindar. He is believed to have died about 450 B.C.

Eleftherios Venizélos
(1864–1936)

The lawyer and statesman Eleftherios Kyriakos Venizélos was born at Mournies (Crete) in 1864. He founded the Greek Liberal Party and became Prime Minister for the first time in 1912, carrying through far-reaching reforms and laying the foundations of the modern Greek State. In foreign policy he sought the unification of all Greeks and the extension of Greek territory by military means. The two Balkan wars (1912–13) did in fact bring considerable territorial gains and the incorporation of Crete in Greece, but later attempts to expand were frustrated by Turkish resistance under Mustafa Kemal Paşa (Atatürk). After an unsuccessful *coup d'état* against the Tsaldaris government Venizélos went into exile in Paris, where he died in March 1936.

History

On the Greek mainland the Sesklo culture is followed by the Dimini culture; on the Aegean islands the Cycladic culture develops, and on Crete the Minoan culture, which reaches its peak about 2000 B.C. and is economically and culturally dominant until its collapse in the 15th c. B.C.

3rd millennium B.C.

Early Minoan culture (Pre-Palatial periods I, II and III).

2600–2000

Middle Minoan, also with three periods:
I (c. 1900): first palaces at Knossós and Phaistós
II (c. 1800): the heyday of Minoan culture (Kamáres ware)
III (c. 1700): rebuilding, after earlier destruction, of the (second) palaces of Knossós (the Labyrinth) and Phaistós; building of the Ayía Triáda Palace.

2000–1600

Late Minoan: collapse of the Minoan Empire about 1400, perhaps as the result of an earthquake; further rebuilding of the (third) palace of Knossós by Mycenaean Greeks.

1600–1400

Sub-Minoan: Dorian migration; the Cyclades and Euboea remain Ionian.

1400–1000

Aeolians and Ionians found colonies on the west coast of Asia Minor and the islands of the eastern Aegean.

c. 1000

Geometric style in pottery.

1000–700

Homer and the Homerids on Chíos.

8th c.

First Messenian War: the Achaeans are driven out of Achaea and settle on the Ionian Islands.

740–720

End of the Dorian migration. Aeolians now begin to settle in the eastern Aegean (Lésbos) and on Cyprus, Ionians in the Northern Sporades, Euboea, the Cyclades (round a central cult site on Delos), Chíos, Sámos and Ikaría, and Dorians on Crete, Melos, Thera (Santoríni), Anaphe, the Dodecanese, Rhodes and the Ionian Islands.

c. 700

The poetess Sappho and the poet Alkaios on Lésbos; flowering of sculpture and architecture on Náxos, Delos and Sámos; invention of hollow casting of bronze.

c. 600

The philosopher Pythagoras born on Sámos (d. 497/496 at Metapontion in southern Italy).

c. 570

Náxos flourishes under the tyrant Lygdamis, Sámos under Polykrates.

from 550

Northern coast of the Aegean occupied by the Persians.

from 512

First Persian campaign against Greece. Aegina submits to Mardonios, and is then laid waste by Sparta and Athens under Miltiades. Persian fleet wrecked on Athos.

492

History

490	Second Persian campaign; Battle of Marathón.
480	Third Persian campaign, ending in the defeat of the Persian fleet in the Battle of Salamis. This great victory arouses the Greeks' consciousness of their common identity, in spite of their political fragmentation into a large number of small city states (poleis, singular polis).
477	Athens takes the lead in forming the Confederacy of Delos, the first Attic maritime league.
c. 460	Birth of the great Greek physician Hippokrates on Kos (d. Larissa 375).
after 450	Legal code of Górtys (Crete).
433	The victory won by Korkyra (Corfu), with Athenian help, over Corinth in the Sybota islands is the prelude to the Peloponnesian War (431–404).
428–427	The island of Lésbos rebels against Athens.
427	Birth of the philosopher Plato in Athens (d. in Athens 347).
425	Kythera occupied by the Athenians.
416	Melos captured by the Athenians.
399	Sokrates (b. 470) is condemned to death.
359	Philip II becomes King of Macedon.
343	Philip II summons the philosopher Aristotle (b. Stageira in Macedonia 384, d. Chalcis on Euboea 322) to be tutor to his son Alexander (b. 356).
336	Alexander the Great succeeds his murdered father and thereafter founds the Macedonia world empire.
334	Chíos and Lésbos temporarily in Persian hands.
323	After Alexander's death the struggles between the Diadochoi (Successors) begin.
from 220	Rome steadily increasing in strength.
146	The Romans destroy Corinth.
48 B.C.	Julius Cæsar defeats Pompey at Pharsalos.
31 B.C.	Octavian (Augustus) defeats Antony at Aktion (Actium) in Epirus.
A.D. 49–54	The Apostle Paul preaches in Salonica, Athens and Corinth.
c. A.D. 170	Pausanias writes his famous description of Greece.
260–268	Gothic incursions into Greece.

Under Constantine the Great Constantinople becomes capital of the Roman Empire; victory of Christianity.	323–337
Division of the Roman Empire.	395
Vandal incursions into Greece.	467–477
The Emperor Basil II defeats the Bulgars. First appearance of Albanians in Greece.	1019
The Normans capture Salonica.	1185
Giovanni Orsini, an Italian nobleman, gains possession of the Ionian islands of Kefallinía, Ithaca and Zákynthos.	1194
The Venetians occupy Crete, Kýthira and the southern tip of the Peloponnese.	beginning of 13th c.
A Venetian, Marco Sanudo, conquers Náxos and founds the Duchy of Náxos or the Archipelago (Dodecanese).	1207
The Venetians occupy Nauplia and extend their rule over the whole of Greece and the islands.	1389
The Turks take Constantinople (Istanbul): end of the Eastern Roman Empire.	1453 (29 May)
The Turks occupy Athens: beginning of almost 400 years of Turkish rule in Greece.	1456
The Venetian Duchy of Náxos falls to the Turks.	1579
As a Turkish province the Dodecanese is granted extensive autonomy in domestic affairs.	16th c.
Unsuccessful Greek rising, supported by Russian forces under Orlov. Many Albanians flee to the islands.	1770
British Protectorate over the Ionian Islands.	1815
War of liberation against the Turks, which ends in victory after the naval Battle of Navarino (1827) and the landing of a French expeditionary corps.	1821–28
First London Protocol: Greece a hereditary monarchy, but required to pay tribute to Turkey.	1829
Second London Protocol: Greece a sovereign kingdom.	1830
Prince Otto of Bavaria is proclaimed King of the Hellenes as Otto I.	1832
First Greek Constitution of modern times.	1843
Catastrophic earthquake on Crete.	1856
After a number of risings King Otto I leaves the country.	1862
A Danish prince, William of Sonderburg-Glücksburg, becomes King as George I.	1863

Territorial Development of modern Greece

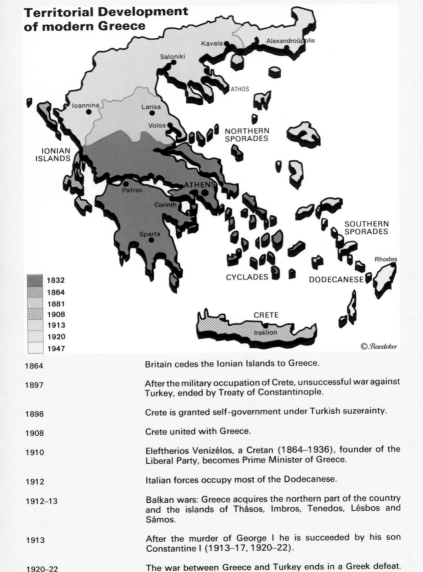

1832	
1864	
1881	
1908	
1913	
1920	
1947	

© Baedeker

1864	Britain cedes the Ionian Islands to Greece.
1897	After the military occupation of Crete, unsuccessful war against Turkey, ended by Treaty of Constantinople.
1898	Crete is granted self-government under Turkish suzerainty.
1908	Crete united with Greece.
1910	Eleftherios Venizélos, a Cretan (1864–1936), founder of the Liberal Party, becomes Prime Minister of Greece.
1912	Italian forces occupy most of the Dodecanese.
1912–13	Balkan wars: Greece acquires the northern part of the country and the islands of Thásos, Imbros, Tenedos, Lésbos and Sámos.
1913	After the murder of George I he is succeeded by his son Constantine I (1913–17, 1920–22).
1920–22	The war between Greece and Turkey ends in a Greek defeat. The Greeks lose the territories in Asia Minor which had been

occupied by Greek settlers since ancient times, together with the islands of Imbros and Tenedos. Over 1,500,000 refugees flee to Greece.

Turkey cedes the Dodecanese to Italy.	1923
Declaration of Republic.	1924
The east coast of Rhodes is devastated by a severe earthquake.	1926
Venizélos again in power.	1928–32
Restoration of the monarchy; King George II (1922–23, 1935–46).	1935
Greek forces repel an Italian attack through Albania.	1940
German and Italian occupation; the King goes into exile in London.	1941–44
Civil war between Government forces and Communists.	1945–49
King George II returns to Athens, but dies in 1947.	1946
George's brother Paul I becomes King. The Dodecanese returns to Greece.	1947
Devastating earthquake in the Ionian Islands.	1953
Greece become an Associate Member of the European Economic Community.	1962
Constantine II succeeds his father Paul I.	1964
Coup d'état, followed by a military dictatorship; the King flees to Rome and later to London.	1967
On Cyprus the National Guard, supported by the Greek military régime, attempt a putsch. Turkey reacts by sending in troops and occupying the northern part of the island. Karamanlis becomes Prime Minister. Referendum in favour of a democratic republic. Tensions with Turkey (Cyprus; Aegean oilfields).	1974
New Constitution.	1975
Treaty on Greece's entry into the European Economic Community signed in Athens (28 May).	1979
Greece rejects any extension of Turkish air control over the Aegean (February). Karamanlis becomes President of Greece and Rallis Prime Minister (May).	1980
Greece becomes the tenth member of the European Community (1 January). In an election on 18 October the Panhellenic Socialist Movement (PASOK) wins an absolute majority. Papandreou becomes Prime Minister, with a programme for the socialisation of major branches of the economy.	1981

History

1983   The Greek Parliament ratifies an agreement on the stationing of American troops in Greece.

1984   Conference in Athens, in which Greece, Yugoslavia, Bulgaria, Romania and Turkey take part, on making the Balkans a nuclear-free zone (January).
Following a controversy between Greece and Turkey over the military status of the island of Lemnos Greece does not take part in the NATO autumn manœuvres.

1985   After a disputed election Sartzetakis becomes President (29 March). In a general election on 2 June PASOK again wins a majority.
Greece ends the state of war with Albania which had existed since 1940.

Art and Architecture

Art, poetry and philosophy were the three fields of ancient Greek achievement which have endured down the ages and won the designation of "classical". While in the 18th c. Johann Joachim Winckelmann, the founder of the study of antiquity, saw the classical period as falling within the 1st millennium B.C., the epoch-making discoveries of Schliemann, Evans and others in the latter part of the 19th c., revealing the Mycenaean and Minoan cultures, have taken our horizons far back into the 2nd and indeed the 3rd millennium, and recent excavations have yielded evidence of human settlement as far back as the 4th millennium. This Sesklo culture (3500–2900 B.C.; named after the type site near Volos) and the Dimini culture which succeeded it produced characteristic decorated pottery; but of much higher quality were the Cycladic culture which flourished on the Aegean islands in the 3rd millennium and is noted in particular for its marble Cycladic idols, and the brilliant Minoan culture on Crete. After an Early Minoan phase beginning about 2600 B.C. this reached its full flowering in the Middle Minoan period (*c.* 2000 B.C.), when large palace complexes were built. This ancient Mediterranean, pre-Indo-European culture also affected the development of art in mainland Greece, exerting a strong influence on the Mycenaean culture (1580–1150 B.C.) of the early (Indo-European) Greeks. To the achievements of Minoan art (fresco-painting, pottery, seal-cutting) the Mycenaeans added structures of monumental scale – Cyclopean defensive walls (Athens, Mycenae, Tiryns) and tholos (domed) tombs such as the so-called Treasury of Atreus at Mycenae.

Sesklo culture
Dimini culture

Cycladic culture

Minoan culture

Greek art in the narrower sense developed in the Dark Age after the incursion of the Dorians. Pottery in the style known from its type of decoration as Geometric now came into favour (after a Proto-Geometric period from about 1050 to 700 B.C.). In the mature Geometric period (mid 8th c.) the purely geometric designs (circles, meanders, chequers) are supplemented by the first figural representations (Dipylon Amphora, National Archaeological Museum, Athens). The first small Greek temples were built during the Geometric period (Perakhora, Thermos, Temple of Artemis Arthia in Sparta, Heraion I on Samos).

Greek art

Geometric style

Of major importance for the further development of Greek art was the Archaic art of the 7th and 6th c. In a short span of time between 650 and 620 B.C. the art of sculpture emerged simultaneouly at a number of different places. Unlike earlier Egyptian sculpture, Greek sculpture sought to represent the free, natural man. Its main theme was the naked figure of a youth (kouros; large collection in National Archaeological Museum, Athens), but there were also figures of goddesses (Nike, Delos; head of Hera, Olympia; Gorgon, Corfu) and the poros (limestone) and marble figures on the Acropolis (pediment figures, Moschophoros, Rampin Horseman and korai in the Acropolis Museum).

Archaic period

Sculpture

In the building of temples the Greeks were now able to achieve monumental scale, at the same time making the transition from

Temples
(see Types of Temple, p. 32)

29

timber to stone construction and evolving the Doric order (temples of Artemis, Corfu; Hera, Olympia; Apollo, Corinth) and the Ionic order (Artemísion, Ephesus; Phoikos' Temple of Hera, Sámos; Treasury of Siphnians, Delphi).

Vase-painting

There was also a great flowering of vase-painting, first in Corinth and then in Athens, which took over the lead; at first in the black-figure technique, then from 530 B.C. red-figure. Since the wall-paintings and panel-paintings of such masters as Polygnotos and Apelles are lost to us we can gain some impression of Greek painting from the vases which have survived in such numbers.

Classical period

The Archaic period ended with the fall of the Peisistratids (510 B.C.) and, even more decisively, with the Persian Wars (490–479 B.C.). The "Archaic smile" disappears, giving place to a more serious expression, as in the "Critian Boy" and the "Fair-Haired Youth", two characteristic works of the early 5th c. (Acropolis Museum). This was the century of classicism, the supreme period of Greek culture, which in the fields of art, poetry and philosophy was now increasingly centred on Athens. Tragedy was a purely Attic creation. The dominant position of Athens as the centre of the Greek World is illustrated by the mingling of styles in the Periclean building programme on the Acropolis, where the Doric and Ionic orders are found side by side (Parthenon, Temple of Nike and Erechtheion), and even in the same building (Parthenon, Propylaia).

High classical period

The Periclean building programme was carried out under the general direction of Pheidias, who also created the bronze Athena Promachos and the chryselephantine statues of Athena Parthenos (Athens) and Zeus (Olympia). These works, succeeding the earlier "severe" style (pediments and metopes of the Temple of Zeus at Olympia, 460 B.C.), mark the full flowering of the classical period. Pheidias had a slightly younger contemporary, but one of equal genius, in Polykleitos of Argos, who does not disown his Dorian origin and magnificently gives expression in his work (Doryphoros, Diadumenos, Apoxyomenos) to the classical canon of proportion and distribution of weight, achieving an equilibrium between opposing tensions by the emphasis given to the supporting leg and the free leg. Other notable sculptors of this period were Myron, Kresilas and Alkamenes. Many works of sculpture were cast in bronze and are now lost, so that we have to depend on later marble copies. The National Archaeological Museum in Athens has a number of fine bronze originals, outstanding among them the figure of Zeus or Poseidon found in the sea off Cape Artemísion (c. 460 B.C.; probably from Salamís).

Late classical period

After Pheidias and Polykleitos, in the "rich" style (425–380) and the late classical period (380–330), sculpture aimed at a closer imitation of nature. Art reflected the individual expectation of salvation of the men of the 4th c. and the humanisation of the gods which ran parallel to it. This trend can be observed in the works of Praxiteles (Hermes, Olympia; Aphrodite of Knidos), Skopas (Stela of Ilissos in National Archaeological Museum, Athens) and Leochares.

In architecture the 4th c. evolved new conceptions of interior space in tholoi (round buildings) with increasingly rich decoration. The tholoi at Delphi (380) and Epidauros (360) have Doric colums on the exterior and Corinthian columns in the interior; the Philippeion at Olympia (after 338) has Ionic columns on the exterior and Corinthian columns in the interior. The structure of theatres also reached its final form during this period (Athens, Epidauros).

The establishment of Alexander the Great's world empire marks the beginning of the Hellenistic period (330–30 B.C.), when regions outside Greece began to play an important part in the development of art and architecture. Architects now began to lay out large complexes into which the individual buildings were fitted. An example of this is the Asklepieion at Kos, which was begun soon after 300 B.C. and was enlarged in the 2nd c. into an extensive complex laid out symmetrically on a series of terraces. The Temple of Athena Lindia on the island of Rhodes was similarly developed into a grandiose composition of staircases and colonnades. In Asia Minor Pergamon, capital of the Attalid kingdom, was designed as an elaborate and deliberately ostentatious complex consisting of temples, a theatre and the Great Altar of Zeus. The sculpture on the altar and other works from Pergamon, including the "Dying Gaul", are examples of the expressive Baroque art of the period, as are such well-known works as the Victory of Samothrace and the Venus de Milo, now in the Louvre, and the Laokoön group by the Rhodian sculptors Agesandros and Polydoros.

Hellenistic period

Mosaics enjoyed great favour in the Hellenistic period. Originally, in the 5th and early 4th c. B.C., they were pebble mosaics (Athens, Olynthos), reaching their peak in the time of Alexander (Pella). From the 3rd c. (e.g. in houses on Delos) coloured tesserae were used.

During the Roman Imperial period (30 B.C.–A.D. 395) new trends emerged – portrait statues showing individual characteristics, historical reliefs (Arch of Galerius, Salonica), large-scale architecture (Olympieion in Athens completed in the reign of Hadrian, 2nd c. A.D.).

Roman Imperial period

In the 4th c. a strictly frontal pose came into favour in relief sculpture (carving on the base of the Egyptian obelisk in the Hippodrome, Constantinople), and this also became predominant in many aspects of Byzantine art, particularly in icons.

In Christian art sculpture in the round gave place to relief carving for the transcendental representation of sacred figures, and a prominent place was occupied by painting, including mosaic work. Byzantine art was above all a religious art, which sought to create buildings in the image of the divine Cosmos. Of central importance in this respect is the cruciform ground-plan of Byzantine churches, represented by the domed cruciform church which in the Middle Byzantine period (9th–12th c.) replaced the older basilican form; and equally significant is the decoration of the churches with figures of Christ Pantokrator (Ruler of All), the Mother of God, saints and Church festivals, to be seen notably in the two 11th c. monastic churches of Osios Loukas and Dafni, the churches at Mistra dating from the Late Byzantine period (1261–1453) and the Early Byzantine mosaics of Salonica. The Byzantine Museum in Athens offers a general survey of Byzantine art in Greece.

Byzantine art

The traditions of Byzantine art were carried on during the Turkish period, for example in the monasteries of Meteora (16th c.) and Athos and the numerous churches of Kastoria.

Art and Architecture

Modern times

After the liberation of Greece in the 19th c. Byzantine art still served as a model in such buildings as the Ophthalmic Hospital and the large New Mitropolis Church in Athens; but the great bulk of the buildings now erected looked back to the art of antiquity, in the work of such architects as Christian and Theophil Hansen, Friedrich von Gärtner, Schaubert and Kleanthes. Examples of this neo-classical architecture in Athens are the University, the Academy, the National Library, the Royal Palace and the marble Stadion, re-erected in its original form.

The Greek Temple

The temple ranks with the theatre as one of the supreme achievements of Greek architecture. It was not designed as a meeting-place of the faithful but as the home of the cult image, and thus of divinity itself. The form was derived from the megaron (principal room) of a residential building, as seen in fully developed form, for example, in the throne-rooms of Mycenaean palaces.

Temple in antis

The simplest type is the temple in antis, in which the naos (cella) is preceded by a pronaos (porch or antechamber) flanked by forward projections (antae) of its side walls. Between the antae are two columns supporting the pediment (Treasury of the Athenians, Delphi). There are also examples of a double anta temple, with a porch at each end.

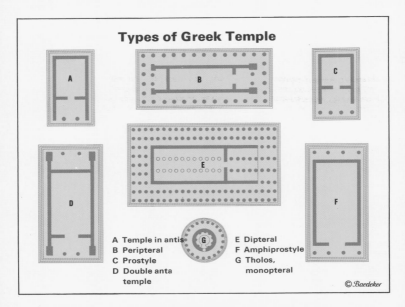

Types of Greek Temple

A Temple in antis
B Peripteral
C Prostyle
D Double anta temple
E Dipteral
F Amphiprostyle
G Tholos, monopteral

© Baedeker

Where there is another row of columns in front of the antae supporting the projecting pediment (one column in front of each of the antae, with two or four columns between) the temple is known as prostyle (eastern temple in the Erechtheion, Athens). If there is a similar row of columns on the rear end of the temple it is known as amphiprostyle (Temple of Nike, Acropolis).

Prostyle

From the second half of the 7th c. B.C. the classical form was the peripteral temple, in which the cella was surrounded on all four sides by a colonnade (peristasis). At one end was the entrance, preceded by a pronaos; at the other end was a rear chamber, the opisthodomos. In the 6th c. an elongated ground-plan was favoured, with 6 columns at the ends and 16 (Temple of Hera, Olympia) or 15 (Temple of Apollo, Delphi) along the sides. In the 5th c. the classical proportions of the temple were developed, with n columns at the ends and $2n + 1$ along the sides (Temple of Zeus, Olympia, 6 by 13 columns; Parthenon, Athens, 8 by 17).

Peripteral

If the temple has a double row of columns on all four sides it is known as dipteral (Olympieion, Athens). If the inner row of columns is omitted to leave room for a wider cella the temple is known as pseudo-dipteral (Temple of Artemis, Magnesia on the Mæander).

Dipteral

A further type of temple is the tholos, on a circular ground-plan (Epidauros, Delphi).

Tholos

The Classical Orders

In the Doric order the shaft of the column, which tapers towards the top and has between 16 and 20 flutings, stands directly, without a base, on the stylobate above the three-stepped substructure. A characteristic feature is the entasis (swelling) of the columns, which together with the frequently applied curvature of the steps of the substructure relieves the austerity of the building. The capital consists of the echinus, curving up from the shaft, and the square abacus. It carries the architrave with its frieze of triglyphs and metopes, which may be either plain or with relief ornament. Between and below the triglyphs are drop-like guttæ. The tympanon is enclosed by the horizontal cornice (geison) and the oblique mouldings which form an angle with it, and usually contains the pediment figures. The sculptured decoration normally consists of the carving on the metopes and the pediment figures, but may extend also to the front of the pronaos.

Doric order

Where limestone and not marble was used it was faced with a coat of stucco. The surface was not left in the natural colour of the stone but was painted, the predominant colours being blue, red and white.

The Ionic order has slenderer and gentler forms than the Doric, the "male" order. The flutings of the columns are separated by narrow ridges. The column stands on a base, which may be either of the Anatolian/Ionian type (with several concave mouldings) or the Attic type (with an alternation between the convex torus moulding and the concave trochilus). The characteristic feature of the capital is the spiral volute on either

Ionic order

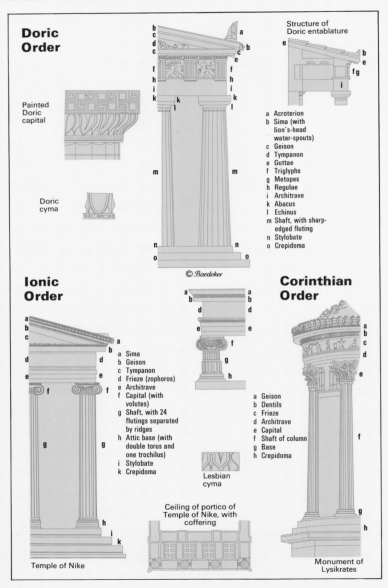

Doric Order

Painted Doric capital

Doric cyma

Structure of Doric entablature

a Acroterion
b Sima (with lion's-head water-spouts)
c Geison
d Tympanon
e Guttae
f Triglyphs
g Metopes
h Regulae
i Architrave
k Abacus
l Echinus
m Shaft, with sharp-edged fluting
n Stylobate
o Crepidoma

© Baedeker

Ionic Order

a Sima
b Geison
c Tympanon
d Frieze (zophoros)
e Architrave
f Capital (with volutes)
g Shaft, with 24 flutings separated by ridges
h Attic base (with double torus and one trochilus)
i Stylobate
k Crepidoma

Lesbian cyma

Ceiling of portico of Temple of Nike, with coffering

Temple of Nike

Corinthian Order

a Geison
b Dentils
c Frieze
d Architrave
e Capital
f Shaft of column
g Base
h Crepidoma

Monument of Lysikrates

side. The architrave is not flat but is made up of three sections, each projecting over the one below. The frieze is continuous, without triglyphs to divide it up.

The Ionic temple, originating in the territories occupied by the Ionian Greeks, was well suited to large-scale buildings, such as the gigantic temples of Sámos and (in Asia Minor) Ephesus, Sardis and Didyma.

The Corinthian order is similar to the Ionic except in the form of the capital. The characteristic feature of this is the acanthus leaves which enclose the circular body of the capital, with tendrils reaching up to the corners of the concave architrave ("master capital" in Epidauros Museum; Olympieion, Athens). The Corinthian order was much favoured under the Roman Empire, which also evolved the "composite" capital out of a marriage of Ionic and Corinthian forms and developed ever more elaborate decorative schemes.

Corinthian order

Church-building

The first churches were built in the 4th c., after the practice of Christianity was authorised in the Roman Empire.

The predominant form was the basilica, with a central aisle or nave flanked by one or two lower aisles on either side. The church was oriented to the east, with an apse at the east end. At the west end was a narthex or porch, which might be preceded by an atrium.
This type is found throughout the whole territory of the Roman Empire, from Rome to Jerusalem.

Basilica

In the 9th c. a new type of church building developed in Greece and thereafter became predominant – the domed cruciform church, with a centralised plan rather than the longitudinal plan of the basilica.
The central dome is borne either on walls or on columns, or sometimes on two side walls and two columns, and spans either the central aisle or – with eight supports – both the central and the lateral aisles.
The east end, with the altar, is separated from the body of the church by a stone screen, which later develops into the iconostasis. On either side are two smaller rooms serving liturgical purposes, the prothesis and the diakonikon.
Corresponding to these three parts, there are usually three apses at the east end. At the west end there is frequently an outer porch (exonarthex) preceding the narthex (then called the esonarthex or inner porch).
The interior of the church was covered with paintings in accordance with a system designed to symbolise the celestial hierarchy. The exterior was of stone or brick, often in elaborate decorative patterns.
In the post-Byzantine period there was an occasional reversion to the basilican type. The churches of this kind were usually small, with either a single aisle or three aisles.

Domed cruciform church

Technical Terms

The upper part or the capital of a Doric column, a square slab above the echinus.

Abacus

Art and Architecture

Abaton	The innermost sanctuary of a temple, to which only priests were admitted.
Acanthus	A spiny leaved plant used in the decoration of Corinthian and Byzantine (Justinianic) capitals.
Acropolis	The upper part or citadel of the Greek city.
Acroterion	A figure or ornament on a roof-ridge or the top of a pediment.
Adyton	= Abaton
Agora	The market-place of a Greek city, the main centre of civic life.
Amphiprostyle	(Temple) with columned portico at each end.
Anathema	Votive offering.
Annulus	A ring round the shaft of a Doric column below the echinus.
Anta	A pillar-like projection at the end of the side wall of a temple cella. *Temple in antis*, a temple with antae at one end, with columns between them.
Apse	A projection, usually semicircular, at the end of a temple cella or church.
Architrave	A horizontal stone lintel resting on the columns of a temple, etc.
Astragal	Knucklebone; applied to the beaded moulding of the Ionic order.
Basilica	1. Originally a royal hall (stoa basilike), usually divided into aisles, used for commercial or judicial purposes. 2. The standard form of Christian church developed in the 4th c., with either three or five aisles.
Bema	1. Platform for orators. 2. Chancel of a Christian church.
Bomos	Square altar.
Bouleuterion	Council chamber; the meeting-place of the council (boule) of a Greek city.
Capital	The top of a column or pillar.
Caryatid	A female figure supporting an entablature.
Cavea	The semicircular auditorium (seating) of a theatre.
Cella	The enclosed central chamber of a temple.
Cenotaph	Funerary momument not containing a body.
Chryselephantine	(Sculpture) of gold and ivory on a wooden core.
Chtonian	(Divinities) of the earth.
Crepidoma	Three-stepped platform of a temple.

(Walls) of large irregular blocks, ascribed in antiquity to the Cyclopes.	Cyclopean
People, community; popular assembly; settlement.	Demos
The right-hand lateral apse of a Byzantine church.	Diakonikon
(Temple) surrounded by a double row of columns.	Dipteral
Double gateway.	Dipylon
Temple with antae at both ends.	Double anta temple
Passage; specifically, passage leading into a Mycenaean tholos tomb.	Dromos
Convex moulding under the abacus of a Dorian capital.	Echinus
The superstructure carried by columns.	Entablature
Swelling in the lower part of a column.	Entasis
A youth who is not yet a full citizen.	Ephebe
= Architrave.	Epistyle
Inner porch of a church.	Esonarthex
A recess, usually semicircular, containing benches.	Exedra
Outer porch of a church.	Exonarthex
Decorative band above the architrave of a temple; in the Doric order made up of metopes and triglyphs, in the Ionic order plain or with continuous carved decoration.	Frieze
Cornice of a temple.	Geison
Fight between gods and giants.	Gigantomachia
A school for physical training or general education.	Gymnasion
A temple (30 m) 100 ft long.	Hekatompedon
Temple or sanctuary of Hera.	Heraion
A square pillar with a head of Hermes or some other god; later with a portrait head.	Herm
Shrine or tomb of a hero.	Heroon
Elliptical course for chariot-races.	Hippodrome
Under-floor heating system for baths, etc.	Hypocaust
Screen in a Byzantine church between the sanctuary and the main part of the church, bearing tiers of icons.	Iconostasis
Principal church of a monastery.	Katholikon

Art and Architecture

Kore (pl. korai)	Maiden, girl; statue of a girl.
Kouros (pl. kouroi)	Youth; statue of a naked youth.
Meander	A continuous fret or key pattern, named after the River Maeander (Büyük Menderes) in Asia Minor.
Megaron	The principal room in a Mycenaean palace; perhaps the basic form of the Greek temple.
Metope	Rectangular panel between the triglyphs in the frieze of a Doric temple, either plain or with relief decoration.
Metroon	Sanctuary of the Great Mother.
Monopteral	(Temple) without a cella, usually circular.
Naiskos	Small temple.
Naos	Cella of a temple.
Narthex	Porch of a Byzantine church.
Necropolis	Cemetery (city of the dead).
Nymphaeum	Shrine of the nymphs; fountain-house.
Odeion	Hall (usually roofed) for musical performances.
Olympieion	Sanctuary of Olympian Zeus.
Opisthodomos	Chamber at the rear end of a temple.
Orchestra	Circular or semicircular area between the stage and the auditorium of a theatre in which the chorus danced.
Orthostat	Large block of stone, set vertically, in the lower part of a temple wall.
Ostracism	A system of voting on potsherds (ostraka) for the banishment of a citizen.
Palaistra	Training school for physical exercises.
Panayia	"All Holy"; the Mother of God.
Pantokrator	"Ruler of All"; Christ.
Parekklisia	Subsidiary church, chapel.
Pediment	Triangular termination of a pitched roof.
Peribolos	Enclosure wall of a sacred precinct.
Peripteral	(Temple) surrounded by a peristyle.
Peristasis	= Peristyle.
Peristyle	Colonnade surrounding a building.

Large storage jar.	Pithos
(Masonry) of irregularly shaped stones.	Polygonal
A kind of limestone.	Poros
Seat of honour in a theatre or stadion.	Prohedria
Entrance portico of a temple.	Pronaos
Monumental form of propylon.	Propylaia
Gateway.	Propylon
Fore-stage, proscenium.	Proskenion
(Temple) with columned portico in front.	Prostyle
Left-hand lateral apse of a Byzantine church.	Prothesis
Human torso or forequarters of an animal as a decorative feature on a building or vase.	Protome
Office of the prytaneis (city councillors).	Prytaneion
Tower, bastion.	Pyrgos
Drinking-vessel, often in the form of an animal's head.	Rhyton
Gutter of building, with lion's-head water-spouts.	Sima
Stage building of theatre.	Skene
Rounded end of a stadion.	Sphendone
Rounded base of cella wall.	Spira
1. Measure of length, a stade or stadium (600 ft (180m)). 2. Running-track 600 feet (180m) long. 3. Stadium, with running-track and enbankments or benches for spectators.	Stadion
Upright stone slab (often a tombstone), usually with an inscription and frequently with carving in relief.	Stela
Portico; hall with pillars along the front.	Stoa
Curved blade used to scrape dust and oil from the body after exercise.	Strigil
The upppermost step of the base of a temple.	Stylobate
Stone benches for clergy in the apse of a Byzantine church.	Synthronon
Sacred precinct.	Temenos
Chancel screen in a Byzantine church.	Templon
Small cube of stone, glass, etc., used in mosaic work.	Tessera

Art and Architecture

Tetrastyle	(Temple) with four columns on the façade.
Thesauros	Treasury.
Tholos	Circular building, rotunda; domed Mycenaean tomb.
Toreutics	The art of ornamental metal-work.
Torus	Convex moulding or semicircular profile.
Triglyph	Projecting member, with two vertical channels, between the metopes of the Doric order.
Trochilus	Convex moulding.
Tympanon	Rear wall of temple pediment.
Volute	Spiral scroll of an Ionic capital.

Quotations

... Wine is a mirror to men ...
Sometimes it is sweet as honey; sometimes the wine you pour
is sharper than thorns.

Alkaios (Alcaeus)
Greek lyric poet
(*c.* 620 B.C.)

Lachon has won from Zeus the Almighty the highest praise as
victor in the race run to the sound of Alpheios' flutes; thus in the
past vine-growing Keos celebrated him, richly decked with
garlands, as victor at Olympia in wrestling and running ... (First
verse of a short ode of 452, probably composed to celebrate the
return to Keos (Kéa) of the Olympic victor Lachon.)

Bakchylides
Greek choral poet
(6th–5th c. B.C.)

When one sails through the Cyclades today it is their bare
sculptured quality that makes them distinctive form all other
Mediterranean islands. It was the blinding light of Delos that
dazzled me when I anchored my small boat in the shadow of
Mount Cynthus, protected by the ancient mole. Across the
white-flecked strait, the sister island of Rheneia harboured a
few sheep, and on Delos itself only a solitary goat-herd and his
flock disturbed my silence. But these sun-devoured islands
which the modern traveller knows are very different from the
islands of the Homeric age. They were thickly forested in those
days, and there were many more springs, green groves, and
grassy places.
Seriphos, Siphnos, Milos, Santorin – I think of sailing past
them, and of being blinded by the glare off their rocks after the
cool, veined marble of the sea. But the islands which Ulysses
knew were as rich and green as Corfu is today, or as the long
valleys of Rhodes where the butterflies seem like specks of fire
in the aquarium light beneath the leaves.

Ernle Bradford
"Ulysses Found"
(1963)

The isles of Greece, the isles of Greece!
  Where burning Sappho loved and sung,
Where grew the arts of war and peace,
  Where Delos rose, and Phoebus sprung!
Eternal summer gilds them yet,
But all, except their sun, is set.
("Don Juan", III, 86,1.)

Lord Byron
(1788–1824)

(Santorin)
I found it a fantastic spot. Picturesque, or romantic, is too mild
a term; the cliff-scenery and the colours of the sea and land
made one catch one's breath. Under a bleak northern sky it
would be a horrific kind of place; drenched in the glittering light
of May it was fabulously beautiful ... Santorin is surely a vision
which can disappoint nobody.

Norman Douglas
"Looking Back"
(1933)

... The whole [Persian] fleet amounting in all to six hundred
triremes, made sail for Ionia. Thence, instead of proceeding
with a straight course along the shore to the Hellespont
[Dardanelles] and to Thrace, they loosed from Samos and
voyaged across the Icarian sea through the midst of the islands;
mainly, as I believe, because they feared the danger of doubling
Mount Athos, where the year before they had suffered so
grievously on their passage; but a constraining cause also was
their former failure to take Naxos.

Herodotus
Greek historian
(5th c. B.C.)

When the Persians, therefore, approaching from the Icarian sea, cast anchor at Naxos, which, recollecting what there befell them formerly, they had determined to attack before any other state, the Naxians, instead of encountering them, took a flight, and hurried off to the hills. The Persians however succeeded in laying hands on some, and them they carried away captive, while at the same time they burnt all the temples together with the town. This done, they left Naxos, and sailed away to the other islands.

While the Persians were thus employed, the Delians likewise quitted Delos, and took refuge in Tenos. And now the expedition drew near, when Datis sailed forward in advance of the other ships; commanding them, instead of anchoring at Delos, to rendezvous at Rhênea, over against Delos . . .

("History", V, 95–97; translation by George Rawlinson.)

Homer
(c. 8th c. B.C.)

Thus we to Tenedos, of home full fain,
Came; but for all our sacrifices slain
Stern Zeus ordained not our return, but there
Stirred evil discord up yet once again.

Then they that had with lord Odysseus gone,
The wise of heart, the subtle-minded one,
Swung round their ships and hastened back to make
Their peace with Agamemnon, Atreus' son.

But I with all the ships that round me drew
Fled in close order: for full well I knew
That God was wroth at us; and with me fled
The valiant son of Tydeus and his crew.

And fair-haired Menelaus late that say
Followed and caught us up in Lesbos bay
Pondering the long sea passage, whether we
Straight for the Psyrian isle our course should lay.

With craggy Chios low on our left hand,
Or coasting Mimas by the windy land
Keep Chios on our starboard; then we prayed
God for a sign that we might understand.

And sign he showed, that bade us cut the sea
Straight forward toward Euboea, so to flee
Quick from destruction; and a wind arose
Shrill-blowing, and before the wind went we.

Swift through the fishes' tracks our ships ran on,
And made Geraestus ere the morning shone:
Where to Poseidon many bulls we slew,
Because we safe through the great deep had gone.

("Odyssey", III, 159–179; translation by J. W. Mackail.)

Longos
Greek writer
(2nd–3rd c. A.D.)
"Daphnis and Chloe"

On the island of Lesbos is Mytilene, a large and beautiful city. It is traversed by channels flowing in from the sea and has handsome bridges of smooth white stone: it seems not so much a city as a world of islands. Some 200 stadia from this city of Mytilene was the estate of a wealthy man, a fine property indeed: mountains full of game, fields of wheat, hillsides covered with vines, grazing for sheep and goats. And the sea washed against the soft sand of a long expanse of shore.

A goatherd named Lamon who was grazing his flock there found a baby boy who was being fed by one of his she-goats.

The child lay on soft grass amid trees and thorny scrub and a rampant growth of ivy. The goat kept running up to the child, disappearing and returning again, while her kid was left to look after himself. Lamon watched this coming and going closely, for he was concerned for the abandoned kid; and when the sun stood high in the sky at midday he followed the goat and saw it standing over the child, its legs spread wide so as to avoid trampling or injuring the boy, who was sucking the goat's milk as if from his mother's breast. Full of astonishment, as well he might be, he went closer and saw that the child was well grown and fair, clad in swaddling clothes which bespoke a better origin than a poor foundling – a purple over-garment with a golden pin and a small sword with an ivory haft.

The goatherd's first impulse was to take these things and concern himself no more with the child; then, feeling ashamed at the thought that a she-goat had more care for the child than he, took him up and returned, along with the goat, to his wife Myrtale. When she, in surprise, asked whether a goat could bring a child into the world he told her the whole story – how he had found the child, left there by his parents, how he had seen the she-goat suckling him and how he had been ashamed to leave him to die. Then they hid the objects found with the child, took him as their own and allowed the goat to continue suckling him. And in order that he might have a name such as a herd might bear they called him Daphnis . . .

Then when autumn was at its fairest and it was almost time for the vintage everyone was busy in the fields. One prepared the wine-presses, another cleaned out the casks, another wove baskets. Still another procured a sickle-shaped knife for cutting off the bunches of grapes, another sought a stone for pressing the grapes, another collected pieces of dry wood so as to have light for carrying in the grape juice at night. Daphnis and Chloe now concerned themselves less with their sheep and goats and helped one another with the vintage. Daphnis brought in the grapes in a basket, threw them into the wine-press and trod them, and then filled the wine into the casks. Chloe prepared food for the workers and dispensed older wine for them to drink, and also gathered the lower bunches on the vines. For the vines on Lesbos are low-growing: they do not reach up high or cling to the stems of trees, but spread out their shoots low down, creeping like ivy: even a child whose hands have just been freed from its swaddling clothes can pick grapes on Lesbos.

. . . In my opinion Neleus' cattle mostly grazed outside the borders [of his land], because the countryside at Pylos is all rather sandy and incapable of producing enough grass for that herd. I can bring Homer as my witness; he always calls Nestor king of sandy Pylos.

The island of Sphakteria lies opposite the harbour, just as Reneia lies opposite the anchorage at Delos. Human fortunes seem to make places famous which were hitherto quite unknown; for example Kaphareus in Euboia where a storm hit Agamemnon and the Greeks on the journey home from Troy, and Psyttaleia at Salamis, which we know only because the Persians perished on it. (Translation by Peter Levi.)

Pausanias
Greek writer
"Description of Greece"
(A.D. 144–170)

Round the moon, the glorious,
The stars hide their clear light
When the full moon sheds it radiance
Over the earth below.

Sappho
Greek poetess
(7th–6th c. B.C.)

Quotations

The moon and the Pleiades have set;
Midnight is past;
And I – I lie alone

(Two fragments of poems.)

Simonides
Greek poet
(6th–5th c. B.C.)

Slight is the strength of men, fruitless their strivings.
In their brief existence trouble is heaped on trouble.
Inescapably death hangs over them –
An equal share falling both to the good and to those who are
evil.

Death catches even the man who flees from the battle.

(From his fragmentary Dirges.)

The "Odyssey"

Seafaring in antiquity

The shores of the Mediterranean and its countless islands and islets were already densely populated in prehistoric times. On these shores and island ended the migrations of many different peoples, whose origins are frequently obscure; and the various peoples brought with them a variety of distinctive cultural, social and religious characteristics. The new settlers soon acquired the skills of seamanship, which carried them to distant and unkown shores. The leading seafarers, after the Phoenicians, were the Greeks, who as early as the 2nd millennium B.C. were undertaking hazardous voyages as far afield as Spain. Thereafter they founded trading-posts and colonies all along the Mediterranean coasts and carried on an extensive trade with foreign peoples.

On their voyages the Greek seafarers encountered peoples and cultures, which often seemed to them mysterious and dangerous, and always strange and marvellous. On their return home they spun their seamen's yarns of incredible adventures, which were preserved by oral tradition and passed on from generation to generation.

The "Odyssey"

The most celebrated work of this kind is Homer's "Odyssey", a heroic epic written in hexameters in an elaborately wrought style. It describes the adventures of the "many-wiled" Odysseus, King of Ithaca, who on his way home from the Trojan War (in which he had devised the stratagem of the wooden horse) is held against his will on the island of Ogygia by the nymph Kalypso. When after ten years, at the behest of the gods, Kalypso at last releases him his raft is caught in a fearful storm and he is cast ashore on the island of Scheria, in the land of the Phaeacians. There he is hospitably received by King Alkinoos and his daughter Nausikaa and tells the story of his adventures, including his encounters with the one-eyed Cyclops Polyphemos and the sorceress Kirke (Circe), his journey into the land of the dead, the Sirens, the sea-monsters Skylla and Charybdis, the loss of all his companions as punishment for killing the cattle of the sun god Helios, and finally his stay with Kalypso. Alkinoos then gives Odysseus a magical ship to take him back to Ithaca. After his return home Odysseus kills the insolent suitors of his wife Penelope and restores order in his kingdom. The "Odyssey" is probably an assemblage of seamen's stories by various authors dating from Mycenaean times (1300 B.C.), incorporating the social circumstances and mythological ideas of the 7th and 6th c. B.C., which was worked into a continuous narrative by Homer. This is suggested by the striking variations and unevennesses in the text as we have it.

Odysseus' route

Repeated attempts have been made to trace Odysseus' route and identify the places to which his wanderings took him, on the basis of Homer's descriptions of these places and evidence obtained by excavation.

It has been suggested, for example, that the little island of Gavdos, off the south coast of Crete, was Kalypso's island of Ogygia. Corfu (Kerkyra) was considered in ancient times to be the island of Scheria, the land of the Phaeacians; and the little

Ithaca, presumed home of Odysseus

offshore islet of Pontikonisi (Mouse Island) was taken to be Alkinoos' ship, turned to stone by Poseidon ("Odyssey", XIII, 163). The Greek geographer Strabo (*c.* 63 B.C.–A.D. 20) interpreted the sea-monsters Skylla and Charybdis as two violent whirlpools on either side of the Straits of Messian.
The German archaeologist Wilhelm Dörpfeld (1853–1940) believed that Odysseus' kingdom of Ithaca was the island of Lefkás, and carried out excavations there which yielded interesting results but no conclusive proof of his theory.

Sights from A to Z

There is no generally accepted system for the transliteration of modern Greek place-names and personal names into the Latin alphabet, and the visitor to Greece will find much diversity and inconsistency of spelling, for example on signposts and in guidebooks and other literature in English. The situation is still further complicated by changes in pronunciation which have taken place since ancient times, so that many familiar old classical names sound very different in modern Greek.

In this guide modern Greek place-names and personal names are transliterated in a form approximating to their pronunciation. Classical names are generally given in their "Greek" rather than their "Latin" form (e.g. Polykleitos rather than Polyclitus). But where there is a generally accepted English form (e.g. Athens, Crete) or where a name is so familiar in its Latinised form that it would be pedantic to insist on the Greek spelling (e.g. Aegina rather than Aíyina) the traditional English names are used.

In the headings of the entries in this section of the guide the name of the island or town in its English form is followed by the Greek name, with a transliteration reproducing its pronunciation as closely as possible; the syllable on which the stress falls is indicated by an acute accent.

Aegina   Αἴγινα/Aíyina   D3

Region: Central Greece
Island group: Saronic Islands
Nomos (administrative district): Attica
Area: 83 sq. km (32 sq. miles)
Altitude: 0–532 m (0–1745 ft)
Population: 9550
Chief place: Aíyina

Boats and hydrofoils several times daily between Athens (Piraeus) and the ports of Aíyina, Souvála, and Ayía Marína, and between Méthana and Aíyina. Local connections with Angístri.

Situation and characteristics

Aegina, lying some 19 km (12 miles) south-west of Piraeus in the Saronic Gulf, is a hilly and fertile island of Tertiary limestones and schists, with isolated rounded hills of volcanic origin. For the most part the coast falls steeply down to the sea, with few sheltered bays. The main occupation of the inhabitants is farming, in particular the growing and export of the island's excellent pistachio nuts. Fishing, sponge-diving and pottery manufacture are also of some economic importance. Aegina is noted for the production of its water-coolers (kannatia) – two-handled wide-necked jars in a porous fabric which keep their contents cool by evaporation. With its mild climate and low rainfall, Aegina has long been favoured as a summer resort by the prosperous citizens of Athens. In recent years it has become increasingly popular with foreign visitors.

Myth and history

The legendary ancestor of the Aeginetans was Aiakos, son of Zeus and Aigina and father of Peleus and Telamon, who was

celebrated for his wise and just rule and became judge in the Underworld together with Minos and Rhadamanthys.

The earliest traces of Pelasgian settlement on the island date from the 3rd millennium B.C. In the 2nd millennium Aegina was already an important trading-station, dealing in pottery and ointments, as finds of Helladic, Cycladic and Minoan material have shown. It is first recorded in history as a colony of the Dorian city of Epidauros, and together with Epidauros was ruled in the 7th c. B.C. by Phaidon of Argos. After shaking off the control of its mother city in the 6th c. Aegina enjoyed a period of some prosperity, which soon brought it into competition with Corinth. The Aeginetans had trading-posts in Umbria, on the Black Sea and in Egypt, and their shipowners were the wealthiest in the Ancient World. Aeginetan coins bearing the effigy of a tortoise are the oldest known, and by 656 B.C. already had a wide circulation, and Aeginetan weights and measures remained current into Roman times.

At the beginning of the Persian Wars this seafaring State ws at the height of its power. After the Battle of Salamís, in which 30 vessels from Aegina took part, an Aeginetan ship was awarded the prize for the highest valour. But Aegina was also led by its commercial interests to offer Darius' envoys earth and water in token of submission, whereupon, on the motion of Athens, it was called to account by Sparta. This was the occasion of further conflicts with Athens, which saw the strong neighbouring island as an obstacle to the expansion of its sea-power. After naval victories at Kekryphaleia (Angístri) and off Aegina itself the Athenians – though simultaneously fighting with Megára and in Egypt – forced Aegina to submit after a nine-month-long siege, and in 456 B.C. the city was compelled to pull down its walls, surrender its warships and pay tribute to Athens.

At the beginning of the Peloponnesian War (431 B.C.) the Aeginetans were expelled from their island and the land distributed to citizens of Attica. After the final defeat of Athens in 404 many of them returned, but the island's great days were over. Athens rapidly recovered and after a series of military campaigns regained control of Aegina, which thereafter shared the fortunes of the Athenian State.

From 12 January to 3 October 1828 Aegina was capital of Greece.

Aíyina town

The chief place on the island, Aíyina (pop. 5000), lies on gently rising ground on a wide bay at the north end of the west coast. It occupies the site of the ancient city, which was larger than the present town. From the harbour, sheltered by a breakwater, there are fine views of the smaller islands of Metópi and Angístri to the south-west and Moní to the south and of the hills round Epidauros. The Archaeological Museum contains material from the temples of Aphaia and Aphrodite, together with pottery and other grave-goods ranging in date from the 3rd millennium B.C. to Roman times.

On the hill of Kolóna, to the north of the town, is an 8 m (26 ft) high Doric column. According to Pausanias this belonged to

Kolóna

◀ *Temple of Aphaia, Aegina*

49

the Temple of Aphrodite by the harbour (460 B.C.): in fact the temple was dedicated to Apollo. Under the temple were found remains of Mycenaean and pre-Mycenaean settlement (3rd millennium B.C.). To the west were two smaller temples, probably dedicated to Artemis and Dionysos. A sphinx (c. 460 B.C.) which was discovered here in 1904 is now in the Archaeological Museum.

Ancient harbour

Below the temple, to the south, was the ancient commercial harbour, now silted up. When the sea is calm the old quays can still be seen under water. The modern habour, on the site of the ancient naval harbour, is still protected by the ancient moles which have been maintained in good condition. On the north mole, the longer of the two, is an early 19th c. chapel dedicated to St Nicholas.

Tomb of Phokas

1·5 km (1 mile) north of the town is a mound (6th c. B.C.), similar to the Sorós at Marathon, traditionally identified as the Tomb of Phokos, who was killed by his half-brothers Peleus and Telamon.

**Temple of Aphaia

The road to the Temple of Aphaia, 13 km (8 miles) east of Aíyina, runs through rolling country, partly wooded and partly cultivated, passing the Church of Ayii Theódori (1289; frescoes), built of stones from ancient temples. In 8 km (5 miles) it reaches Palaiokhóra, the medieval capital of the island, which was abandoned about 1800. Above the village, which has some 20 chapels ranging in date between the 13th and 18th c., is a ruined medieval castle.

Farther on the road passes the scattered houses of the village of Mesagró. Soon afterwards a steep footpath leads up to the temple.

The Temple of Aphaia (5th c. B.C.), a goddess associated with Artemis as a protectress of women (foundation inscription; terracotta decoration), is built on the foundations of a 6th c. temple, which itself succeeded a pre-Greek cult site. It is

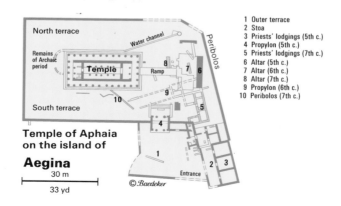

1 Outer terrace
2 Stoa
3 Priests' lodgings (5th c.)
4 Propylon (5th c.)
5 Priests' lodgings (7th c.)
6 Altar (5th c.)
7 Altar (6th c.)
8 Altar (7th c.)
9 Propylon (6th c.)
10 Peribolos (7th c.)

Temple of Aphaia
on the island of
Aegina
30 m
33 yd
© Baedeker

peripteral in type, with 6 by 12 columns. The pronaos and opisthodomos were enclosed by antae, between which were two columns. The roof of the cella was borne on two rows of columns. In the opisthodomos is a stone altar-table. The temple preserves 23 columns of yellowish limestone, with fragments of their stucco facing, particularly at the east and along the sides; some of the columns are monolithic. The roof and the sculptural decoration were of Pentelic marble. Unusual features are irregularities in the floor of the cella and the subdivision of the opisthodomos. In the floor are holes for fixing a grille.

The sculpture in the pediments was bought by Crown Prince Ludwig of Bavaria and is now in the Glyptothek in Munich. Other sculpture from the temple can be seen in Athens and Aíyina museums.

At the east end of the temple, extending across its whole width and connected with it by a ramp, was the sacrificial altar. To the south of the ramp was a small propylon with octagonal columns. The sacred precinct had been banked up to form a level surface and was supported partly on the natural rock and partly on retaining walls of dressed stone.

In the surrounding area the remains of Late Neolithic houses (4th–3rd millennium B.C.) were found by the excavators. From the temple there is a superb view, covering much of the Saronic Gulf and extending to the coast of the mainland, from Athens to Cape Soúnion.

Ayía Marína

3 km (2 miles) south of the Temple of Aphaia, in a wide bay on the east coast of the island, lies the busy little modern resort of Ayía Marína.

*Oros

The most prominent feature in the Saronic Gulf is the Oros (Hill; 532 m (1745 ft)), also known as Mount Profítis Ilías after the chapel on its summit. It can be climbed on a fairly arduous footpath from the village of Marathon, 6 km (4 miles) south of Aíyina. In Mycenaean times (13th c. B.C.) there was a considerable town built on the terraces round the summit, supported by Cyclopean retaining walls. The view extends over almost the whole of the island and the Saronic Gulf, with Salamís, the Methourides (Troupika and Revitousa), Diaporia, Angístri, the Methana Peninsula, the island of Póros and, beyond this, Hýdra.

*View

On the north side of the hill, near the Chapel of the Taxiarchs (Archangels), was a Sanctuary of Zeus Hellanios (5th c. B.C.).

Angístri

5 km (3 miles) south-west of Aíyina is the wooded island of Angístri (12 sq. km (4½ sq. miles); 0–216 m (0–709 ft)), with a population of 700, the descendants of Albanians who settled here in the 16th c.

Agathonisi 'Αγαδονησι/Agathonísi D5

Region: Aegean Islands
Island group: Dodecanese
Nomos: Dodecanese
Area: 13 sq. km (5 sq. miles)
Altitude: 0–212 m (0–696 ft)
Population: 180
Chief place: Megálo Khorió

Boat services

Local connections with Sámos, Pátmos, Lipsí and Arkí.

Situation and characteristics

Agathonísi (formerly known as Gaidouronísi), the most northerly island in the Dodecanese, lies approximately half-way between Sámos and Léros, off the coast of Asia Minor. It was the ancient Tragia, where the young Caesar was captured by pirates in 76 B.C. This barren karstic island (7 km (4½ miles) long by up to 3 km (2 miles) wide), surrounded by steep rocky coasts, offers little in the way of sheltered anchorages. Off the north, east and south coasts are seven uninhabited islets, some land on which is worked by the inhabitants of Agathonísi, who make a modest living by farming and fishing. Agathonísi, with neither sandy beaches nor ancient monuments to attract visitors, has remained entirely untouched by the tourist and holiday trade, and accordingly has preserved its original character unspoiled to an extent equalled by few other Aegean islands.

Alonnisos 'Αλόννησος/Alónnisos C3

Region: Thessaly
Island group: Northern Sporades
Nomos: Magnesia
Area; 72 sq. km (28 sq. miles)
Altitude: 0–476 m (0–1562 ft)
Population: 1350
Chief place: Patitíri

Boat services

Regular boat and hydrofoil services several times weekly from Vólos, Ayios Konstantínos and Kými (Euboea), via Skíathos and Skópelos.

Situation and characteristics

The long rocky island of Alónnisos (formerly Khiliondrómia; ancient Ikos), still one of the remoter places in Greece, lies half-way along the chain of the Northern Sporades, which extends north-east from Skíathos at its western end. A ridge of hills runs along the island from end to end, reaching its highest point in Mount Kouvoúli (476 m (1526 ft)). The north-west coast is edged by steep cliffs and has few indentations, but the south-east coast is more hospitable, with a number of sheltered bays. In this area there are many traces of human settlement reaching back to Neolithic times.

Patitíri Alónnisos (Khorió)

The population, mostly farmers and fishermen, live almost exclusively in the fertile southern part of the island. On this side are the little port of Patitíri and Alónnisos (Khorió), formerly the chief place on the island, which was largely abandoned after an earthquake in 1965. Commandingly situated above the sea, with extensive views, the village is now increasingly being developed as a holiday centre.

1 km (¾ mile) east of Patitíri lies the modest little fishing village of Vótsi, with simple holiday homes.

Vótsi

Ancient Ikos is believed to have been at Kokkinókastro, half-way along the south-east coast, where remains of town walls and tombs have been brought to light.

Ikos

Peristéra

Off the south-east coast of Alónnisos, separated from it by a wide sound, is the bare island of Peristéra or Xeró (14 sq. km (5½ sq. miles); 0–250 m (0–820 ft)).

Skántsoura

The island of Skántsoura (7 sq. km (2¾ sq. miles); 0–107 m (0–351 ft)), which belongs to the Monastic Republic of Athos (Chalcidice) and is used for the grazing of goats, lies 20 km (12½ miles) south-east of Alónnisos. It is occasionally visited for the sake of its sea-caves and its underwater fishing grounds.

Pélagos

13 km (8 miles) north-east of the northern tip of Alónnisos is the wooded island of Pélagos (25 sq. km (9½ sq. miles); 0–302 m (0–991 ft)), known in antiquity as Euthyra. It is also called Kirá Panayía, after the monastery of that name on its east coast, a dependency of Athos. The 12th c. monastic church contains a number of old icons.

Yioúra

The next in the chain of islands curving north-east is the former monastic island of Yioúra (9 sq. km (3½ sq. miles); 0–570 m (0–1870 ft)), now a reserve for wild goats. On the south side of the island are the Caves of the Cyclops, traditionally believed to have been the home of Polyphemos.

Farther east is the little island of Pipéri (7 sq. km (2¾ sq. miles)), in a seal reserve.

Psathoúra

The volcanic island of Psathoúra (6 sq. km (2¼ sq. miles); 0–20 m (0–65 ft)) is the last in the string of the Northern Sporades. Just off the coast, under water, are the remains of buildings belonging to an ancient city engulfed by the sea.

Alónnisos

Amorgós

Amorgos ’Αμοργός/Amorgós   D4/5

Region: Aegean Islands
Island group: Cyclades
Nomos: Cyclades
Area: 130 sq. km (50 sq. miles)
Altitude: 0–826 m (0–2710 ft)
Population: 1800
Chief place: Amorgós (Khóra)

Boat services

Weekly connections with Piraeus; several times weekly with Náxos, Ios and Santoríni.

Situation and characteristics

Amorgós is an island of bare rocky hills 33 km (21 miles) long and up to 6.5 km (4 miles) wide. For the most part the south-east coast falls steeply down to the sea, but the north-west coast is gentler, with two deep inlets – the sheltered Katápola Bay near the south end, with the island's principal harbour, and Aiyiáli Bay at the north end. The population – much reduced by emigration – lives by farming and fishing.

History

The remains of several ancient cities, extensive cemetary areas, finds of coins and rock inscriptions bear witness to the importance of the island in Minoan and Hellenistic times as a port of call on the sea route between Melos and the south-eastern Aegean. Used in Roman times as a place of exile and in subsequent centuries frequently harried by pirates, Amorgós has remained since then an island of no economic or political importance and has in consequence retained much of its

The Monastery of Panayía Khozoviótissa, Amorgós

distinctive character. Unfortunately, however, this very beautiful island, like many other islands in the Aegean, has suffered from the attentions of backpacking holiday-makers of a rather undesirable kind.

Sights

Amorgós (Khóra), the chief place on the island, is situated on the slopes of a hill, huddling round a ruined 13th c. Venetian castle with its typical whitewashed Cycladic houses, its many barrel-vaulted family churches and its windmills. From the town it is a half-hour walk (or donkey-ride) to the Byzantine Monastery of Panayía Khozoviótissa (1088), clinging to a sheer rock face at a height of 367 m (1204 ft). From the lower terrace there is a magnificent view over the sea.

Amorgós

*Monastery of Panayía
Khozoviótissa

4 km (2½ miles) west of Khóra is the port of Katápola. On Moundiliá Hill on the south side of the bay are remains of the ancient settlement of Minoa, which is believed to have been founded by Cretans as early as the 2nd millennium B.C.

Katápola

Minoa

At the south end of the island, at the pretty village of Arkesíni, is the site of Kastrí, with remains of a settlement occupied from Mycenaean to Roman times.

Kastrí

At the north end of Amorgós, in Aiyiáli Bay, are traces of a settlement established by Milesians. From here there is a very rewarding climb to the summit of Mount Kríkelos (826 m (2710 ft)), the highest point on the island.

Mount Kríkelos

Levíta group

North-east of Amorgós lies the Levíta group, which consists of the two principal islands of Levíta (5 sq. km (2 sq. miles); 0–167 m (0–548 ft)) and Kínaros (9 sq. km (3½ sq. miles); 0–320 m (1050 ft)), together with several smaller islands, mostly uninhabited. Here there are beautiful solitary beaches, since the islands have no regular boat services and no accommodation for visitors.

Anafi 'Ανάφη/Anáfi   D4

Region: Aegean Islands
Island group: Cyclades
Nomos: Cyclades
Area: 36 sq. km (14 sq. miles)
Altitude: 0–584 m (0–1916 ft)
Population: 300
Chief place: Anáfi (Khóra)

Boat services

Several times a week from Athens (Piraeus). Passengers are brought ashore in small boats.

Situation and characteristics

The hilly Cycladic island of Anáfi lies 22 km (14 miles) east of Santorin. According to the myth Apollo caused it to emerge from the sea to provide a refuge for the Argonauts on their return voyage from Kolkhis. The inhabitants earn a modest subsistence by farming and some fishing.

A typical Cycladic village on Anáfi

On the south side of the island is its chief place, Anáfi (Khóra), which is now increasingly being abandoned by its inhabitants. Above the village, on a spur of rock, are remains of a 14th c. Venetian castle.

North-east of Khóra, on the round-topped hill of Kastélli, is the site of the ancient city, with remains of walls and fragments of sculpture.

At the east end of the island is the Monastery of Zoodókhos Piyí or Káto Kalamiótissa, built with stones from a Temple of Apollo which had previously occupied the site. Farther north are the ruins of another Venetian castle.

At the extreme eastern tip of the island, prominently situated on a limestone crag (Mount Kálamos, 396 m (1299 ft)) falling sheer down to the sea, is the little Church of Panayía Kalamiótissa (1715). From the top of the hill there are far-ranging views, extending in clear weather to Crete.

South-east of Anáfi are the rocky islets of Ftená, Pakhiá and Makrá.

Andros Ἄνδρος/Ándros   D4

Island group: Cyclades
Nomos: Cyclades
Area: 374 sq. km (144 sq. miles)
Altitude: 0–994 m (0–3261 ft)
Population: 10,500
Chief place: Ándros (Khóra)

Daily from Rafína (Attica).

Boat services

The thickly wooded island of Ándros, the most northerly and, after Náxos, the largest of the Cyclades, is a kind of south-easterly continuation of Euboea, from which it is separated by the busy but sometimes stormy Pórthmos Kafiréfs, a channel some 12 km (7½ miles) wide. To the south-east, beyond the narrow Stenó Channel (1200 m (1300 yd) wide), is the island of Tínos. In the island's four ranges of hills, the highest of which is Mount Pétalon (994 m (3261 ft)), are marble quarries which were already being worked in antiquity. Thanks to its unusual abundance of water Ándros has a flourishing agriculture. It is the home island of several large shipowners.

Situation and characteristics

In antiquity the island was sacred to Dionysos, and its festivals in his honour were widely famed. Originally settled by Ionians, Ándros came under the control of Erétria at an early stage. In the 7th c. B.C. it sent settlers to Chalcidice (Thrace). After the Battle of Salamís, when it had supported the Persians, it was unsuccessfully besieged by Themistokles. Later it became an ally of Athens; then in 338 B.C. it fell into the hands of the Macedonians, and thereafter became Roman.

From A.D. 1207 Ándros was ruled by Venetian dynasts, who built the watch-towers still to be seen on the island. At the beginning of the 15th c. Albanian incomers settled in the north of the island, preserving their language into the 20th c. In 1566 Ándros was occupied by the Turks, and remained in Turkish hands until the establishment of the Greek State in the 19th c.

Myth and history

Sights

Ándros (Khóra)

The chief place on the island, Ándros or Khóra (pop. 2000), lies in the middle bay on the east coast, which offers little shelter for shipping. From the harbour a picturesque flight of steps leads up to the old part of the town, on a rocky promontory, with the ruins of a Venetian castle. Extending inland is the newer part of the town with its broad and busy main stret and its market square. The main features of interest are the Orthodox Church of Zoodókhos Piyí (iconostasis of 1717), the Catholic Church of St Andrew (15th c., rebuilt in 18th c.) and the little Maritime Museum.

'Zoodókhos Piyí

5 km (3 miles) north-west of Khóra is the Apíkia Spring, the source of "Sáriza" mineral water.

Mesariá

5 km (3 miles) west of Khóra, in the fertile Mesariá Valley with its picturesque old dovecots, lies the attractive village of Mesariá. The church dates from 1158.

Kórthion

10 km (6 miles) south of Khóra is Kórthion, with a Venetian castle.

The ancient capital of the island, which flourished into Byzantine times, lay 16 km (10 miles) west of present-day Ándros at the little village of Palaiópolis, in a wide bay on the west coast. There are remains of the acropolis, the harbour, etc.

Palaiópolis

Gávrion

In sheltered Gávrion Bay is the fishing village of Gávrion, with the island's main harbour. There was a harbour here in late antiquity, and remains of the medieval harbour can be seen at the Monastery of Ayía Moní. 2 km (1¼ miles) north-west, at the village of Ayios Pétros, is a Hellenistic watch-tower (beautiful view).

Batsí

8 km (5 miles) south east of Gávrion we come to the seaside resort of Batsí, from which Mount Kouvári (975 m (3199 ft)) can be climbed (4–5 hours).

Argolic Islands   'Αργολιχαὶ Νῆσοι/Argolikaí/Nísi   D3

The Argolic Islands are the islands off the coast of the Argolid and in the Argolic Gulf. They include Hydra (see entry), Dokós, Spétsai (see entry), the smaller islands of Tríkeri, Psilí and Platía, and numerous isolated rocks and stacks. They are the most southerly and most westerly group of the Saronic Islands (see entry).

Arki   'Αρχοί/Arkí   D5

Region: Aegean Islands
Island group: Southern Sporades
Nomos: Dodecanese
Area: 7 sq. km (2¾ sq. miles)
Altitude: 0–115 m (0–377 ft)
Population: 50
Chief place: Arkí (Khóra)

Boat services

Occasional service from Pátmos and Lipsí.

Situation and characteristics

The barren and desolate island of Arkí (ancient Akrite) lies 12 km (7½ miles) north-east of Pátmos. The few inhabitants live in primitive conditions, without any modern infrastructure, gaining a modest subsistence from farming and fishing. Round Arkí are numbers of smaller islets, some of which are used for the grazing of goats.

Astypalaia 'Αστνπάλαια/Astipálaia   D5

Region: Aegean Islands
Island group: Dodecanese
Nomos: Dodecanese
Area: 99 sq. km (38 sq. miles)
Altitude: 0–482 m (0–1581 ft)
Population: 1100
Chief place: Astypálaia (Khóra)

Regular service twice a week from Athens (Piraeus); local services in the Dodecanese (Kos – Kálymnos – Astypálaia), weekly.

Boat services

The arid karstic island of Astypálaia, the most westerly in the Dodecanese, lying between Kos (40 km (25 miles)), Amorgós (35 km (22 miles)) and Anáfi (40 km (25 miles)), shows clear affinities in both landscape and culture with the Cyclades. Two wide bays on the north-west and south-east sides divide the island into a higher western half (up to 482 m (1581 ft)) and a lower eastern half (up to 366 m (1201 ft)), joined by the Ayios Andréas Isthmus, which is only 110 m (120 yd) wide. Stock-farming (cheese), fruit- and vegetable-growing and fishing bring the inhabitants a modest degree of well-being.

Situation and characteristics

Astypálaia

Sights

Astypálaia (Khóra)

The picturesque village of Astypálaia (Khóra), dominated by a Venetian castle (13th–16th c.), is situated on a bare rocky hill above its little port of Skála.

Livádia Valley

Below Khóra, to the west, is the fertile Livádia Valley, the island's main agricultural area.

Scattered over the island are some 200 little churches and chapels, most of them founded by private citizens and many of them in a state of disrepair.

Some of the many neighbouring rocky islets are used for the grazing of goats, as are the lonely islets of Seírena and Tría Nisía, 35–45 km (22–28 miles) to the south-east.

Athens   'Aθῆναι/Athínai   C/D3

Region: Central Greece
Nomos: Attica
Altitude: 40–150 m (130–490 ft)
Population: 3,030,000

Since many trips to the Greek Islands will start from Athens the city's principal sights are described in this guide. The description has been deliberately kept short, however, since a fuller account is availabe in the Athens city guide in this series.

Situation and characteristics

Athens, a city which has grown enormously since it became capital of Greece in 1834 – when it had a population of only 6000 – lies on the north side of the Gulf of Aegina (Saronic Gulf), extending over the main plain of Attica, which is bounded on the north and west by Mounts Párnis and Aigaleos, on the north-east by Mount Pentéli (ancient Pentélikon, famous for its Pentelic marble) and on the east and south-east by Mount Imittós (Hymettos) and is watered by the rivers Kifissos and Ilissos.

Modern Athens, like the ancient city, is a great intellectual and artistic centre, and with its port of Piraeus (see entry) is also the economic centre of Greece. Its importance in the life of the country is indicated by the fact that almost a quarter of the total population of Greece live within the conurbation of Athens.

Culture and art

With its University, College of Technology, Academy of Sciences, Commercial College and Academy of Art, Athens is the cultural centre of Greece. It has several libraries and eight theatres, which provide a varied repertoire, and the annual Athens Festival (July–September) offers a full programme of opera, drama and music. The city's many museums and galleries cater for a wide range of interests – the world of ancient Greece, Byzantine culture, art, natural history.

Commerce and industry

Athens is a great commercial and industrial centre, with the headquarters of all the country's banks, most of its business firms and shipping lines and many insurance corporations. Major contributions are made to the economy by the industrial installations round the Bay of Eleusis and by the port of Piraeus. The tourist trade also plays an important part in the city's economy. The attractions for visitors include not only the

The Acropolis, landmark and emblem of Athens ▶

ancient remains in and around Athens but the popular resorts in the Saronic Gulf.

Transport

The international and domestic airport, the coach services to all parts of Greece, the rail system and the shipping lines centred on Piraeus make Athens the focal point for travel anywhere in Greece.

In recent years traffic conditions within the city have become chaotic, making a major contribution to the perennial problem of air pollution.

History

Finds on the southern slope of the Acropolis have shown that the history of Athens goes back to the 3rd millennium B.C. The union (synoecism) of the various settlements in Attica under the leadership of Athens was traditionally believed to have been achieved by a king, Theseus, in the 10th c. B.C.; but this early period in the history of Athens remains completely obscure. All that is known is that during the 8th and 7th c. B.C. monarchy gradually gave place to aristocratic rule, the functions of the king being taken over by archons appointed annually.

During the 7th c. B.C. severe social tension in Athens were temporarily resolved by the reforms of the great legislator Solon (594–593 B.C.), but after his death they broke out again, leading to the establishment of the tyranny (rule by a single ruler) of Peisistratos and his sons (560–510 B.C.). During this period the power of the aristocracy was weakened – an important precondition for the emergence of democracy in Attica. A further decisive step in this development was represented by the reforms of Kleisthenes (508–507 B.C.).

Under the leadership of Themistokles the city emerged victorious from the Persian Wars (500–479 B.C.), during which it supported the Greek cities in Asia Minor. After the system of Attic democracy was finally established by the reforms of Ephialtes (462–461 B.C.) the way was clear for Athens to become the leading economic and cultural force in Greece. It reached its peak in the time of Perikles, who was elected strategos (general) almost continuously from 443 to 429 B.C., and it was during this period that the great buildings on the Acropolis were erected.

The Peloponnesian War (431–404 B.C.) was a grave setback for Athens, which now lost the leadership of Greece to Sparta. In 371 B.C. it shook off the hegemony of Sparta, but from 338 B.C. onwards it fell increasingly under Macedonian control. In subsequent centuries Athens was no longer of any political significance.

Athens fell to the Romans under the leadership of Sulla in 86 B.C. Other splendid buildings were erected in Athens by the Emperors, particularly by Hadrian. This period of renewed prosperity, however, was brought to a sudden end in A.D. 267 when the city was captured and looted by the Heruli, an East Germanic people. In the Age of the Great Migrations it was plundered by Alaric's Goths (A.D. 395) and other raiders, and thereafter declined into a provincial town of no consequence in the East Roman and later the Byzantine Empire.

In the 13th c. Athens had a further brief period of prosperity under Frankish rule, then in 1458 it was captured by the Ottomans, and thereafter remained Turkish until the 19th c. After the achievement of Greek independence in 1834 the city regained importance as capital of the new kingdom of Greece and the residence of the King. Subsequent decades saw the planned development of Athens into a modern city and a rapid increase in population.

Between 1923 and 1928, as a result of the war with Turkey, some 300,000 refugees from Asia Minor flocked to Athens, creating serious problems and leading to a considerable extension of the city. Athens and Piraeus have long formed a single conurbation, and Greater Athens, with its 9 city wards and 38 outer communes, now extends far into the Plain of Attica.

Ancient Athens

**Acropolis

The limestone crag of the Acropolis, situated in the middle of the Plain of Attica, was a site well suited for the "upper city", originally a royal fortress and a precinct enclosing the most ancient shrines of Athens. In 480–479 B.C. the buildings of the early period were destroyed by the Persians. The walls were rebuilt by Themistokles and Kimon, and the great building programme carried out by Perikles gave the Acropolis the architectural splendour which can still be recognised today.

In recent years the buildings that have survived so many centuries have increasingly been destroyed by exhaust fumes and other forms of air pollution and by the 3,000,000 visitors who tramp over the Acropolis every year. It remains to be seen whether the Unesco conservation programme will make it possible to preserve this incomparable monument of antiquity.

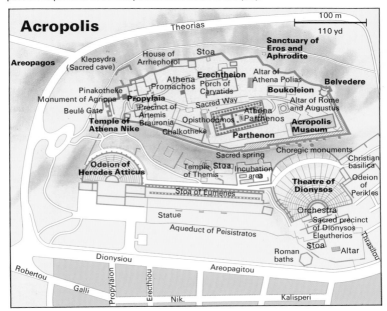

Athens

The Parthenon, a master-work by Iktinos and Pheidias

Beulé Gate

The Acropolis is now entered by the Beulé Gate (ticket-office), built after the Herulian raid of A.D. 267, using stone from destroyed buildings.

Propylaia

From the Beulé Gate a flight of marble steps, now largely destroyed, led up to the Propylaia, built by Mnesikles in 437–432 B.C. He had conceived a monumental and symmetrical structure consisting of three wings, but the original plan had to be modified to take account of the old Temple of Athena Nike on the projecting spur of rock to the right, the Pyrgos of Nike. The central structure consists of a portal with five gateways, increasing in width and height towards the centre. The architrave of the central gateway is extended by the addition of a metope – a device used here for the first time. In front of the portal is a deep vestibule with six Doric columns along the front and six slender Ionic columns flanking the central carriageway. On the far side is a shorter and lower portico, also with six Doric columns.

The west portico was flanked by side wings. On the left was the Pinakotheke, which housed a collection of pictures; on the right was a vestibule giving access to the Temple of Athena Nike.

*Temple of Athena Nike

The Temple of Athena the Bringer of Victory, built in 432–421 B.C., had four Ionic columns at each end. In front of the little temple the remains of the altar can be identified, and opposite this a fragment of the Mycenaean defensive walls.

**Parthenon

Beyond the Propylaia the bare rock of the Acropolis rises in a gentle slope. Numerous cuttings in the rock mark the positions

Detail from the Parthenon

of the cult images and votive monuments which once stood here. Passing the Sanctuary of Artemis Brauronia and the Chalkotheke, in which works of art in bronze were kept, we come finally to the Parthenon, at present in course of restoration and part rebuilding.

The Temple of the Maiden Athena (Athena Parthenos) was built between 447 and 438 B.C., the master-work of Iktinos and Pheidias, to whom Perikles had entrusted the overall direction of the building work on the Acropolis. Building had previously begun on an earlier Parthenon, standing on a substructure up to 10·75 m (35 ft) high, and some of the material prepared for it (column drums, metopes) was used in the construction of the new temple on a different plan. As can be seen from the foundations of this "Pre-Parthenon" on the south side, the earlier temple was narrower and extended farther east.

The new Parthenon was larger than the earlier one, with 8 columns instead of 6 at each end and 17 instead of 16 along the sides. Its Doric columns are 10·43 m (34 ft) high, with a diameter at the base of 1·90 m (6 ft 3 in) and at the top of 1·48 m (4 ft 10 in). The columns have a distinct swelling in the middle (known as entasis), while the substructure shows a gentle curve, rising in the middle – both features designed to avoid any impression of heaviness or rigidity.

The architraves and pediments of the Parthenon were splendidly decorated with sculpture (most of it now in the British Museum, with some pieces in the Acropolis Museum and some in the Louvre). The 92 metopes depicted a battle of giants (east), a fight with centaurs (south), fighting with Amazons (west) and the Trojan War (north). The pediments (completed in 432 B.C.) depicted the birth of Athena from Zeus' head (east end) and the contest between Athena and Poseidon for the possession of Attica (west end). The frieze, 1 m (3 ft) high and 160 m (525 ft) long, which extended along the top of the outer wall of the cella was devoted not to a historical or mythological scene but to one of the great ceremonial occasions in Athenian life, the procession which made its way up to the Acropolis on the Panathenaic Festival. On the west side of the Parthenon the frieze, badly weathered is still *in situ*. The interior of the temple (now closed to visitors) is in two parts. The western half, with a roof borne on four Ionic columns, housed the State Treasury. In the eastern half stood Pheidias' chryselephantine statue of Athena Parthenos, which was surrounded on three sides by a two-storey colonnade.

Temple of Rome and Augustus

Outside the east end of the Parthenon stood a round Temple of Rome and Augustus dating from the Early Imperial period, with decorative forms modelled on the Erechtheion.

**Erechtheion

The Erechtheion, on the north side of the Acropolis, was built between 421 and 406 B.C. It has a complex ground-plan, since it had to be accommodated to a number of earlier shrines on the site. At the east end was the temple housing the old wooden cult image of Athena Polias, patroness of Athens; at the west end were the Tomb of Erechtheus, the Tomb of Kekrops, first King of Attica – below the Porch of the Caryatids which projects on the south side, its entablature borne by six figures of maidens (now replaced by copies) – and, in the floor of the north porch, the marks left by Poseidon's trident. The east and north porches each have six Ionic columns. On the cella wall, above a band of elegant palmette ornament, is a frieze of grey Eleusinian marble on which white marble figures were applied. The thorough restoration of the Erechtheion which has been in progress for some years is now almost complete.

Old Temple of Athena

Immediately south of the Erechtheion can be seen the foundations of the old Temple of Athena, also known as the Hekatompedon, built at the beginning of the 6th c. B.C. on the site of the Mycenaean palace (from which two column bases survive).

**Acropolis Museum

The Acropolis Museum, built in 1949–53 and inconspicuously sited low down at the south-east corner of the Acropolis, contains one of the world's finest collections of Greek sculpture. The left-hand end contains material of the Archaic period (6th c. B.C.) recovered by excavation in 1885–86 – pediments of temples and treasuries, votive statues and, extending into the right-hand end, figures from the marble pediment of the old Temple of Athena (Rooms I–V). The other rooms (VI–XI) are mainly devoted to sculpture of the classical period (5th c. B.C.).

*Theatre of Dionysos

In association with the cult of Dionysos – the god of drunkenness, of transformation, of ecstasy and the mask – the Theatre of Dionysos was built in a natural hollow on the south side of the Acropolis. Although the earliest of the theatre's nine building phases is dated to the 6th c. B.C. the tiers of stone seating (accommodating some 17,000 spectators) which are still to be seen date only from about 330 B.C. In the front row are seats of honour for the priests, identified by inscriptions, and above these is a throne for the Emperor Hadrian (A.D. 117–138). The orchestra is paved with marble slabs and is surrounded by a stone barrier to provide protection from the wild beasts which took part in shows during the Roman period. The stage building on the south side was several times reconstructed. Here there are striking reliefs of Dionysiac scenes.

The Theatre of Dionysos, in which the earliest tragedies – the works of Aeschylus, Sophocles and Euripides – were performed, can be seen as the place of origin of the European theatre.

Stoa of Eumenes

Adjoining the Theatre of Dionysos on the west is the 163 m (535 ft) long Stoa of Eumenes, built by King Eumenes II of Pergamon (197–159 B.C.). It differed from the Stoa of Attalos (see entry) in having no rooms behind the double-aisled colonnade. It was thus not designed for the purposes of business but was merely a spacious promenade for visitors to the temple and Theatre of Dionysos.

*Odeion of Herodes Atticus

At the west end of the group of imposing buildings on the south side of the Acropolis stands the Odeion of Herodes Atticus, built by the great art patron of that name in A.D. 161 after the death of his wife. Its proximity to the Theatre of Dionysos provides a convenient demonstration of the differences between the Greek and the Roman theatre. In a Roman theatre the auditorium was exactly semicircular, while in a Greek one it extended round more than semicircle; the side entrances were vaulted over and the stage, which in the later period was raised, was backed by an elaborate stage wall of several tiers, lavishly decorated with columns and statues.

The 32 steeply raked tiers of seating, which can accommodate an audience of some 5000, have recently been refaced with white marble, and the Odeion is now used for dramatic performances and concerts during the Athens Festival in summer.

Asklepieion

On a narrow terrace above the Stoa of Eumenes and immediately under the precipitous rock face of the Acropolis is the Asklepiein, the shrine of the healing god Asklepios (Aesculapius), established here in 420 B.C., when the cult of Asklepios was brought to Athens from Epidauros. The sanctuary is centred on two springs.

Areopagos

To the west of the Acropolis is the Areopagos (115 m (377 ft)), on which the ancient judicial council of that name used to meet. It was here, on Mars' Hill, that the Apostle Paul addressed the men of Athens (Acts 17:22 ff.).

*Agora

To the north of the Acropolis lay a number of large open squares. Notable among these was the Agora, which was not only the city's market square but, from the 6th c. B.C. onwards, the centre of civic life, embellished over the centuries with a succession of new colonnades and stoas, temples and other buildings.

Panathenaic Way

The Panathenaic Way, still retaining some of its original paving, cuts diagonally across the Agora. This was the route followed by the great Panathenaic procession on its way from the Kerameikos quarter (see entry) to the Acropolis.

Stoa of Attalos and *Agora Museum

Conspicuous on the east side of the Agora stands the 116 m (380 ft) long Stoa of Attalos, faithfully reconstructed at American expense in 1953–56. It is two-storeyed, with Doric columns on ground-level and Ionic columns on the upper level. It now houses the Agora Museum. The most striking feature is a colossal statue of Apollo Patroos. The long main hall displays a large collection of material, most of it notable not so much for its artistic quality as for the evidence it gives of life in ancient Athens.

Odeion of Agrippa

A well-preserved Corinthian capital of considerable size marks the position of the Odeion of Agrippa, in the centre of the Agora. Built about 20 B.C. by the Roman General Agrippa, it was a square building with a stage and 18 tiers of seating which could accommodate an audience of 1000 (some remains of the seating have been preserved). The original building was

Panorama of Athens, with the Stoa of Attalos and the Hill of the Nymphs

destroyed by the Heruli in A.D. 267, and a Gymnasion was built on the site about A.D. 400.

One of the most important buildings on the west side of the Agora was the Tholos, a circular building 18·30 m (60 ft) in diameter which housed the sacred hearth.

Tholos

To the north of the Tholos is the Metroon (Sanctuary of the Great Mother), with the Bouleuterion (Council Chamber; 5th c. B.C.) to its rear. In the 2nd c. B.C. a colonnade was built in front of the vestibule of the Bouleuterion and the Metroon in order to unify the façade facing the Agora.

Metroon
Bouleuterion

The next building, also surviving only in the form of foundations, is the Temple of Apollo Patroos (4th c. B.C.), the cult image from which is now in the Stoa of Attalos.

Temple of Apollo Patroos

Immediately beyond the temple, extending to the Piraeus railway line, is the Stoa of Zeus (5th c.), in a style reminiscent of the Propylaia on the Acropolis.

Stoa of Zeus

Recent excavations on the north side of the railway have brought to light the Royal Stoa (mid 6th c. B.C.), seat of the Archon Basileus who took over the cultic functions of the kings. This may have been the scene of Sokrates' trial in 399 B.C., when he was condemned to death by drinking hemlock.

Royal Stoa

Medieval Athens – (see entry)

Ayii Apóstoli

On a low hill on the west side of the Agora stands the Temple of Hephaistos, often wrongly called the Theseion.

**Temple of Hephaistos

The building of the temple was begun about 449 B.C. Its almost perfect state of preservation is due to its conversion, in Christian times, into a church dedicated to St George. This Doric peripteral temple, with 6 by 13 columns, was built about the same time as the Parthenon but is considerably smaller. Unusual features are the extension of the porch and pronaos at the east end by two bays each and the porch and opisthodomos at the west end by one and a half bays each. The east end is also given greater emphasis by carved metopes on the outside wall and by a frieze on the pronaos which is carried across into the north and south peristyles. The cella contained cult images of Hephaistos and Athena by Alkamenes (420 B.C.). In a later building phase, following the model of the Parthenon, columns were set round the side and rear walls of the cella, creating a rather cramped effect.

When the temple was converted into a church a new entrance was broken through the rear wall of the cella and the original timber roof was replaced by the present barrel-vaulted stone roof.

Roman Market

On the east side of the Agora is the beginning of an ancient road which led to the Roman Market. Unlike the Agora, which grew and developed over the centuries, the Roman Market was laid out on a unified plan within a rectangular area measuring 112 m (367 ft) by 96 m (315 ft).

During the Turkish period a mosque, the Fethiye Camii, was built on the north side of the market; this now serves as an archaeological store.

Mosque

Just beyond the east end of the Roman Market is the octagonal Tower of the Winds (c. 40 B.C.), which housed a water-clock.

Tower of the Winds

National Archaeological Museum
Omonia

Deutsch
Arch
Insti

Kolou
Menandru
Sokratus
Eolu
Stadiu
Veniz

Alesilau
Town Hall   Kotzia

Sophokleus
Pireos
Athinas

Eleftheria
Evripidu
Market
Sophokleus

Dipilu
Sari
**Ajios
Athanasios**
Kyriaki
**Ministry of
Interior**

Al. Anargiron
Palados
Ajios Chrysospel
Evripidu
Praxitelus
Ajii Theodori
Klafth-
monos
City Museum

KERAMEIKOS
Sari
Athinas
Eolu

Ajii Asomati
Karaiskaki
Ajios Jeorji

Ermu
Kolokotroni

**Theseion
Station**
Ajia Irini
Lekka
Perikleus

**Monastiraki
Church**
Ermu
Athinaidos

**Stoa of
Zeus**
Adrianu
**Folk Art
Museum**
Kapnikarea
Ermu

**Hephaisteion
(Theseion)**
**Temple of
Ares**
**Stoa des
Attalos**
**Library of
Hadrian**

Metróon
Mitropolis

Buleuterion
Odeion
Yrissakiu
Mikri Mitropolis
Apollonos

A g o r a
Roman Market
Ajii Apostoli
**Tower
of Winds**
Ajios Andreas

Nikodimu

Pritaniu
Flessa

**Kanellopulos-
Museum**
P L A K A

Metamorphosis
Sotir tu Ko

Hill of Nymphs
Tripodon
Kidathine

Areopagos
Beulé Gate **Propyläen**
Erechtheion
Ajios Jeorji os

Apostolu
Temple of Nike
Acropolis
Museum
Ajia Ekaterini

Pavlu
Phyx
**Odeion of
Herodes
Atticus**
Parthenon
**Monument of
Lysikrates**
Lissikratus

Thespidos
Virronos

**Theatre of
Dionysos**
**Arch o
Hadria**

**Ajios Dimitrios
Lombardiaris**
Dionissiu
Areopajitu

Rov. Galli

© *Baedeker*

===== Presumed line of ancient walls

Airport, Soú

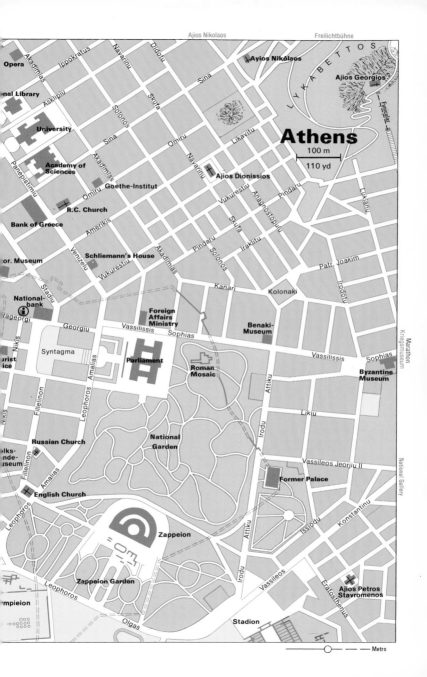

Athens

100 m
110 yd

It owes its present name to the carved representations of the eight wind gods below the cornice.

Hadrian's Library

Parallel to the Roman Market, only 16 m (52 ft) away, can be found another complex of similar character but different function – Hadrian's Library, founded by the Emperor of that name in A.D. 132. At the west end is a handsome Corinthian propylon. The courtyard was laid out as a garden, with a central pool, over which the Church of Megáli Panayía was built in the 5th c.

Kerameikos

Bordering the Agora on the north-west was the potters' quarter of ancient Athens, named Kerameikos (hence the modern term ceramics) after Keramos, the patron of potters.
From the 12th c. B.C. this area, on both sides of the little River Eridanos, was used for burial, and a continuous sequence of tombs can be traced from sub-Mycenaean times to late antiquity.

*Museum

The Kerameikos Museum, near the entrance to the site, displays the most recent finds; material recovered in earlier excavations is in the National Archaeological Museum (see entry). Of particular interest is the large collection of pottery, which illustrates the history of the area and the development of Greek pottery.

Excavated area

The excavated area is traversed by three roads – the road to the Academy, the Sacred Way to Eleusis and the Street of Tombs. Along all three roads are numerous funerary monuments – single tombs, burial precincts and terraces of tombs (some original, some copies). The most notable tombs date from the 5th and 4th c. B.C.

Dipylon, Sacred Gate

At this point there are two gates through the Themistoclean walls of Athens, the Dipylon and the Sacred Gate.
The more northerly of the two, and architecturally the more impressive, is the Dipylon the largest of the city gates of ancient Athens. As its name (Double Gate) indicates, it consists of two gates with an enclosed court between them. On the inner side of the gate can be seen an altar dedicated to Zeus, Hermes and Akamas and a fountain-house.

Pompeion

Between the Dipylon and the Sacred Gate a Gymnasion was built in the 5th c. B.C., known as the Pompeion after the procession (pompe) which formed up here during the Panathenaic Festival. Destroyed by Sulla in 86 B.C., it was replaced in the 2nd c. A.D. by a three-aisled hall, which in turn was destroyed by the Heruli in A.D. 267.

*Olympieion

The area to the east of the Acropolis is dominated by the largest temple in Athens, the Olympieion. It was begun in the time of the Peisistratids but left unfinished. Work was resumed by the

Seleucid Antiochos IV (175–164 B.C.), but the building was completed only in the reign of Hadrian, about A.D. 130.

From the entrance to the site a number of column drums from the temple of the Peisistratid period can be seen to the north, in the old defensive ditch of Athens. Farther west are the remains of Roman baths. Through the partly reconstructed propylon we enter the large rectangular precinct in which the temple stands. Although most of the original 104 columns have disappeared, the surviving remains – a group of 13 columns and part of the entablature at the south-east corner, two isolated columns on the south side and another column which collapsed in 1852 – are still of imposing grandeur.

Below the south wall of the temple precinct, in an excavated area on a lower level, the foundations of the Temple of Apollo Delphinios can be traced.

Delphinion

Hadrian's Arch

Immediately west of the Olympieion is Hadrian's Arch (A.D. 131–132), which marks the boundary between the "city of Theseus" and the "city of Hadrian", as an inscription on the arch records.

Monument of Lysikrates

In a little square at the far end of Lysikrates Street stands the Monument of Lysikrates, a rotunda 6·50 m (21 ft) high surrounded by Corinthian columns. The frieze round the top depicts scenes from the life of Dionysos. The stone acanthus flower on the roof originally bore a bronze tripod, the prize received by Lysikrates when the choir which he had financed was victorious in the tragedy competition in 334 B.C.

*Stadion

To the east of the Olympieion, between two hills, lies the Stadion. Although this large marble structure, with seating for 70,000 spectators, is modern (rebuilt for the first Olympic Games of modern times in 1896), it has the same form and occupies the same site as its ancient predecessor, in which the Panathenaic Games were held.

Medieval Athens

Although in the Christian period Athens was a place of little importance, it has preserved a number of Early Christian and Byzantine Churches which are of considerable interest. The churches of the Middle Byzantine period are predominantly of the domed cruciform type. The ground-plan is in the form of a Greek cross (i.e. with four arms of equal length), with a central dome and sometimes smaller subsidiary domes over the arms.

A good example of this type is Ayios Nikodímos (St Nicodemus) in Filellínon Street, built, as an inscription records, in 1045. It has been a Russian Orthodox church since 1852, when the church (which had been damaged during the Wars of Liberation) was purchased by the Tsar of Russia.

Ayios Nikodímos

Athens

Kapnikaréa

The Kapnikaréa Church in Hermes (Ermoú) Street also dates from the 11th c. When this new street was laid out it was preserved from destruction through the intervention of King Ludwig I of Bavaria. It is now the University church.

Ayii Apóstoli

When the old quarter of the town on the site of the Agora was pulled down to enable excavations to be carried out the only building left standing was the Church of the Ayii Apóstoli (Holy Apostles), built in the 11th c. on the site of a semicircular nymphaeum.

Ayii Theódori
Ayía Ekateríni

Another typical 11th c. church is Ayii Theódori (SS. Theodore) in Platía Klafthmónos. In Lysikrates Street stands Ayía Ekateríni (St Catherine), which dates from the 12th or 13th c.

Ayios Ioánnis Kolóna

In Euripides (Evripídou) Street is the tiny Chapel of Ayios Ioánnis Kolóna (St John of the Column), named after a Roman column which rises above its roof. The assistance of St John the Baptist is invoked here for the cure of ailments affecting the head.

°Little and Great Mitrópolis

In Mitrópolis Square are two very different churches, the Little and the Great Mitrópolis.

The Little Mitrópolis is a 12th c. church of the greatest interest. The builder incorporated in the structure a variety of ancient and medieval fragments, including part of an ancient calendar frieze (arranged in the wrong order) over the entrance, pilaster capitals and figural reliefs.

The Great Mitrópolis (1842–62), designed by Schaubert, met the need for a suitably imposing church in the new capital of Greece. Here the principal festivals of the Greek Orthodox Church are celebrated in the presence of leading figures in the State.

Great and Little Mitrópolis

Little Mitrópolis (detail)

Two monasteries on the outskirts of Athens are of great beauty and interest.

The Monastery of Dafní, 10 km (6 miles) west of the city centre, is famed for its 11th c. mosaics. The name refers to a Shrine of Apollo, to whom the laurel (daphne) was sacred, which stood on the site. It was succeeded by an Early Christian monastery dedicated to the Dormition of the Mother of God which gave place in 1080 to the present building.

* * Dafní

Kaisarianí Monastery lies in a valley on the slopes of Mount Hymettos (Imittós) outside the eastern suburb of Kaisarianí. It has a domed cruciform church, built about the year 1000 on the site of an earlier church. The dome is borne not on the walls but on four columns with Ionic capitals, giving the interior an air of lightness. The wall-paintings are much later than the church, dating only from the 16th c.

* Kaisarianí

Modern Athens

The modern city of Athens dates from the reign of King Otto I (1834–62). The plan which was to convert a sleepy little town into the new capital of Greece was the work of a number of Germans, two Danes, a Frenchman and a Greek. The general lines of the new town to be built north of the old city were laid down in 1832–33 by a German architect, Schaubert, and his Greek friend Kleanthes.

Syntagma Square

The focal point of modern Athens is Syntagma (Constitution) Square.

On the east side of the square stands the Old Palace, built by Friedrich von Gärtner in 1834–38, which is now occupied by the Greek Parliament.

Old Palace

To the south and east of the Old Palace lies the National Garden, originally laid out by Queen Amalia, Otto I's wife.

National Garden

Adjoining the National Garden on the south is the Záppion Garden, in which is the Záppion, an exhibition hall (designed by Ernst Ziller) on a semicircular plan with a Corinthian colonnade on the main front.

Záppion Garden

Venizelos Street (University Street)

A general impression of the modern city can be gained by walking along Venizelos Street (University Street) from Syntagma Square.

On the right, fronted by loggias, is the Ilíou Mélathron, built by Ernst Ziller for Heinrich Schliemann and his Greek wife Sophia. It now houses the Schliemann Museum.

Schliemann's house

A dominant position, farther along the street, is occupied by the University, designed by the Danish architect Christian Hansen (begun 1837). In front of the entrance can be seen statues of Kapodistrias, who as Governor of Greece (1827–31) proclaimed the establishment of the University, and the writer and scholar Adamantios Korais. King Otto, who initiated the

University

building of the University, appears in a painting over the entrance, surrounded by the Muses.

The University is flanked on the right by the Academy of Art (1859–85) and on the left by the National Library (begun 1887). In front of the Academy rise two columns bearing figures of Athena and Apollo, and on either side of the steps leading up to the building are seated figures of Plato and Sokrates.

Omónia Square

The rest of University Street is made up of modern shops and offices, with occasional remnants of the two-storey neo-classical buildings of the 19th c. It ends in Omónia (Concord) Square, a busy traffic intersection with an elaborate fountain in the centre.

Pláka

The Pláka is the old part of Athens lying between the north side of the Acropolis and Hermes (Ermoú) Street and extending almost to Amalia Avenue (Leofóros Amalías). In the narrow lanes and little squares of the Pláka are a number of old churches and modest houses in neo-classical style; but, like the old tavernas, they are steadily becoming rarer as the district is increasingly taken over by the showier and noisier establishments which cater for the tourist trade.

The Museums of Athens

*National Archaeological Museum

The National Archaeological Museum in Leofóros Patissión, built by the German architect Ludwig Lange in 1860 and considerably enlarged since then, contains the world's finest collection of Greek art. It would take repeated visits to get anything approaching a complete idea of its full range and

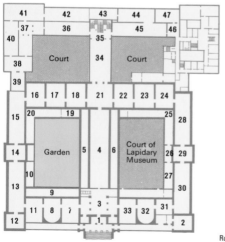

National Archaeological Museum

1 Entrance
2 Shop
3 Entrance hall
4 Mycenaean art
5 Neolithic art
6 Cycladic art
7–13 Archaic art
14, 15 First half of 5th c.
16–20 Classical period (5th c.)
   21 Diadumenos and other statues
   22 Sculpture from Epidauros
23, 24 Funerary stelae (4th c.)
25–27 Votive reliefs (4th c.)
   28 Ephebe of Antikythira
   29 Themis (3rd c.)
   30 Hellenistic art
   32 Stathatos Collection
   34 Votive reliefs
   35 Stairs to upper floor
   36 Karapanos Collection
   37 Small bronzes
   45 Bronze statues

Rooms not listed are not at present open to the public

richness, including such outstanding items as the gold mask of a Mycenaen king (Room IV), the Dipylon Vase from Kerameikos, which dates from the time of Homer (Room VII), and the two 3 m (10 ft) high kouroi from Soúnion (Room VIII).

The Byzantine Museum, in the former palace of the Duchesse de Plaisance in Leofóros Vasílissis Sofías, contains a valuable collection of Byzantine art, including large numbers of icons. The rooms on the ground floor illustrate the development of the church interior, with reconstructions of an Early Christian basilica, a Middle Byzantine domed cruciform church and a post-Byzantine chapel.

'Byzantine Museum

The Benáki Museum, in Leófóros Vasílissis Sofías, grew out of the private collection assembled by Antonios Benakis. On its three floors it displays manuscripts and icons (including two attributed to El Greco), costumes from the different regions of Greece, ancient pottery and Islamic and East Asian material.

Benáki Museum

The Historical Museum in the Old Parliament Building in Stadion Street is devoted to the history of Greece in the 18th and 19th c. The main emphasis is on the period of the struggle for the liberation of Greece (1821).

Historical Museum

The Museum of Folk Art in Kydathinéon Street gives some impression of the richness, variety and distinctive character of Greek folk art, the inheritor of Byzantine traditions (embroidery, wood-carving, painting, etc.).

Museum of Folk Art

The recently opened Museum of Cycladic and Ancient Art in Neofytou Street illustrates the distinctive Cycladic culture of the 3rd and 2nd millennia B.C. and the development of ancient Greek art from 2000 B.C. to Roman times.

Museum of Cycladic and Ancient Art

See Agora

Agora Museum

See Acropolis

Acropolis Museum

See Kerameikos

Kerameikos Museum

Surroundings of Athens

Popular places of resort, particularly in summer, are two suburbs of Athens which lie in the hills and accordingly have a very agreeable climate – Amaroússion (230 m (755 ft)) and the even more attractive Kifissiá (267 m (876 ft)). Other pleasant places to stay are Mount Párnis and Mount Pentéli, north and north-east of the city.

Amaroússion, Kifissiá

Párnis, Pentéli

A popular and attractive holiday area extends along the south coast of Attica from Athens to Cape Soúnion, 64 km (40 miles) from the capital. Cape Soúnion itself, at the south-eastern tip of Attica, is famous for its Temple of Poseidon, magnificently situated on the edge of a precipitous crag. The marble temple with its exceptionally slender Doric columns stands on a terrace, artificially enlarged, to which a propylon gave access.

''Cape Soúnion

Ayios Efstratios   ῾Αγιοζ Ένστράτιοζ/Ayios Efstrátios   C4

Region: Aegean Islands
Nomos: Lesbos
Area: 43 sq. km (16¼ sq. miles)
Altitude: 0–303 m (0–994 ft)
Population: 500
Chief place: Ayios Efstrátios

Boat services

Several times weekly Ayios Konstantínos or Kymi (Euboea) – Skópelos – Ayios Efstrátios – Lemnos; also local connections with Lemnos and Lesbos.

Situation and characteristics

Ayios Efstrátios, known in antiquity as Alonesos and in the Middle Ages as Neon (Turkish Hagiostrati), is a rocky island of volcanic origin some 30 km (19 miles) south of Lemnos. In antiquity it guarded the sea route from Athens to the islands of Lemnos and Imbros and to the Hellespont. The chief place on the island, the port of Ayios Efstrátios, lies in the largest bay on the west coast; above the village are a castle and windmills.

Ayios Yeoryios   ῾Αγιοζ Γεώργιοζ/Ayios Yeóryios   D3

Region: Central Greece
Island group: Saronic Islands
Nomos: Attica
Area: 9 sq. km (3½ sq. miles)
Altitude: 0–329 m (0–1079 ft)

Situation and characteristics

The barren rocky islet of Ayios Yeóryios (lighthouse), some 20 km (12¾ miles) south of Cape Soúnion, was used in antiquity as a penal colony, and is still a closed island.

Chíos   Χίοζ/Khíos   C4/5

Region: Aegean Islands
Nomos: Chíos
Area: 842 sq. km (325 sq. miles)
Altitude: 0–1267 m (0–4157 ft)
Population: 52,000
Chief place: Chíos

Communications

By air, several flights daily from Athens. By sea, several times a week from Athens (Piraeus); local connections with the neighbouring islands of Inoúsai and Psará. Ferry service to Çeşme (Turkey).

Situation and characteristics

The craggy island of Chíos (in Turkish Sakız Adası, Mastic Island) lies in the eastern Aegean, only 8 km (5 miles) off the Çeşme Peninsula (on the south side of the Gulf of Izmir) on the mainland of Asia Minor, from which it is separated by the Chíos Strait. Most of the island is occupied by a range of rugged limestone hills running from north to south, reaching their highest point in Mount Profítis Ilías (the ancient Mount Pellinaon; 1267 m (4157 ft)) at the north end of the island and forming impressive cliffs, particularly on the east side, as they fall steeply down to the sea.

The population is concentrated mainly in the fertile southern part of the island, where olives, vines, figs and citrus fruits are grown, in addition to the mastic tree or lentisk (*Pistacia lentiscus* L.), the source of the island's major product, the mastic gum which was already being exported in ancient times and contributed – as it still does – to the prosperity of Chíos. The aromatic resin is also used to produce mastíkha, a sweetish liqueur, and confections of rather cloying sweetness. Commerce and shipping also make important contributions to the economy of the island; roughly a third of the Greek commercial shipping fleet is based on Chíos.

The earliest archaeological evidence goes back to the 4th millennium B.C. In the 8th c. B.C. Ionian Greeks settled on Chíos and made it one of the wealthiest and most powerful members of the Panionic League, which was established about 700 B.C. In the 6th c. an important school of sculptors was active on Chíos.

From 512 to 479 B.C. the island was under Persian rule. It then joined the first Attic maritime league but was able to preserve its independence. At this period it was said to have a population of 30,000 free men and 100,000 slaves, who prospered through the wine trade, commerce and industry (producing beds and couches which were much sought after). In 412 B.C.

History

79

Chíos broke away from Athens, and in 392 it severed its alliance with Sparta. In 377 B.C. it became a member, for a brief period, of the second Attic maritime league. Under the Romans, with whom it formed an alliance in 190 B.C., it still contrived to maintain its independence.

Chíos was held by the Venetians from 1204 to 1304 and subsequently by the Genoese. It became Turkish in 1566. The island's mastic and the sweets made from it were so popular in the Sultan's harem that Chíos enjoyed a special status; no Greeks, however, were allowed to live in the citadel. The weaving of silk also contributed to the island's fame and prosperity.

Throughout their eventful history the men of Chíos were renowned for their skill in seamanship and trade. During the War of Greek Independence Chíos was sympathetic to the cause of liberation, and suffered for it when the Turks sent a punitive expedition to the island in 1822 and carried out the bloody massacres depicted in a famous painting by Delacroix. In 1881 the island was devastated by a violent earthquake. In 1912, during the Balkan War, a Greek squadron captured the island from the Turks after a brief resistance. After the First World War Chíos lost its economic hinterland on the mainland of Turkey and thereafter had to give asylum to many Greeks expelled from Asia Minor.

Sights

Chíos Town

The island's capital and principal port, Chíos (pop. 24,000), occupies approximately the same site as the ancient city, half-way down the east coast. Its houses extend in a semicircle

A sheltered harbour on Chíos

round the harbour bay, which is dominated on the north by the ruined medieval Kastro or citadel (13th–16th c.; renovation planned). Of the old town little remains; the few houses that survived the Turkish punitive expedition of 1822 were destroyed in the 1881 earthquake.

Features of interest in the modern town are the Archaeological Museum (pottery from prehistoric times onwards, coins, some sculpture), the Folk Museum and the Korais Library, the third largest in Greece (140,000 volumes), named after the Chíos-born scholar Adamantios Korais (1748–1833), who later worked in Paris.

In the fertile Kampos area to the south of the town is the mansion of the Argentis family, now open to the public. The house with its marble fountains and painted water-wheels, set in a large orange grove, gives a good idea of the way of life of the Genoese and native aristocracy.

From Chíos town a road runs north-west, through the colourful village of Karyés (5 km (3 miles)) and over a pass, to the Convent of Néa Moní, a straggling complex of buildings in a verdant setting now occupied only by a handful of nuns. The convent, founded by the Emperor Constantine IX Mono-machos (1042–55), is notable for its magnificent mosaics on a gold ground – undoubtedly the work of artists from the Imperial capital of Constantinople – which rank with those at Dafní (see Athens) and Osios Loukás near Delphi as the finest surviving examples of 11th c. religious art.

*Convent of Néa Moní

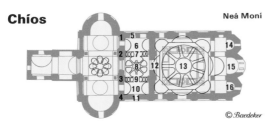

Chíos

Neá Moní

© *Baedeker*

ICONOGRAPHY

1 Symeon Stylites
2 Stylite, Isaiah, Jeremiah
3 Daniel, Ezechiel, Symeon Stylites
4 Daniel Stylites
5 Washing of the Feet
6 Before the Washing of the Feet, Entry into Jerusalem
7 Stephen the Yr, Ephraim, Arsenius, Nicetas, Antony, Maximus, John Calybites
8 Joachim, Anna, Stephen, Panteleimon, Theodore Stratelates, Bacchus, Orestes, Mardarius, Eugenius, Auxentius, Eustatius, Sergius, Mary
9 John Studites, Theodosius,
Euthymius, Menas, Pachomius, Sabbas, John Climacus
10 Pentecost
11 Gethsemane, Betrayal
12 Pantocrator
13 Nativity, Presentation in Temple, Baptism, Transfiguration, Crucifixion, Descent from Cross, Descent into Hell, Annunciation, Cherubim, John the Divine, Andrew, Luke, Bartholomew, Seraphim, Philip, Mark, Matthew, Angels, Pantocrator
14 Archangel Michael
15 Mother of God Orans
16 Archangel Gabriel

The church

The dome of the convent church is borne, like the one at Dafní, on eight piers, and spans the full width of the church, not merely the central aisle or nave. The walls still have their original facing of red marble. The mosaics were partly destroyed in the 1881 earthquake; in particular those on the dome, which collapsed, were lost. In subsequent restoration work the dome was rebuilt and the surviving mosaics made safe. Among the principal scenes are the Baptism of Christ, the Crucifixion, the Descent from the Cross and the Descent into Hell. In the main apse is the Mother of God, flanked by the archangels Michael and Gabriel in the lateral apses.

There are also fine mosaics in the esonarthex (inner porch) – the Washing of the Feet, the Mother of God with local saints, the Betrayal.

All these mosaics date from the period of the foundation of the convent (c. 1050) and are thus rather later than those at Osios Loukás and rather earlier than the mosaics at Dafní. The frescoes in the exonarthex (outer porch; among them a Last Judgment) date from the Late Byzantine period (14th c.).

The other conventual buildings were damaged during the Turkish punitive expedition in 1822, and many of them are now in a state of some dilapidation, as are the hostels for pilgrims round the convent. By the gateway of the convent is a chapel commemorating the victims of the 1822 massacre. Other features of interest are the old refectory (trápeza) and a large cistern a few yards to the right of the main gateway.

From the terrace of the new refectory, the one now used by the nuns, there is a very beautiful view.

The north of the island

Going north from Chíos town, we come in 6 km (4 miles) to the villa suburb of Vrondádes (pop. 4700). At the north end of the little town, at the Pasha's Spring (Basávrysi), near the sea, is a large block of dressed stone which was probably a Shrine of Kybele. This is popularly known as the Daskalópetra (Teacher's Stone) or Skholí Omírou (School of Homer) – recalling the island's claim to be the birthplace of Homer.

Continuing along the coast, we come to Langada (15 km (9 miles)), near which are the excavated remains of Delphinion, a strong point established by the Athenians in 412 B.C. At Kardámyla (27 km (17 miles); pop. 1300) a road branches off on the right to the little port of Mármaron (25 km (16 miles); pop. 2400; sandy beach). Beyond Kardámyla the main road continues round the north of the island, passing through Víki and the picturesque village of Kéramos to reach Ayion Gála (50 km (31 miles)).

Another road runs north-west from Kardámyla along the northern slopes of Mount Aepos to Vólyssos (40 km (25 miles)) and its port of Límnia, from which there is a motor-boat service to the island of Psará (see entry).

The south of the island

30 km (19 miles) south of Chíos town, in the centre of the mastikhokhoriá, the mastic-gum-tree-growing area, is the small town of Pyryí, a picturesque little place dominated by a Genoese castle. The 12th c. Church of the Ayii Apóstoli (frescoes) follows the pattern of the Néa Moní, which also served as a model for other churches on the island. Many of the houses have attractive sgraffito decoration.

8 km (5 miles) south-west of Pyryí lies the archaeological site of Káto Fána, with remains of a Temple of Apollo. 7 km (4½ miles) south-east is the site of Emborió. The road

north-west from Pyryí leads to the port of Ayía Anastasía or Basalimáni (43 km (27 miles) from Chíos town), from which we can return to Chíos by way of Eláta and the medieval village of Vésa.

Inoúsai Islands

To the north of the island of Chíos, at the north end of the Chíos Strait, are the Inoúsai Islands (formerly known as the Spalmatori Islands), an archipelago extending from south-east to north-west. The principal island is Inoúsai (nautical school), to the east of which are the islets of Pásas, Gaváthion and Váton, together with many isolated rocks.

South-west of Chíos, off Eláta Bay, are the little islands of Pelagonísos, Ayios Yeóryios and Ayios Stéfanos, with the remains of Hellenistic watch-towers.

Corfu Κέρχνρα/Kérkira   C1/2

Region: Ionian Islands
Island group: Ionian Islands
Nomos: Corfu (Kérkyra)
Area: 592 sq. km (229 sq. miles)
Altitude: 0–906 m (0–2973 ft)
Population: 100,000
Chief place: Corfu town (Kérkyra)

Airport 5 km (3 miles) south of Corfu town. Scheduled flights several times a day from Athens (50 minutes); regular weekly flights and many charter flights from London.

Air services

Ferry Igoumenitsa – Corfu 10 times a day; Patras – Corfu weekly; also ferry services from Italy (Brindisi, Bari, Ancona and Otranto) and Yugoslavia (Dubrovnik). Local services: Corfu – Paxí; Corfu – Erikoúsa – Mathráki – Ottonian Islands; Kefallinía (Sámi) – Ithaca – Patras.

Boat services

Corfu (Kérkyra), the most important and the most northerly of the Ionian Islands, lies only 2·5–20 km (1½–12½ miles) off the coast of Albania and the Greek region of Epirus. It offers a varied range of attractions to visitors – the beauty of its scenery, with gentle green uplands in the south and rugged limestone hills in the north, rising to 906 m (2973 ft) in the double peak of Pantokrátor, its mild climate, the southern luxuriance of its vegetations and its excellent tourist facilities and amenities. Its main economic resources are agriculture and, increasingly, the tourist and holiday trade.

Situation and characteristics

Corfu (ancient Korkyra, Corcyra) is identified as the Homeric Scheria, the land of the Phaeacians and their King Alkinoos. The oldest traces of human settlement on the island point to the presence of farming peoples who may have come from Italy. Corfu was colonised by Corinth in 734 B.C., but developed into a powerful State which threatened the mother city. A naval victory by the Corinthians over the Corcyraeans in the Sybota Islands (probably round the mouth of the River Kalamas, which is now silted up) was a major factor in the outbreak of the Peloponnesian War. In 229 B.C. the island was captured by

Myth and history

83

Rome, and when the Empire was finally split in two in A.D. 395 became part of the Byzantine Empire.

The medieval name of the island, now the accepted English name, is believed to be derived from the Greek Koryphi (Peaks). From 1386 to 1797 Corfu was held by Venice; thereafter it was briefly part of the Napoleonic empire; and in 1815, together with the rest of the Ionian Islands, it was assigned to Britain. It was reunited with Greece in 1864.

In the course of its eventful history the island was frequently devastated and plundered, so that it has preserved few relics of ancient or medieval times.

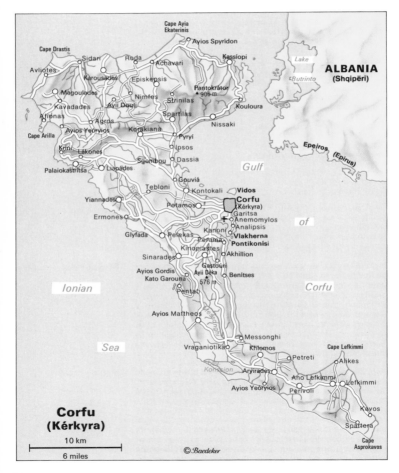

Corfu (Kérkyra)

10 km

6 miles

© Baedeker

Vlakernai Monastery and Moúse Island (Pontikonísi)

Corfu town (Kérkyra)

The island's capital, Corfu town (Kérkyra; pop. 30,000), is beautifully situated on a promontory on the east coast, dominated by the Néo Froúrio (New Fortress). The ancient city lay farther south on the Kanóni Peninsula. Corfu is the seat of both a Greek Orthodox and a Roman Catholic archbishop.

On the north side of town lies the Harbour, above which is the massive New Fortress (16th c.). From the harbour we can go either east on the road running above the seafront (view), passing the old royal palace, or south-east along Odós Nikifórou, the town's busy main street, to the Esplanade Gardens, between the town and the Old Fortress. On the north side of the square stands the former residence of the British Governor, a neo-classical building of 1816 which later became the royal palace and now houses the Museum of Byzantine and Eastern Asiatic Art. From the east side of the Esplanade, with a monument to Count Matthias von der Schulenburg, who defended the town against the Turks in 1716, a bridge leads over an artificial canal, the contrafossa, to the rather dilapidated Old Fortress, rising in stages up a steep-sided double hill (70 m (230 ft); lighthouse) on a small islet; *son et lumiére* performances in summer.

North-west of the Esplanade is the Church of Ayios Spyrídon, which contains the silver sarcophagus of the town's patron saint (processions on Palm Sunday, Easter Saturday, 1 August and the first Sunday in November). To the north extends the old

New Fortress

*Museum of Asiatic Art

Old Fortress

Old town

town of Corfu with its narrow lanes (many silversmiths' shops) and its Venetian-style houses.

To the west of the Esplanade, in Town Hall Square, are the old Venetian theatre (1663–93), which in 1902 became the Town Hall, and the Roman Catholic Cathedral (16th c.), with a later neo-classical façade. To the west stands the former Roman Catholic Archbishop's Palace (18th c.), now occupied by the National Bank of Greece.

Archaeological Museum, with 'Gorgon Pediment

From the Esplanade Leofóros Vasiléos Konstantínou runs south, following the seafront. 200 m (220 yd) along this street, just beyond the Corfu Palace Hotel, is the Archaeological Museum; its greatest treasure is the Gorgon Pediment (c. 585 B.C.) from the Sanctuary of Artemis (see below).

Some 500 m (550 yd) farther on, off to the right in the garden of a police station, is the Tomb of Menekrates (7th or 6th c. B.C.), a low circular structure which was discovered in 1843 when the old Salvator Bastion was demolished.

The Leofóros Vasiléos Konstantínou ends at the Mon Repos bathing station, at the south-east end of the suburb of Garítsa.

Monrepos, with 'park

Some 500 m (550 yd) south, in a beautiful park, is the Villa Monrepos, in which the Duke of Edinburgh was born in 1921. To the north of the park, near the ancient harbour of Anemomylos, now silted up, is the Byzantine Church of SS. Jason and Sosipater (11th–12th c.), which incorporates stones from ancient buildings. 500 km (550 yd) farther south-west are the ruins of the Church of Ayía Kérkyra (originally

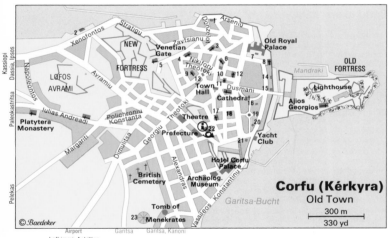

Corfu (Kérkyra)
Old Town

300 m
330 yd

© Baedeker

1 Tourist Police
2 Yacht Supply Station
3 Mitropolis (Cathedral)
4 Ayios Antonios
5 Panayía Tenedou
6 Ayios Spyrídon
7 Statue of Adam
8 Panayía Mandrakina
9 Ayii Peteres
10 Ionian Bank
11 Ayios Ioannis
12 Panayia ton Xenon
13 National Bank of Greece
14 Guilford Statue
15 Schulenburg statue
16 Enosis Monument
17 Anglican church
18 Bandstand
19 Maitland Rotunda
20 Douglas Obelisk
21 EOT, Post Office
22 Prison

Street scene in Corfu town

Beach, Glyfada

5th c.; much damaged and rebuilt), formerly the Basilican Church of Palaiopolis, on the site of the Late Hellenistic agora (2nd–1st c. B.C.). Near by are the remains of Roman baths.
1 km (¾ mile) west, beyond the Monastery of Ayios Theodóros, can be seen the scanty remains of a Sanctuary of Artemis (6th c. B.C.). The Gorgon Pediment now in the Archaeological Museum came from the west end of this temple.

From Garítsa a beautiful road (3 km (2 miles)) runs south to Kanóni (view), at the southern tip of a peninsula between the sea and Lake Khalikiópoulos, which is now largely silted up. In the bay are two little islets. On the nearer one is the Monastic Church of Vlakhérnai; to the rear is Pontikonísi (Mouse Island; Byzantine chapel), held to be the Phaeacian ship which took Odysseus back from Scheria to Ithaca and was turned to stone by Poseidon ("Odyssey", XIII, 163). On the west side of the Kanóni Peninsula is Lake Khalikiópoulos, in antiquity the island's principal harbour but now partly reclaimed (airport) and partly silted up and marshy (wild duck). Odysseus is said to have been cast ashore and discovered by Nausikaa on the south-west shore of the lake. *Kanóni

*Pontikonísi

An attractive excursion from Corfu town is to the villa of Akhíllion, 16 km (10 miles) south beyond the village of Gastoúri. This villa in Italian Renaissance style, situated at an altitude of 145 m (475 ft), was built in 1890–91 for the Empress Elisabeth of Austria (d. 1898) and bought in 1908 by Wilhelm II of Germany. It was acquired by the Greek Government in 1928 and is now a casino. It contains mementoes of its two previous owners. In the beautiful park (magnificent *Akhíllion views) are numerous statues and a miniature temple commemorating the 19th c. German poet Heinrich Heine.

Benítses

3 km (2 miles) south of the Akhíllion, at the charming fishing village of Benítses, are the remains of a Roman villa.
From here, or from the Akhíllion, the east coast road brings us back to Corfu town (17 or 20 km (10½ or 12½ miles)).

Ayii Déka

13 km (8 miles) along the road to Gastoúri a side road diverges on the right to the village of Ayii Déka (Ten Saints; 206 m (676 ft)). From here it is an hour's climb (with guide and stout footwear) to the summit of the hill of Ayii Déka (576 m (1890 ft)), from which there are fine far-ranging views.

Corfu town to Palaiokastrítsa

Leaving Corfu town, the road runs close to the coast. On a hill to the left is the old Fortress of Abramo; farther on, on the right, Lazaretto Island.
10 km (6 miles): Gouviá, with a Venetian arsenal of 1716. Beyond the village a road (20 km (12½ miles)) goes off on the right to Ipsos and Pyryí, where a road on the left leads inland to Spartílas (424 m (1391 ft)) and Strínilas; then on foot (1 hour) or on a bad road to a small rest-house, from which it is a 10

'Mount Pantokrátor

minutes' climb to the summit of Mount Pantokrátor, the highest peak on the island (906 m (2973 ft); view). On the summit of the hill is an abandoned monastery of 1347.
Beyond Pyryí the coast road follows a winding course northward, running close to the sea along the steep lower

Beach near Palaiokastrítsa

slopes of Mount Pantokrátor, with side roads to various little fishing villages and beaches. In 20 km (12½ miles) it comes to the little coastal village of Kassiópi, with the ruins of a medieval castle.

From the road fork beyond Gouviá the main road continues across the island, descends to Liapádes Bay and then climbs again.

10 km (6 miles): side road on right (3·5 km (2 miles)) to the picturesquely situated village of Lákones and, 1 km (¾ mile) farther on, the Vella Vista viewpoint.

*Bella Vista

6 km (4 miles): Palaiokastrítsa, a lively and attractive tourist resort, dominated by the Monastery of Panayía Theotokós on a high crag (view). Near the village are sea-caves. From here it is a 1½ hours' climb (with guide; stout footwear required) to the ruined Angelokástro Castle (13th c.; panoramic views); it can also be reached in half an hour on a steeper and more direct route from Kríni (10 km (6 miles) north-west of Palaiokastrítsa).

Crete Κρήτη/Kríti

E3–5

Region: Crete
Nomi: Chaniá, Réthymnon, Iráklion, Lasíthi
Area: 8331 sq. km (3217 sq. miles)
Altitude: 0–2456 m (0–8058 ft)
Population: 460,000 (about 12,000 Turks)
Chief place: Iráklion

Iráklion Airport, 5 km (3 miles) east; Chaniá Airport, 12 km (7½ miles) north-east at Stérnes on the Akrotíri Peninsula; Sitía Airport, 5 km (3 miles) north. Scheduled services several times daily Athens – Iráklion; several times weekly Rhodes – Iráklion and Salonica – Iráklion; several times daily Athens – Chaniá; several times weekly Rhodes via Kárpathos and Kásos to Sitía. Direct flights London – Iráklion.

Air services

Regular services Athens (Piraeus) to Iráklion and to Chaniá twice daily (10–14 hours; cars carried); several services weekly to Cyclades and Rhodes (via Kásos and Kárpathos).

Boat services

On the approach to Chaniá Cape Spátha (on the northern tip, remains of the Diktynaion, an ancient sanctuary) is seen on the right and Akrotíri Peninsula (known in antiquity as Kyamon) on the left. Between the two promontories extends the wide Bay of Chaniá (frequently exposed to northerly gales), with the Lefká Ori (White Mountains) to the rear. Ships anchor in the open roadsteads, the large ferries in Soúda Bay beyond the Akrotíri Peninsula – the island's only good harbour, which can provide shelter for a whole fleet in any weather.

Approach by sea

On the approach to Iráklion Cape Stávros, an important landmark, is seen on the right; on the left is the bare island of Día (known to the Venetians as Standia; 265 m (869 ft); wild goat reserve), which provides shelter in a northerly gale. Ahead can be seen Iraklion Bay, bounded on the west by Cape Panayía.

Crete (Kríti), the largest of the Greek islands and the fourth largest in the Mediterranean, lies some 100 km (60 miles)

Situation and characteristics

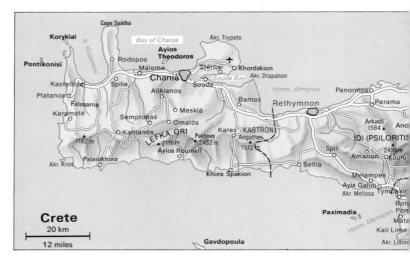

Crete

20 km

12 miles

south-east of the Peloponnese on the southern verge of the Aegean. It is the most southerly outpost of Europe and one of the main elements in the arc of islands which links southern Greece with Asia Minor. The island, celebrated for its great Minoan sites, is roughly 260 km (160 miles) long from west to east and ranges in width between 12 km (7½ miles) and 57 km (35 miles). It is broken up by three karstic mountain massifs – in the west the Lefká Ori (White Mountains; 2452 m (8045 ft)), which are usually covered with snow; in the centre the Psilorítis range (Ídi Óros, better known as Mount Ida, 2456 m (8058 ft)), which also has an abundance of snow; and in the east the Díkti range (2148 m (7048 ft)). These rugged and barren mountains are the home of the wild goat (*Capra aegagrus*), an ancestral form of the domestic goat. Agriculture is possible in these regions only in the karstic collapse depressions (poljes). Between the mountain ranges are fertile plains (Mesará; Omalós, Lasíthi), with plantations of palms, olives, bananas and oranges, vineyards and, in the south, early vegetables.

While the south coast generally falls steeply down to the sea, the north coast is flatter and more indented. On the north coast are Chaniá, Iráklion, the island's capital and its largest town, and Réthymnon, Crete's third largest town. The climate is Mediterranean, with comparatively mild and rainy winters and absolutely dry and subtropically hot summers (lasting 6–7 months). The island's main source of income is agriculture, with the tourist trade now making an increasing contribution to the economy.

History

The earliest traces of human settlement, by incomes from North Africa, date back to the 7th millennium B.C. From the 3rd millennium onwards there developed in Crete a pre-Greek Bronze Age culture which reached its peak about 2000–1600 B.C. and is known as the Minoan culture (named after the

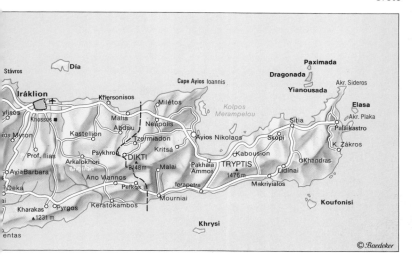

legendary King Minos). The cultural and economic influence of the Minoan kingdom – the first Mediterranean sea-power – extended as far afield as the Iberian Peninsula. Then about 1400 B.C. the Minoan civilisation suddenly collapsed. The cause of the collapse is not known; one possibility is that the Cretan cities were destroyed by a catastrophic earthquake, perhaps associated with the explosion of the volcanic island of Santorín (see entry). It is possible also that the island was devastated by invaders. But whatever the cause of the catastrophe, Crete never recovered its earlier importance.

Towards the end of the 12th c. B.C. Dorian Greeks conquered the greater part of the island. In 66 B.C. Crete was taken by the Romans, who thus gained a base of major importance in the Mediterranean. When the Roman Empire was divided into two in A.D. 395 Crete became part of the Byzantine Empire, and remained in Byzantine hands until it was taken by the Arabs in 824.

Between 961 and 1204 it was again part of the Byzantine Empire. Thereafter followed the long period of Venetian rule (1204–1669), which saw bitter struggles by the Cretans to recover their independence but also brought the island a considerable cultural flowering. The great painter and sculptor Domenikos Theotokopoulos (b. 1541 in the village of Fódele near Iráklion, d. 1614 in Toledo), better known as El Greco, lived and worked during this period.

In 1669 Crete was captured by the Turks, who held it until 1898, when they were forced out by Greek and western European military action. After a period of independence Crete was incorporated in the kingdom of Greece on 5 October 1912, through the initiative of Eleftherios Kyriakos Venizélos (1864–1936), the Cretan-born lawyer and liberal politician who later became Prime Minister of Greece.

In the spring of 1941 German airborne troops occupied the

Cretan mountain goat

91

island, which was of great strategic importance because of its situation between southern Europe and Africa. German forces were evacuated from Crete in May 1945.

Chaniá

Chaniá (pop. 55,000), chief town of the nomos of the same name, lies in the south-east corner of Chaniá Bay, which opens off the Sea of Crete on the north coast of the island. The present town, on the site of ancient Kydonia, was founded by the Venetians in the 13th c. under the name of La Canea. It suffered severe damage during the Second World War.

The old town of Chaniá is surrounded by a 3 km (2 mile) long circuit of 16th c. walls. On the north side of the town is the Venetian harbour (marina; lighthouse at end of pier), with arsenals of about 1500 (now used as boat-sheds) and remains of the old fortress. The Gothic Church of San Lorenzo now houses the Archaeological Museum (material of the Dorian period). Other features of interest are the Church of San Salvatore (16th c.), the Janissaries' Mosque (1645), a number of handsome Venetian patrician houses and the large modern Market Hall.

Old town

`San Lorenzo
Archaeological Museum

To the south of the old town are the Historical Archives (Odós I. Sfakianáki 20), with interesting manuscripts, documents, weapons and icons.

Historical Archives

1·5 km (1 mile) east of the town is the villa suburb of Khalépa, with the residence of the Prefect and various foreign consulates.

Khalépa

4 km (2½ miles) south-east of the old town is Soúda Bay, the largest and most sheltered natural harbour on the island (Chaniá's commercial harbour; naval base).

Soúda Bay

Excursions from Chaniá

8 km (5 miles) east of Chaniá on Mount Profítis Ilías are a statue of Freedom and the tombs of two men who fought for Cretan freedom, Sophokles and Eleftherios Venizélos. – 6 km (4 miles) farther east, at Maráthi, can be seen the remains of the ancient city of Minoa. – 17 km (10½ miles) north-east, on the Akrotíri Peninsula, is the Monastery of Ayía Triáda (1631), and 4 km (2½ miles) (north of this is the Monastery of Gouvernéto (16th c.), near which, on the coast, are the cave-dwelling and church of a hermit named John (Venetian façade).

Mount Profítis Ilías

Maráthi
Akrotíri

At Máleme, 16 km (10 miles), west of Chaniá, is a large German military cemetery. 21 km (13 miles) farther west, on the south side of Kísamos Bay, lies the little town of Kastélli Kisámou, from which there are attractive excursions to the ancient port of Kísamos (2 km (1¼ miles) north-west) and the island of Gramvoúsa (20 km (12½ miles)), off the peninsula of that name, at the extreme north-westerly tip of Crete; at a height of 135 m (443 ft) above the steep west coast of the island stands a 16th c. Venetian fort. Other rewarding excursions are to the ancient port town of Falasarna (9 km (5½ miles) west), with the

Máleme

Falasarna

◄ The Samariá Gorge

remains of buildings and harbour installations, tombs and rock sculptures, and to the site of the Dorian city of Polyrheneia (Polyrínia), 6 km (4 miles) south.

Kándanos

60 km (37 miles) south-west of Chaniá is Kándanos, the inhabitants of which were shot by German forces in a reprisal action during the Second World War.

**Samariá Gorge

42 km (26 miles) south of Chaniá we come to the village of Omalós, on the edge of the fertile Omalós Plateau. This is the starting-point of a 7-hour walk through the Samariá Gorge (Farángi Samariás), 18 km (11 miles) long, up to 300 m (1000 ft) deep and,at the Iron Gate (Sideroportes), only 2–3 m (6–10 ft) wide, in which the Cretan wild goat (kri-kri) can still be found. Walkers must be fit, well shod and provided with sufficient food and water. At the south end of the gorge is the village of Ayía Rouméli, from which there are boats (and a footpath) to Khóra Sfakíon (10 km (6 miles) west), with the Venetian Fort of Frangokástello or Castelfranco (14th c.). From Khóra Sfakíon the return to Chaniá (75 km (47 miles)) is by bus.

Réthymnon

Réthymnon (pop. 15,000), Crete's third largest town, lies half way between Chaniá and Iráklion on the north coast of the island, with the Psilorítis range rearing above it to the south-east. It shows an attractive mingling of different cultures, with relics of both the Venetian and the Turkish periods.

Lentas, on the south coast

The old part of the town contains many Venetian palazzos, Turkish houses with latticed wooden balconies, a number of small mosques (18th c.) and the Venetian citadel (Fortezza; 14th c., enlarged in 16th c.), with a mosque spanned by a massive dome. The 17th c. Loggia now houses the Municipal Museum.

Old town

Excursions from Réthymnon

Some 10 km (6 miles) east of Réthymnon, in the Piyí area, is the largest olive grove in the Mediterranean area, with 1,500,000 trees.

23 km (14 miles) south-east of Réthymnon are the ruins of the Early Byzantine Monastery of Arkádi, the scene of a bloody rising against the Turks in 1866.

˙Arkádi

Some 30–40 km (20–25 miles) south-east of Réthymnon, round Amári, are a number of typical Cretan villages, some of which have interesting old churches – particularly Apóstoli, Méronas, Yerakárion, Vrýses, Áno Méros and Fourfourás. In this area, too, is the Asomáton Monastery (17th c.), near which a Minoan country house has been excavated.

Still farther south-east (62 km (39 miles) from Réthymnon) lies the charming fishing village of Ayía Galíni (Holy Peace), with a beautiful beach.

36 km (22 miles) south of Réthymnon near Préveli Monastery (17th c.) is a beautiful beach.

Réthymnon

Iráklion

Iráklion (pop. 85,000), situated half-way along the north coast of Crete, is the island's administrative centre, its largest town and principal port, and the see of an Orthodox archbishop. In ancient times it was the port of Knossós, but under the Romans it declined; then in A.D. 824 it was captured by the Arabs and given a new lease of life under the name of Kandak. In 1204 it was taken by the Venetians, who called it Candia; and from 1538 onwards it was surrounded by a massive circuit of walls 5 km (3 miles) long designed by the celebrated Italian military engineer Michele Sammicheli. In the 16th and 17th c. there was an important school of painters in Iráklion, one of whom, Domenikos Theotokópoulos, was to become better known as El Greco.

Archaeological Museum

The principal features of interest in Iráklion, and one of the great tourist attractions of Crete, is the Archaeological Museum (Kretikón Mousíon) in the eastern part of the old town, which contains the magnificent finds from the palaces and houses of Knossós, Phaistós, Ayía Triáda and other sites on the island, giving a remarkable picture of its rich pre-Greek culture from the 5th millennium B.C. onwards.

Ground floor. – Section A, Room I: Neolithic (5000–2600 B.C.) and Early Minoan period (2600–2000 B.C.): stone vessels from the island of Mókhlos (north-east of Crete) and seals. – Section B, Rooms II and III: material of the Middle Minoan (Proto-Palatial) period (2000–1700 B.C.); in particular vases in Kamáres style (after the village of that name) from

Knossós, Mália and Phaistós. – Section Γ, Rooms IV, V, VII and VIII: material of the Middle Minoan (Neo-Palatial) period (1700–1450 B.C.): libation vessels, inscribed tablets, statuettes, an ivory gaming-board, jewellery. – Section Δ, Room VI: jewellery and other valuable grave-goods of the Late Minoan (Post-Palatial) period (1400–1250 B.C.). – Section Z, Room IX: Middle Minoan material from eastern Crete. – Section H, Room X: Late Minoan/Helladic material (1400–1100 B.C.). – Section Θ, Rooms XI and XII: Sub-Minoan/Geometric period (Dorian; 1100–650 B.C.) and later developments. – Section I, Room XIII: Minoan sarcophagi from Ayía Triáda, Tylisós, Gourniá, etc. – Section N, Room XIX: Archaic period (7th–6th c. B.C.). – Section Ξ, Room XX: Hellenistic and Roman sculpture (5th c. B.C.– 4th c. A.D.).

First floor. – Section K, Rooms XIV (long hall) to XVI: wall-paintings and reliefs from Minoan palaces; a magnificent stone sarcophagus from Ayía Triáda. – Section Λ, Room XVII: Giamalakis Collection of Dorian sculpture (700–500 B.C.). – Section M, Room XVIII: material of the Archaic to Roman periods (7th c. B.C.–4th c. A.D.).

**Wall-paintings
**Ayía Triáda sarcophagus

To the north of the old town is the charming Venetian harbour, with a fort on the outer breakwater. In Venizélos Square are the Morosini Fountain (1628), with 14th c. figures of lions, and St Mark's Church (1303), now housing the Museum of Byzantine Painting. Near the church, in 25th August Street,

*Morosini Fountain

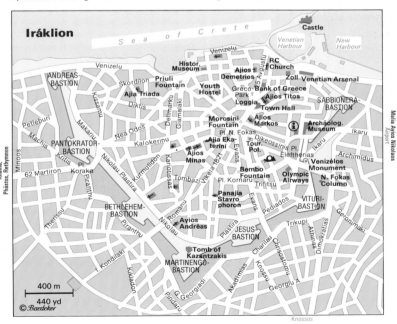

Iráklion Harbour

Treasures from Knossós: the snake goddess and a bull's-head rhyton

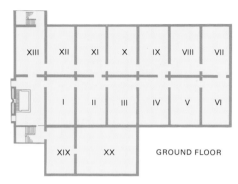

GROUND FLOOR

FIRST FLOOR

I	Neolithic and Pre-Palatial (2500–2000 B.C.)
II	Proto-Palatial: Knossós, Mália (2000–1700 B.C.)
III	Proto-Palatial: Phaistós (2000–1700 B.C.)
IV	Neo-Palatial: Knossós, Phaistós, Mália (1700–1450 B.C.)
V	Late Neo-Palatial: Knossós (1450–1400 B.C.)
VI	Neo-Palatial and Post-Palatial: Knossós, Phaistós (1400–1350 B.C.)
VII	Neo-Palatial: central Crete
VIII	Neo-Palatial: Káto Zákros (1700–1450 B.C.)
IX	Neo-Palatial: eastern Crete
X	Post-Palatial (1400–1100 B.C.)
XI	Sub-Minoan and Early Geometric (1100–800 B.C.)
XII	Late Geometric and Orientalising (800–650 B.C.)
XIII	Sarcophagi
XIX	Archaic period (7th–6th c. B.C.)
XX	Classical and late (5th c. B.C.–4th c. A.D.)

XIV–XVI	Neo-Palatial: wall paintings
XVII	Giamalakis Collection
XVIII	Archaic to Roman periods: minor arts (7th c. B.C.–4th c. A.D.)

Iráklion Archaeological Museum

which leads north to the harbour is the Venetian Loggia (1627), now the Town Hall. Close by, to the north-east, stands St Titus's Church, dedicated to the Apostle who accompanied Paul and according to tradition became the first Bishop of Crete; the Saint's skull is preserved in a reliquary.

In St Catherine's Square are the 19th c. Cathedral of St Menas and the little Church of St Catherine (18th c.), now a Museum of Sacred Art (16th c. icons by Michael Damaskinos).

The Historical Museum, in the northern part of the old town, contains examples of Cretan folk art and mementoes of the period of Turkish rule.

*Historical Museum

Knossós

5 km (3 miles) south-east of Iráklion (15 minutes by bus), near the village of Makrítíkhos, is the site of Knossós, the island's earliest capital, with the Minoan Royal Palace, which was excavated and partly reconstructed by Sir Arthur Evans (1859–1941) from 1899 onwards. This extensive complex of buildings, laid out on four levels on Mount Kefála and originally of two and three storeys, was several times destroyed, presumably by earthquakes, and subsequently rebuilt. The palace was occupied from about 2000 to 1400 B.C., and during this period three phases can be distinguished – the First Palace about 2000–1800, the Second Palace about 1800–1700 and

**Royal Palace

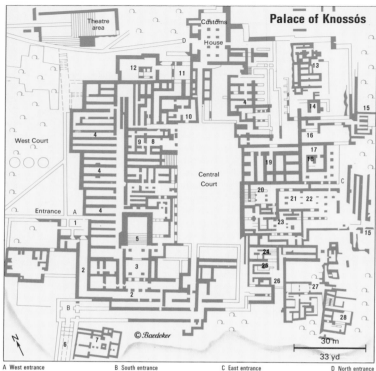

Palace of Knossós

Theatre area

Customs House

West Court

Central Court

Entrance

West Court

© Baedeker

30 m

33 yd

A West entrance   B South entrance   C East entrance   D North entrance

1 West Propylaia	9 Inner shrine	16 Workshops	24 Bathroom
2 Processional corridor	10 Prison	17 Potter's workshop	25 Shrine of the Double Axes
3 South Propylaia	11 North-west Portico	18 Lapidary's workshop	26 Lustral basin
4 Store-rooms	12 Lustral basin	19 Water channel	27 High altar
5 Grand Staircase	13 Pottery stores	20 Grand staircase	28 South-east House
6 Stepped Porch	14 Store-rooms with	21 Hall of the Double Axes	
7 South House	giant pithoi	22 King's Megaron	
8 Throne-Room	15 Bastions	23 Queen's Megaron	

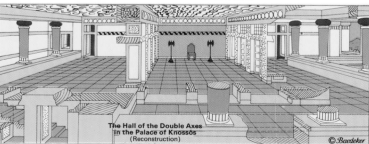

**The Hall of the Double Axes
in the Palace of Knossós**
(Reconstruction)

© Baedeker

Palace of Knossós (partly reconstructed)

the Third Palace about 1700–1400. The remains now visible belong mainly to the Third Palace, built after 1700 B.C., and although there were various alterations and enlargements in subsequent centuries the remains broadly represent the condition of the palace in the 16th c. B.C. The complicated layout of the palace provided a basis for the belief that this was the legendary Labyrinth of King Minos, particularly in view of the frequent occurrence in the palace of the double axe (labrys) which was the emblem of Minoan Crete.

Tour of the palace. – Entering the palace from the West Court (on the left, remains of a theatre), we pass along the Processional Corridor (so called from the frescoes with which it was decorated), through the South Propylaia and along a long passage with numerous store-rooms containing large pottery storage jars (pithoi) into the spacious Central Court, which may have been the scene of the contests with bulls depicted in finds from Knossós in the Archaeological Museum in Iráklion.

On the west side of the court are the Grand Staircase and the Throne Room, with a stone throne of about 2000 B.C.; on the east side are domestic offices and residential apartments, with bathrooms and flushing lavatories. Adjoining the Hall of Double Axes (named after the emblems carved on the pillars) are the King's and Queen's Apartments. The many frescoes are copies; the originals are in the Archaeological Museum in Iráklion.

Round the palace is the site of the Minoan city of Knossós, which may have had a population of up to 100,000. Most of the site is still unexcavated, but the remains of a number of villas and of the Little Palace (200 m (220 yd) north-west) can be seen.

Iráklion to Mátala via Górtys, Faistós and Ayía Triáda

Leave Iráklion on the road to Réthymnon, going west, and in 2 km (1¼ miles) take a road on the left, which in 31 km (19 miles) reaches the large village of Ayía Varvára. The road then climbs to the Askífou Pass (700m (2300 ft)) and descends (fine views) into the fertile Mesará Plain with its large plantations of olives, oranges, sugar-cane, bananas, etc.

16 km (10 miles): Ayii Déka. 1 km (¾ mile) south-east is a small archaeological museum.

°Górtys

1 km (¾ mile) farther on are the remains of the city of Górtys (Górtyn), once the rival of Knossós and later chief town of the Roman province of Crete and Cyrenaica, which survived until the Arab incursion in A.D. 826. Among the remains in the olive grove on the left of the road are the foundations of the Temple of Apollo Pythios, the palace: of the Roman Governor, with baths (2nd c. A.D.), a theatre, an amphitheatre and a circus 374 m (409 yd) long. 500 m (550 yd) beyond this, on the right of the road, below the acropolis, can be seen the ruins of the Basilica of St Titus (6th c. A.D.), the remains of an ancient theatre and a building which was converted into an Odeion (concert hall) in Roman times. Inscribed on slabs in the ambulatory of this building is the Code of Gortyn, a legal code of about 450 B.C. The text is written boustrophedon (i.e. as the ox ploughs, with alternate lines running left to right and right to left).

Excavations, Górtys

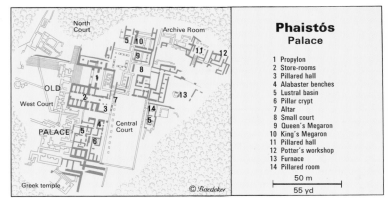

Phaistós
Palace

1 Propylon
2 Store-rooms
3 Pillared hall
4 Alabaster benches
5 Lustral basin
6 Pillar crypt
7 Altar
8 Small court
9 Queen's Megaron
10 King's Megaron
11 Pillared hall
12 Potter's workshop
13 Furnace
14 Pillared room

50 m
55 yd

14 km (8½ miles) beyond Górtys a road goes off on the left, crosses the River Yeropótamos and climbs up to the site of ancient Phaistós, a city founded by King Minos and destroyed during the 2nd millennium B.C. At the east end of the hill, laid out in terraces, is a palace of the same type as the one at Knossós. Built soon after 1650 B.C. on the site of an earlier palace of about 1800 B.C. which was destroyed a century later by an earthquake, this palace, like Knossós, was in turn destroyed by an earthquake about 1450 B.C. Of the palace buildings, which were laid out round a central court, there survive only the remains of the west and north wings, the south and east wings having collapsed in the earthquake. On the west and north sides of the surviving structures are remains of the first palace.

*Faistós (Phaistós)

The palace is entered from the west side on a monumental staircase 13·75 m (45 ft) wide leading up to the propylon. In front of this, to the left, are the tiers of seating of a theatre. From a bastion on the highest terrace there is a magnificent view of the Mesará Plain with its surrounding hills.

2 km (1¼ miles) west of Faistós, on the northern slope of the hill, are the remains of the Minoan Summer Palace of Ayía Triáda, originally linked with the Phaistós Palace by a paved road. The site takes its present name from a Byzantine chapel on a neighbouring hill; its ancient name is not known. Like Festós, it dates mainly from the 16th c. B.C., but was rebuilt after the earthquake of 1450 B.C. and was occupied until Dorian times. The frescoes and pottery recovered from the site are now mostly in the Archaeological Museum in Iráklion. From the west side of the palace there are superb views of the sea, 3 km (2 miles) away, and the south coast of Crete.

*Ayía Triáda

Higher up the hill is the Venetian Chapel of Ayios Yeóryios (14th c.; frescoes and inscriptions). Lower down, to the north-east, can be seen remains of a Late Minoan settlement (14th–11th c. B.C.). At the foot of the hill is a necropolis, with a large circular domed tomb.

10 km (6 miles) beyond Phaistós, on the south coast, is Mátala, the port of Phaistós in Minoan times and of Górtys in Roman

Mátala

times. The sandy bay is edged by cliffs containing caves which in the Early Christian period were used as burial-places and dwellings.

Other excursions from Iráklion

Amnisós

7 km (4½ miles) east of Iráklion, at Amnisós, are remains of a two-storey Minoan villa (frescoes, now in Iráklion Museum) and a harbour building, both dating from about 1660 B.C. 3 km (2 miles) farther east are the remains of another Minoan villa at the ancient port of Nírou Kháni, with a sanctuary of the double axe. There are remains of other Minoan villas at Týlisos (14 km (9 miles) south-west), Slavókampos (22 km (13½ miles) south-west) and Vathýpetro (20 km (12½ miles) south).

Nírou Kháni
Týlisos
Slavókampos
Vathýpetro

*Mount Ida

The ascent of Mount Ida (Ídi Óros; Psilorítis, 2456 m (8058 ft)) is a very rewarding but strenuous climb (warm clothing and provisions essential; guide advisable). The best approaches are from Kamáres (9 hours) by way of the Kamáres Cave (where large numbers of painted vases of the type known as Kamáres ware were found) or from Anóyia (8 hours).

On the north side of Mount Ida, at a height of 1280 m (4200 ft), is the Idéon Antron, a Minoan cult cave.

15 km (9 miles) south of Iráklion lies Arkhánes (pop. 4000), a little country town noted for its rozakí table grapes and its wine.

Ayios Nikólaos (in the foreground Lake Voulisméni)

Sporadic excavation has suggested that this was a place of some importance in Minoan times.

Ayïos Nikólaos

The little town of Ayios Nikólaos, charmingly situated on the slopes above the Gulf of Mirabello, with beautiful beaches and much of interest to see in the surrounding area, has developed into a popular tourist resort. The harbour is linked with the small inland freshwater Lake of Voulisméni, in which legend has it that the goddess Athena once bathed. Offshore is the island of Ayía Pántes (wild goat reserve).

Excursions from Ayios Nikólaos

6 km (4 miles) north of Ayios Nikólaos is the holiday village of Eloúnda, near which are remains (partly under the sea) of the Dorian city of Oloús.

*Eloúnda

Just off Eloúnda is the island of Spinalonga (originally a peninsula), at the northern tip of which is a Venetian fortress (1571; enlarged 1585), used for some years (1897 onwards) as a leper colony.

On the island of Psíra, on the east side of the Gulf of Mirabello, are remains of a Middle and Late Minoan settlement.

Psíra

Venetian fort, Spinalonga

Byzantine church, Kritsá

Mokhlós	Farther east is the island of Mokhlós, which in ancient times was joined to the mainland. Numerous tombs on this island yielded various utensils and grave-goods of the Early Minoan period which are now in the Iráklion Museum.
Dréros	22 km (13½ miles) north-west of Ayios Nikólaos and 2 km (1¼ miles) north-east of the village of Neápolis is the site of the Minoan settlement of Dréros, with a Sanctuary of Apollo (8th–7th c. B.C.; bronze cult images).
°Mália	34 km (21 miles) north-west of Ayios Nikólaos the village of Mália lies in a fertile low-lying area irrigated with the help of windmills. Near the village, which has a fine beach, are the remains of a Minoan palace similar to Knossós and Faistós but smaller in size. Built about 1800 B.C., it was rebuilt after the earthquake of about 1700 B.C. but later fell into ruin. Round the palace are remains of the Minoan city of Mália and of a necropolis.
°Lasíthi Plain	30–40 km (20–25 miles) west of Ayios Nikólaos is the fertile karstic Lasíthi Plain (850 m (2790 ft)), almost exactly circular in shape. Its 12,000 windmills (now increasingly going out of use) have earned it the name of the Valley of Windmills. On the south-western verge of the plain, near the village of Psykhrón, is the Dictaean Cave (Diktaíon Ántron), the legendary birthplace of Zeus.
°Kritsá	11 km (7 miles) south-west of Ayios Nikólaos, amid ancient olive groves, is the picturesque hill village of Kritsá. In this area

Gourniá, a Minoan town

are a number of beautiful Byzantine churches, in particular Panayía tis Kerás (12th–14th c.; frescoes) and Ayios Yeóryios (14th c.).

4 km (2½ miles) farther north-west are the overgrown remains of the city of Lato, probably built between the 7th and 4th c. B.C. From the terraces of the site and from the two acropolis hills there are magnificent views of the surrounding hills and the Gulf of Mirabello.

30 km (19 miles) south-west of Ayios Nikólaos, above a south-facing valley in the Díkti range, lies the village of Máles, with remains of the Dorian settlement of Málla. 15 km (9 miles) farther south is Mýrtos (beach), with Roman remains.

Máles

36 km (22 miles) south of Ayios Nikólaos on the south coast of Crete, in a fertile vegetable-growing area, Ierápetra, the most southerly town in Europe, occupies the site of the ancient port of Hierapydna. Venetian fort defending the harbour; small museum in the Town Hall, with material of the Roman and Venetian periods.

Ierápetra

18 km (11 miles) south-west of Ierápetra are the Gaidouronísi islands. Farther east, some 5 km (3 miles) from Cape Goudoúra, is the island of Koufonísi.

20 km (12½ miles) south-east of Ayios Nikólaos is the site (only partly excavated) of the Minoan settlement of Gourniá, which with its narrow paved lanes, small dwelling houses and palace and sanctuary on a higher level gives an excellent impression of the aspect of a town of the Late Minoan period (2600–1400 B.C.).

Gourniá

Sitía

Sitía (ancient Eteia), near the east end of the island, is a picturesque little port town (beach) dominated by a Venetian castle, with many recently built houses. Along the harbour quay can be found a string of typically Greek restaurants.

Excursions from Sitía

Ayía Fotiá Toploú Monastery

5 km (3 miles) east of Sitía, at Ayía Fotiá, is a Minoan necropolis. 16 km (10 miles) farther east is the fortified Monastery of Toploú (17th c.), which was a stronghold of resistance to the Turks and a place of refuge from the German occupying forces during the Second World War. It has a fine collection of Bibles and icons.

Palaíkastro

23 km (14 miles) east of Sitía is the Minoan site of Palaíkastro.

° Vái Bay

26 km (16 miles) north-east of Sitía lies the little village of Vái in its beautiful sandy bay, with the only palm grove on Crete.

Itanós

3 km (2 miles) north is the Minoan site of Itanós, near Ermoúpolis.

° Káto Zákros

46 km (29 miles) south-east of Sitía on a good road, the last section of which is a magnificent scenic road high above the sea, is the Minoan site (only partly excavated) of Káto Zákros. The city, which flourished from about 1600 to 1450 B.C., was a base for trade with Egypt and the rest of North Africa.

Praisós

15 km (9 miles) south of Sitía, at Praisós, are the remains of a Minoan villa and a Hellenistic necropolis.

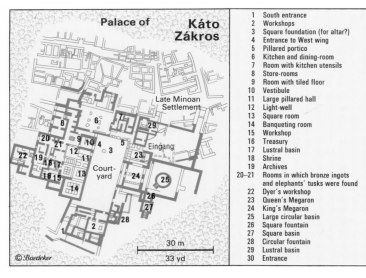

Palace of Káto Zákros

1 South entrance
2 Workshops
3 Square foundation (for altar?)
4 Entrance to West wing
5 Pillared portico
6 Kitchen and dining-room
7 Room with kitchen utensils
8 Store-rooms
9 Room with tiled floor
10 Vestibule
11 Large pillared hall
12 Light-well
13 Square room
14 Banqueting room
15 Workshop
16 Treasury
17 Lustral basin
18 Shrine
19 Archives
20–21 Rooms in which bronze ingots and elephants' tusks were found
22 Dyer's workshop
23 Queen's Megaron
24 King's Megaron
25 Large circular basin
26 Square fountain
27 Square basin
28 Circular fountain
29 Lustral basin
30 Entrance

Late Minoan Settlement
Eingang
Court-yard
30 m
33 yd
© Baedeker

Among the many other archaeological sites in the neighbourhood of Sitía are the Minoan villas of Piskokéfalon, Zoú and Ríza (all to the south-east) and a Mycenaean domed tomb at Akhládia (to the south).

Gávdos

Some 37 km (23 miles) off the west end of the Crete's south coast lies the flat wooded island of Gávdos, the most southerly point in Europe, which was traditionally held to be Kalypso's island of Ogygia ("Odyssey", VII, 244).

Cyclades Κυκλάδες/Kikládes

D4/5

The Cyclades, a group of islands mainly settled by Ionians, were so named because they lay in a circle (Greek kyklos) round the sacred island of Delos, the birthplace of Apollo. According to the ancient legend Poseidon with his trident had thrust the mountains into the sea, where they took root.

The archipelago, consisting of 23 large islands and some 200 smaller ones, is based on a submarine plateau which extends in an arc from the most easterly points of Attica and Euboea towards the coast of Asia Minor. All the islands are hilly. The more northerly ones consist predominantly of Cretaceous limestones, micaceous schists, gneisses and marbles; those to the south consist in part of volcanic rocks. With the exception of Náxos the islands have no perennial rivers, and as a result of the prevailing sharp sea-winds (the meltemi in summer) are lacking in trees. Characteristic features of the landscape are the cube-shaped whitewashed Cycladic houses and the thatch-roofed windmills with their light-coloured sails.

The original occupants of the islands are believed to have been Carians, who developed the Early Bronze Age culture known as Cycladic (2400–1200 B.C.), producing the characteristic Cycladic idols (mostly female figures carved from stone) which have been found on all the islands. At the end of the 2nd millennium B.C. the indigenous inhabitants were displaced by Ionians in the northern islands and Dorians in the islands to the south. Most of the Cycladic islands joined the first and later the second Attic maritime league. In the latter part of the 1st millennium B.C. they fell under Macedonian control and thereafter were ruled by the Ptolemies. They then became Roman, and after the division of the Empire became part of the Byzantine Empire.

During the Middle Ages there followed centuries of Venetian and Frankish rule, a period of flourishing artistic and intellectual life. Even after the Turkish occupation (1579) the Cyclades largely preserved their religious (predominantly Roman Catholic) and cultural identity. They were reunited with Greece in 1834.

History and culture

For descriptions of the individual islands, consult the Index.

The new Museum of Cycladic and Ancient Art in Athens (see entry) is devoted to the very distinctive Cycladic culture of the 4th and 3rd millennia B.C.

Delos Δῆλος/Dílos

Region: Aegean Islands
Island group: Cyclades
Nomos: Cyclades
Area: 3·6 sq. km (1½ sq. miles)
Altitude: 0–113 m (0–371 ft)
No villages and no permanent inhabitants

Boat services

Connections, subject to demand and to weather, with Mýkonos; occasionally also with Tínos, Náxos and Páros.

Situation and characteristics

Delos, a rocky island 5 km (3 miles) long and only 1300 m (1400 yd) wide, lies 10 km (6 miles) south-west of Mýkonos. Although it is one of the smallest of the Cyclades, and much smaller than its nearest neighbours Mýkonos and Rínia, Delos was of great importance in antiquity as the birthplace of Apollo, and the Cyclades were so called because they were seen as lying in a circle (kyklos) round the sacred island. The extensive area of remains excavated under the direction of French archaeologists from 1873 onwards is one of the most important archaeological sites in Greece.

Delos will appeal particularly to those interested in Greek antiquity. Apart from the ancient remains it has no other tourist attractions or amenities.

History

According to the ancient myth Delos was the birthplace of Apollo and Artemis. The destinies of the island turned on its importance as a pan-Hellenic shrine.

The earliest settlers, in the 3rd millennium B.C., were Phoenicians and Carians. After their displacement by Ionians in the 1st millennium B.C. the island became the main centre of the cult of Apollo, and splendid games – said to have been originally established by Theseus – were held annually in honour of the god. In the 6th c. B.C. Peisistratos carried out a purification (catharsis) of the island by removing all tombs from the area round the sanctuary, and in a second purification in 426–425 B.C. all births, deaths and burials on the island were prohibited and the existing tombs were removed to the neighbouring island of Reneia (Rínia).

When the Panionic League was founded after the Persian Wars, the Temple of Apollo was selected as the treasury of the League. In 454 B.C., however, Athens carried off the contents of the treasury and reduced Delos and the other islands to a condition of dependence. In 314 B.C. Delos asserted its independence of Athens and thereafter developed a prosperous trade which made it the economic centre of the archipelago. Foreign trading guilds including the Hermaists (Romans) and the Poseidoniasts (Syrians from Berytos, present-day Beirut) established themselves on the island.

In 166 B.C. the Romans gained control of Delos, and thereafter assigned it to Athens. This brought a revival of the island's prosperity, particularly after the destruction of Corinth. The end came with the devastation of Delos by Mithridates in 88 B.C., followed by its complete destruction by pirates in 69 B.C. Thereafter the island was almost uninhabited, and when Pausanias visited it in the 2nd c. A.D. he saw only the custodians of the deserted sanctuary. A fresh settlement was established in Christian times, but this had only a brief life.

*The Site

On the west side of the island is the Sacred Harbour (landing-stage), now some distance inland as a result of silting up, where envoys attending the sacred festival landed. To the south of this is the old commercial harbour. At a later period the shoreline betwen the Sacred Harbour and Fourni Bay was lined with quay walls (completed in 111 B.C.) and warehouse, remains of which can still be seen under water.

Sacred Harbour

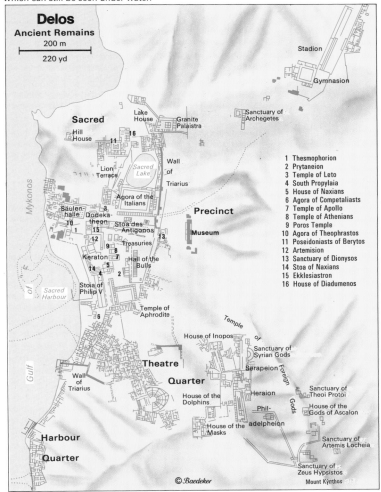

Delos

Ancient Remains

200 m
220 yd

Stadion

Gymnasion

Sacred

Hill House

Lake House

Granite Palaistra

Sanctuary of Archegetes

Wall of Triarius

Lion Terrace

Sacred Lake

Säulen-halle

Agora of the Italians

Dodeka-theon

Stoa des Antigonos

Precinct

Museum

Treasuries

Keraton

Hall of the Bulls

Stoia of Philip V

Sacred Harbour

Temple of Aphrodite

Temple of Foreign Gods

House of Inopos

Sanctuary of Syrian Gods

Serapeion

Theatre

Quarter

Wall of Triarius

House of the Dolphins

Heraion

Sanctuary of Theoi Protoi

House of the Gods of Ascalon

Phil-adelpheion

House of the Masks

Harbour

Quarter

Sanctuary of Artemis Locheia

Sanctuary of Zeus Hypsistos

Mount Kýnthos

Mykonos

Gulf   of

© *Baedeker*

1 Thesmophorion
2 Prytaneion
3 Temple of Leto
4 South Propylaia
5 House of Naxians
6 Agora of Competaliasts
7 Temple of Apollo
8 Temple of Athenians
9 Poros Temple
10 Agora of Theophrastos
11 Poseidoniasts of Berytos
12 Artemision
13 Sanctuary of Dionysos
14 Stoa of Naxians
15 Ekklesiastron
16 House of Diadumenos

Delos

The Sacred Precinct, which was surrounded by walls and stoas, was approached from the south on a paved way running above the present harbour between two stoas. The 87 m (285 ft) long Stoa of Philip (on the left), of the Doric order, is open on both the east and the west sides and has a dedicatory inscription on the architrave recording that it was built by Philip V of Macedon about 210 B.C. On the east side of the street is a smaller portico, along the rear of which were eight shops. Beyond this, to the east, is the almost square South Agora (1st c. B.C.). To the north of this lies a square, on the east side of which are the South Propylaia. Opposite, on the west side of the square, is a passage through the small portico. The whole area between here and the Hall of the Bulls was occupied in medieval times by the fortifications built by the Knights of St John.

From the South Propylaia (2nd c. B.C.), approached by three marble steps, with four Doric columns on the front and rear, the ceremonial way continued north, over a small esplanade paved with bluish marble and flanked by altars, statues and exedras, passing the west ends of three parallel temples and then curving round to the east fronts of the temples. A shorter route to the east side of the precinct was provided by a long Ionic portico, with narrow columned porches at each end, running east immediately inside the South Propylaia. On the north side of the portico can be seen the base of a colossal statue of Apollo; the inscription (6th c. B.C.) indicates that the statue and the base were hewn from a single block of stone. The dedication on the west side, The Naxians to Apollo is a later addition.

Beyond the esplanade, on the left of the ceremonial way, is a court with a stoa and two temples. The larger of the two, the Keraton (at the south-west corner), was dedicated to Apollo and once contained the Horned Altar (so called after the rams' horns which were set round it), celebrated as one of the Seven Wonders of the World. The Keraton is thought to be older than the smaller Artemision in the centre of the court, an Ionic temple on granite foundations with a peristyle, probably built on the site of an earlier 7th c. temple.
In front of the south-facing entrance to the Keraton, towards the harbour, are a number of bases for equestrian statues, the most northerly and the smallest of which bore a statue of Sulla (inscription on rear ramp).
North-west of the Precinct of Artemis is the Thesmophorion, dedicated to Demeter.

To the east of the Artemision the ceremonial way curves round the three parallel temples of Apollo. The south temple (4th–3rd c. B.C.), similar in layout to the Theseion in Athens, is the largest of the three, covering an area 26·40 m (87 ft) by 13·55 m (44 ft). It can be seen from the massive foundations, laid on a layer of greyish-blue schist, that this was a peripteral temple with 6 by 13 columns. The pronaos (entrance portico) and opisthodomos (rear chamber), at the east and west ends, seem to have had two columns between the antea. The cella measured 11·50 m (38 ft) by 5·60 m (18 ft). Of the structure of the temple little is left apart from fragments of the frieze of triglyphs and the Doric columns; of the sculptural decoration there survive only the palmette ornament and the lions' heads of the sima.
To the north are the poros foundations of the second temple,

dedicated by the Athenians (late 5th c. B.C.; Doric); this is also oriented to the east, with narrow antechambers at the east and west ends and a two-part cella.

The third temple, also built of poros, is the oldest of the three (first half of 6th c. B.C.).

On the north side of the curve described by the ceremonial way are five small buildings, four of them facing the three temples, which from their similarity to the corresponding buildings at Delphi and Olympus are thought to be treasuries. The fifth (to the south), with a pronaos and opisthodomos was probably a temple. Opposite its entrance is the Prytaneion (5th c. B.C.), the office of the city's chief official.

To the east is the long hall (67·20 m (220 ft) by 8·86 m (29 ft)) extending from north-east to south-west known as the Hall of the Bulls or Ship Hall. Dated to the Hellenistic period, it is one of the best-preserved buildings on Delos. Over a granite foundation three marble steps, still partly preserved, lead up to an enclosure wall round the two sides and the north end; The entrance front, at the south end, probably had Doric columns between antae. In the centre of the hall is a rectangular cavity. Of its sculptural decoration only a Nereid and a dolphin remain *in situ*. The core of granite blocks becomes narrower at the north end, in the manner of a ship's prow, and may have held the mast of the votive ship housed in the hall. At the entrance are pillars with Doric half-columns in front of them, their capitals carved with recumbent figures of bulls. The step-like structure to the south-east of the hall was part of an Altar of Zeus Polieus.

° Hall of the Bulls

On the east side of the Precinct of Apollo was the Sanctuary of Dionysos, with a number of marble phalluses. On one of the bases are reliefs of Dionysiac scenes (*c.* 300 B.C.).

At the north end of the Sacred Precinct is the Stoa of Antigonos (3rd c. B.C.), with bull's-head triglyphs. The rooms to the rear served for the accommodation of envoys attending the festivals. In front of the stoa is a semicircular structure dating from Mycenaean times, the Tomb of the Hyperborean Maidens who attended Leto at the birth of the divine twins.

From the west end of the Precinct of Apollo a side propylaion (gateway) leads into the business quarter of the city. On the right-hand side of the street, which was lined with shops, is the Agora of the Italians (2nd c. B.C.), a large square court surrounded by two-storey Doric colonnades with shops, workshops and niches for votive gifts (mosaics). These were the business premises of a corporation of Roman merchants, known as Hermaists after their patron divinity Hermes. To the north-west of the Sacred Lake was a similar building belonging to the Poseidoniasts of Berytos (Beirut). To the north, beside the entrance to the Agora of the Italians, is the Temple of Leto; farther west is the Stoa of Antigonos Gonatas (3rd c. B.C.).

Business quarter

Immediately north of the Agora of the Italians is the Sacred Lake (now filled in), on the shores of which Leto was said to have given birth to Apollo. On a terrace to the west of the lake is a row of lions in Naxian marble (Archaic period, 7th c. B.C.). To the north of the lake were the Old and the New Palaistra, and to the north-east were the Sanctuary of the hero Archegetes, which could be entered only by citizens of Delos, the Gymnasion and the Stadion, the north-west side of which was

Sacred Lake

° Marble lions

Delos

Lion Terrace, Delos

built against the rock. A building to the east of the Stadion may have been a synagogue.

To the north and north-west of the Sacred Lake are the remains of dwelling-houses.

°Museum

To the east of the Sacred Precinct stands the Museum (at present closed). The two central rooms contain works of art of the Archaic period, including (on the left) a triangular marble base with a ram's head and Gorgons (7th c. B.C.), a sphinx, several kouroi and korai (6th c. B.C.), a hand of the Naxian Apollo (on the right) and three seated female figures (7th c. B.C.). The room to the left of the entrance contains fragments from the Temple of the Athenians (akroteria, figures from the pediments), herms, funerary stelae, small sculpture, terracottas and pottery. In the room to the right are votive gifts from the Temple of Artemis, fragments of sculpture and inscriptions.

Other important finds from Delos are in the National Archaeological Museum and the new Museum of Cycladic Art in Athens.

Theatre Quarter and residential area

In the southern part of the Sacred Precinct is the Agora of the Competaliasts (the Roman merchants who had as their patrons the Lares Competales), decorated with statues and small shrines. Farther south, between Mount Kýnthos and the commercial harbour, lies the so-called Theatre Quarter (3rd–2nd c. B.C.), which gives a vivid impression of a town of the period. The narrow winding streets are paved with slabs of schist. The houses, frequently preserved to a height of 4–5 m (13–16 ft), had at least one upper storey; the internal decoration is reminiscent of the First Pompeian style. Of particular interest is the House of the Trident, with a mosaic pavement.

To the south-east of this quarter is the Theatre (3rd c. B.C.), with an auditorium of Greek type, extending round more than a semicircle. The four lowest rows have preserved their marble seating, and the first row still has its marble backs at the right-hand end. The orchestra was surrounded by a narrow drainage channel and the stage building by a colonnade, the east side of which served as a proscenium. Under the stage building was a large cistern.

Mount Kynthos

From the Sacred Precinct an ancient road runs south-east to the dry bed of the River Inopós, a meagre watercourse even in ancient times. On the west side of the gorge is the Inopós House (2nd c. B.C.). To the south, higher up the valley, are the House of the Dolphins, with a dolphin mosaic in the peristyle, and the House of the Masks. On a terrace above the east side of the gorge are temples of Serapis, Isis, Anubis and Harpokrates, in which these foreign divinities were worshipped from the 2nd c. B.C. onwards. From here the ancient road climbs, with steps at some points, to the sumit of Mount Kýnthos (113 m (371 ft)), on which stood a Temple of Zeus Kynthios and Athena Kynthia (3rd c. B.C.), the successor to an earlier temple of the 7th c.

View

From the top of the hill there are wide views – to the south the hills of Náxos, to the west Sýros with the sea of houses of its chief town Ermoúpolis, to the north the mountainous island of Tínos, to the east the neighbouring island of Mýkonos with its innumerable chapels.

On the way down a visit can be paid to a cave on the west side of the hill which is enclosed by massive stone slabs and contains a statue base; it is called, without any justification, the Grotto of Apollo.

Rínia

To the west of Delos is the island of Rínia, also known as Megáli Dílos (area 17 sq. km (6½ sq. miles)), the ancient Reneia. After the second purification (see History) it became the burial-place for Delos.

In the strait (1 km (¾ mile) wide) between Delos and the southern part of Rína are two barren rocks, Mikrós Revmatiáris and Megálos Revmatiáris.

Dodecanese Δωδεχάνησα/Dodekánisa   D5

The Dodecanese (Twelve Islands) is the most southerly group of islands in the Southern Sporades, lying off the south-west coast of Asia Minor. It includes the 14 larger islands of Lipsí, Pátmos, Léros, Kálymnos, Kos, Astypálaia, Nísyros, Sými, Tílos, Rhodes, Khalkí, Kárpathos, Kásos and Kastellórizo (see individual entries, except Khalkí), together with some 40 smaller islets and rocks.

With the exception of Rhodes the islands, which belong culturally to Greece but geologically to the mainland of Anatolia, are arid and largely barren. Their inhabitants live by farming, sponge-fishing (the Dodecanese is the base of the

A fisherman of Pátmos, in the Dodecanese

Greek sponge-fishing fleet), silkworm culture, the manufacture of pottery, tanning, carpet-weaving and, increasingly, the tourist trade.

History

Neither in Greek nor in Roman times was the Dodecanese a separate political entity. It was an administrative region of the Byzantine Empire, and it was only when the islands came under Turkish rule in the 16th c. that they were given extensive rights of self-government in domestic affairs and gained a common political status. In 1912 most of the islands were occupied by Italy as a counter-measure to the Turkish occupation of Libya. Under the Treaty of Lausanne in 1923 Turkey formally ceded the whole of the Dodecanese to Italy. After being occupied by German forces during the Second World War the islands were reunited with Greece in 1947.

The Dodecanese group enjoys certain customs privileges (e.g. in relation to alcohol).

Ekhinades Ἐχινάδες/Ekhinádes C2

Region: Ionian Islands
Island group: Ionian Islands
Nomos: Kefallinía

The Ekhinádes (also called the Kourtsolares) are a fertile group of islands lying north-east of Ithaca near the mouth of the River

Akhelóos. The principal islands are Dragonéra, Petalá and Oxiá, now partly joined to the mainland as a result of extensive silting up.

In this area was fought the Battle of Lépanto (1571), in which the 26-year-old Don John of Austria, with 250 Venetian and Spanish galleys, defeated a Turkish fleet of equal strength and destroyed almost 200 Turkish vessels.

Lépanto

Elafonisos 'Ελαφόνησος/Elafónisos   D3

Region: Peloponnese
Nomos: Laconia
Area: 18 sq. km (7 sq. miles)
Altitude: 0–277 m (0–909 ft)
Population: 600

Weekly from Athens (Piraeus). Local connections with Neápolis (Peloponnese).

Boat services

Elafónisos (Italian Cervi, ancient Onougnathos) lies just off the south-eastern tip of the Peloponnese. It has two sheltered anchorages. At the north end of the island is the village of Elafónisos. Off its west coast are a number of limestone islets and rocks.
Elafónisos is separated from the larger island of Kýthira to the south by the 10 km (6 mile) wide Elafónisos Channel.

Situation and characteristics

Erimonísia

Erimonisia   'Ερημονήσια/Erimonísia   D4

Region: Aegean Islands
Island group: Cyclades
Nomos: Cyclades

Boat services   No regular services.

Situation and characteristics   The Erimonísia or Nisídes (Islets) are a chain of lonely and
barren island within the triangle formed by Náxos, Amorgós
and Íos. To the north are the Voidonísi, a group of small islets;
to the south of these are the island of Donoúsa (pop. 200; alt.
to 488 m (1601 ft)) and the Makáries Islands, between
Donoúsa and Náxos; and farther south again are the Koufo
Islands – Presoúra and Áno Koufónisi (8 sq. km (3 sq. miles))
to the north, Káto Koufónisi (5 sq. km (2 sq. miles)) to the south
and Kéros (14 sq. km (5½ sq. miles)), on which an acropolis of
the 3rd c. B.C. has been brought to light, Antikéros and Dríma to
the east. To the south-west, also belonging to the Koufo group,
is Skhinoúsa (10 sq. km (3¾ sq. miles); pop. 200), with the
village of Skhinoúsa in the interior of the island. The most
southerly of the Erimonísia is Iráklia (18 sq. km (7 sq. miles);
pop. 250), with the village of Iráklia above the bay (anchorage)
of Áyios Yeóryios.

Euboea   Εΰβοια/Evvia   C3/4

Region: Central Greece
Nomos: Euboea
Area: 3654 sq. km (1411 sq. miles)
Altitude: 0–1743 m (0–5719 ft)
Population: 165,000
Chief pace: Khalkís

Boat services   Ferry services between Glyfa and Ayiókampos, Arkítsa and
Loutrá Aidipsoú, Skála Oropoú and Erétria, Ayía Marína and
Néa Stýra, Rafína and Néa Stýra, Marmári and Kárystos. –
Cruise (recommended) from Khalkís through the Northern
Bight of Euboea to Péfki. – Regular services from Vólos via
Kými to the Northern Sporades and to Kavála and Alexan-
droúpolis.

Access by road and rail   Euboea is connected with the mainland by a toll-bridge at
Khalkís. – Bus services: Athens–Khalkís, frequent services
(1½ hours), and on to Kými (several services daily; total time
3¾ hours); Athens to Skála Oropoú, hourly, then ferry to Erétria;
Athens–Rafína, frequent services, then ferry to Néa Stýra,
Marmári and Kárystos; Athens to Loutrá Aidipsoú, several
services daily (3½ hours). – By rail: Athens – Khalkís, several
services daily (1¾ hours).

Situation and characteristics   Euboea, the second largest of the Greek islands (170 km (105
miles) long by 5·5 km (3½ miles) wide), lies off the north-east
coast of Boeotia and Attica, forming two enclosed sheets of
water, the North and South Bights, joined by the narrow
Évropos Channel, only 35 m (40 yd) wide and 8·50 m (30 ft)
deep, half-way along the island. The north-east coast of

Khalkís, chief town of Euboea

Euboea is rocky, usually falling steeply down to the sea; the principal harbours are on the gentler south-west side facing the mainland. There are four main groups of hills, some of which are densely wooded: in the north-west the Telétrion range (Mount Xerón, 991 m (3251 ft)); farther south-east the Kandíli range (rising to 1225 m (4019 ft)); to the east of this the Dírfys range (Mount Delfí, 1743 m (5719 ft)); and at the south-eastern tip of the island the Okha range (Mount Okhi, 1398 m (4587 ft)). Below the hills, particularly on the west side of the island, are small fertile alluvial plants. Euboea's minerals (magnesite, lignite) provide the basis for its metal-working industries, particularly round Khalkís. The island's main attraction to visitors lies in the beauty of its scenery.

The earliest inhabitants of Euboea were Ellopians from Thessaly at the north-west end of the island, Abantes from Thrace in the centre and Dryopes in the south-east. Ionians from Attica merged with the Abantes and gained control of the whole island, achieving power and prosperity between the 8th and 6th c. B.C. The two chief towns, Chalkis and Erétria, established numerous colonies in Greater Greece, Sicily and the Thracian Chersonese (Chalcidice).

The continuous history of the island begins with the conquest of the city of Chalkis in 506 B.C. by Athens, which saw possession of this fertile island as a vital necessity. Towards the end of the Peloponnesian War, in 411 B.C., Euboea recovered its independence, but in subsequent wars was usually allied with Athens, the destinies of which it shared.

After the Latin conquest of Constantinople in A.D. 1204 Euboea was divided into three baronies under Veronese rulers, but the

History

ports were held by the Venetians, who eventually succeeded, after a series of wars with the Frankish nobles, in gaining possession of the whole island, now known as Negroponte. The most important Venetian stronghold in the eastern Mediterranean after Crete, it fell to the Turks in 1470. It was reunited with Greece under the Second London Protocol of 1830.

Khalkís

The port of Khalkís (or Khalkída; pop. 37,000), chief town of the nomos of Euboea, which also includes the Petalií Islands and Skýros, is charmingly situated on a number of hills on the Évripos Channel, to the west of the site of the ancient city. At this convenient crossing to the mainland a port was established at an early stage, and in 411 B.C. a wooden bridge was built over the narrowest point of the channel. At that time, too, the channel was still further narrowed by the deposit of soil to reclaim land from the sea, thus securing the connection with Boeotia, always subject to the threat of attack by enemy warships.

A rocky islet with the Turkish Fort of Karábaba (1686) divides the Évripos into a narrow western half, now filled up, and a broader eastern half spanned by a swing bridge. The currents in the channel change direction frequently, at least 4 times daily and sometimes as many as 20 times – a tidal phenomenon which puzzled ancient scientists.

The Latin alphabet was based on the alphabet of ancient Chalkis.

Kástro

At the east end of the bridge lies the old Venetian and Turkish town of Kástro, largely surrounded by the sea and still preserving part of its circuit of walls. On the south side of the town is the Church of Ayía Paraskeví (originally 5th–6th c.), rebuilt by the Crusaders in the 14th c. in Gothic style (rare in Greece), which was the principal Venetian church. There are some remains of the Venetian aqueduct which brought water to the town from Mount Dírfys.

Proastion

To the north of the old town is the busy district known as the Proastion (suburb), in which are the main square of Khalkís, the Archaeological Museum (material mainly from Erétria), the Museum of Medieval Art, housed in a mosque (restored) converted in 1470 from the Church of San Marco di Negroponte, and a handsome Turkish fountain.

Kastélli

On a rocky spur of hill above Fýlla, 3 km (2 miles) east of Khalkís, is the well-preserved 13th c. Venetian fort of Lilanto (now Kastélli).

Erétria

In antiquity Erétria, a site occupied since the 3rd millennium B.C., was the most important city on the island after Chalkis. In the 8th c. B.C. it prospered after being settled by Ionians from Attica. When Miletus was under threat from the Persians in 500 B.C. Erétria joined Athens in going to its support; for this the city was destroyed on the orders of Darius and the inhabitants carried off to Susa as slaves. It seems, however, to have been rebuilt soon afterwards, and contributed seven vessels to the Greek fleet in the naval battles of Artemísion and Salamís and several hundred hoplites to the Greek army which fought at Plataia. In 411 B.C., after a naval battle between Athens and Sparta, Erétria made a major contribution to the liberation of Euboea from Athenian domination by destroying the Athenian warships which sought refuge in its harbour in the belief that this was a friendly port. Later the Eretrians joined the Attic maritime league (378 B.C.) and also took part in the struggle against the Macedonians. In 198 B.C. the city was taken by storm by the Romans.

Erétria was the birthplace of Menedemos, a pupil of Plato.

The remains of ancient Erétria are the most considerable on the island. Here and there among the houses of the modern town can be seen ancient foundation walls, and the museum displays finds of the Roman period. To the north-east are the remains of the theatre, constructed in the plain. The oldest part is a stone stage building, on the level of the original orchestra; the seating for the spectators was no doubt on wooden stands. In the 4th c. B.C. a stone theatre was constructed with the orchestra on a lower level, the seating for spectators on ground built up for the purpose and a stone stage building. The action took place on the orchestra in front of a movable wooden proscenium, which was replaced in the Early Roman period by a permanent proscenium of white marble.

South-west of the theatre are the remains of a Temple of Dionysos and one of the town gates. To the east of the theatre is the gymnasion, with baths in its north-east corner. At the north-east end of the town are the foundations of a Temple of

A harbour on the Orei Channel

Apollo Daphnephoros (the Laurel-Bearer); sculpture from its pediments (including a representation of Theseus carrying off the Amazon Antiope of 520 B.C.) can be seen in the Khalkís Museum. 1 km (¾ mile) north-west of the theatre is a tomb with a vaulted roof.

The acropolis hill was surrounded for much of its circumference by polygonal walls. On the north side of the acropolis is a tower (fine view). Two walls, traceable only for part of the way, lead down to the shore from the east and west ends of the acropolis, and there are further remains of walls on the shore itself.

The north-west of the island

From Khalkís via Artemísion to Loutrá Aidipsoú: 151 km (94 miles). The road heads north-east from Khalkís, running close to the Évripos and passing ancient tombs.

9 km (5½ miles): Néa Artáky, where a road branches off on the right and runs north-east to Sténi Dírfyos (26 km (16 miles)). From there Mount Delfí, the highest peak in the Dírfys range (1743 m (5719 ft); view), can be climbed (4 hours, with guide).

8 km (5 miles): Psakhná, 3 km (2 miles) north of which is the Venetian Castle of Kástri. The road now turns away from the Évripos through rugged country and crosses a saddle between Mount Kandílion (1209 m (3967 ft)) and Mount Pisariá (1352 m (4436 ft)); magnificent panoramic views. The road then continues through beautiful hill scenery, passing close to an ancient fort rebuilt by the Venetians, and runs down to the Monastery of Ayios Yeóryios and the valley of the River Kyréfs, amid a luxuriant growth of arbutus and myrtle.

36 km (22 miles): Prokópion, a prosperous village and place of pilgrimage, near the old Turkish country house of Ahmet Aga, in a beautiful wooded setting.

10 km (6 miles): Mantoúdi, a small industrial town (magnesite-mining). To the north, near the mouth of the Kyréfs, are the remains of ancient Kerinthos.

8 km (5 miles): Strofylliá, from which a road runs south-west to the little port of Límni.

8 km (5 miles): Ayía Anná, a prosperous little village.

32 km (20 miles): Agriovótano, to the south of Cape Artemísion (also called Cape Amoni), with a view of the little islet of Pontikonísi.

Artemísion

12 km (7½ miles): Artemísion, a village on the north coast, notable as the scene of the first Greek naval victory over a much larger Persian fleet in 480 B.C. Near the village are the remains of a Temple of Artemis Proseoa. To the west lies the fishing village of Péfki, the base in summer of the anchovy-fishing fleet.

Istiaía

'Marble Bull

13 km (8 miles): Istiaía (pop. 5000), the chief place in the north-western part of the island, in fertile farming country. To the west of the town is the site of ancient Histiaia, conquered in 446 B.C. by Perikles, who ensured its submission to Athens by founding the nearby colony of Oreoi; medieval castle, incorporating ancient masonry. – In the main square of present-day Orei can be seen a massive marble figure of a bull (4th c. B.C.) recovered from the sea.

22 km (13½ miles): Loutrá Aidipsoú, a popular seaside resort and spa, with hot sulphureous springs (32–82 ° C (90–180 °F)) which were already frequented in Roman times. The largest of the springs is on the shore (remains of ancient baths).

The south-east of the island

Khalkís to Erétria, Alivéri and Kárystos (128 km (80 miles)) or Kými (96 km (60 miles)). The road runs south-east from Khalkís, keeping close to the shore.
2·5 km (1½ miles): Chapel of Ayios Stéfanos, on the site of ancient Chalkis, with the Fountain of Arethusa which was famed in antiquity. The bay of Ayios Stéfanos was the ancient harbour. The road continues over the well-cultivated Lelantian Plain, with the village of Vasilikó. Off the road to the left, on the way to the medieval Castle of Fýlla (1·5 km (1 mile)), are three Venetian watch-towers.
19 km (12 miles): Néa Psará (Erétria), with the remains of ancient Erétria. The marshland in this area, a relic of a prehistoric bay, was drained in ancient times by a system of canals. Beyond Erétria the road passes a number of ancient cemetery areas.
9 km (5½ miles): Amárynthos, a small fishing port. To the north-east is the tile-clad Monastery of Ayios Nikólaos (16th c. frescoes; view).
15 km (9 miles): Alivéri, a prosperous little industrial town (lignite-mine; thermal power-station) which is believed to occupy the site of ancient Tamynai. 1 km (¾ mile) away is the port of Skála Alivériou, probably the ancient ferry harbour of Porthmós. The road continues east; just beyond Lépoura the road to Kými (below) diverges to the left.
9 km (5½ miles): road on right to Dýstos. It runs past a marshy and often flooded depression, on the west side of which is the acropolis of ancient Dýstos, with the modern village of the same name at the foot of the hill (fragments of ancient masonry). Farther on are other remains of ancient buildings.
15 km (9 miles): Záraka, with a view of a long inlet of the sea, at the mouth of which is the island of Kavalianí, probably the ancient Glaukonnesos. From the hill beyond the village there are views extending down the east coast of Euboea as far as Cape Kafaréfs and south-west to Stýra Bay with the irregularly shaped island of Stýra (ancient Aigleia).

26 km (16 miles): Stýra, with the whitewashed church of the Panayía, built on the slopes of a double-topped hill. There are scanty remains of ancient Styra at Néa Stýra, 1 km (¾ mile) away on the coast.

From Stýra the so-called dragon's houses can be visited. A stiff half hour's climb leads to a saddle above the village and past ancient quarries, with partly hewn columns and dressed blocks of stone. From here it is another 15–20 minutes' walk to the foot of Mount Ayios Nikólaos, where there are three well-preserved ancient stone buildings, probably huts for quarry workers. On the hill are the imposing Frankish Castle of Larména and a chapel dedicated to St Nicholas (magnificent views).
Half-way between Stýra and Kárystos is the Bey's Fountain.
21 km (13 miles): road on right to Marmári (4 km (2½ miles) south), a popular summer resort. Off the coast, to the south-

west, lie the Petalií, a privately owned group of islands; on some there are houses, others are deserted.

Kárystos

11 km (7 miles): Kárystos (pop. 2000), the chief place in southern Euboea, founded after the Wars of Liberation and now a summer holiday resort. The site of ancient Kárystos, famed in the Roman Imperial period for its cipollino marble (banded white and green), is half an hour's walk inland on the slopes of its acropolis hill, now crowned by the Venetian Fort of Castel Rosso (view). North-east of Kárystos are the ancient marble quarries of Myli.

From here Mount Ayios Nikólaos or Ókhi (1398 m (4587 ft)), to the north-east, can be climbed (3½ hours; fine views).

On the north-east side of the hill is an ancient building (arkhampolis or kharkhambolis) similar to the dragon's houses of Stýra. Farther north-east is Cape Dóro or Kafiréfs, associated with the story of Nauplios, father of the unfortunate Palamedes, who lured the returning Greek ships on to the rocks by lighting beacons but threw himself into the sea on learning that his principal enemies, Agamemnon and Odysseus, had escaped.

9 km (5½ miles) east of Kárystos and 1 km (¾ mile) from the village of Platanistós (well wooded with oaks and planes) is the Hellenikon, a terrace with massive retaining walls. Two hours' walk beyond this, on the coast, is the site of the ancient port of Geraistos, which had a celebrated Temple of Poseidon. From the road junction near Lépoura the road to Kými runs north.

1 km (¾ mile): road on the right to Avlonári, with the 12th c. Church of Ayios Dimítrios (ancient column drums built into the walls), and beyond this to the Church of Ayía Thekla (15th c. frescoes), in the village of that name.

13 km (8 miles): Konístres, from which it is half an hour's walk to the ruined Castle of Episkopí (remains of ancient and medieval walls).

17 km (10½ miles): Kými (pop. 3000), a prosperous little place in fertile rolling countryside, the only port on the inhospitable north-east coast of Euboea. The ancient city was probably on Cape Kymis, to the north, or in the neighbourhood of the Monastery of Ayios Sotír (to the north-west of which is a Byzantine fort). North-west of Kými are lignite-mines (fossils of the Tertiary period).

Farmakonisi   Φαρμαχονήσι/Farmakonísi   D5

Region: Aegean Islands
Island group: Southern Sporades
Nomos: Dodecanese
Area: 4 sq. km (1½ sq. miles)
Altitude: 0–106 m (0–348 ft)
Population: 5

Situation and characteristics

Farmakonísi, an almost uninhabited islet of gentle, partly grass-covered, hills, lies 12 km (7½ miles) south-west of the Cape of Tekağaç Burun, on the Turkish coast near Didyma. Here in 77 B.C. Caesar was captured by pirates and released only on payment of a ransom of 50 talents.

There are remains of a number of Roman villas and the ancient harbour, now partly under the sea.

Folegandros Φολέγανδρος/Folégandros   D4

Region: Aegean Islands
Island group: Cyclades
Nomos: Cyclades
Area: 34 sq. km (13 sq. miles)
Altitude: 0–411 m (0–1348 ft)
Population: 700
Chief place: Folégandros (Khóra)

Regular service Piraeus – Páros – Santoríni – Folégandros – Síkinos – Ios – Náxos – Piraeus.

Boat services

The long straggling island of Folégandros, between Melos and Santoríni, is still barely touched by the tourist trade. The cliff-fringed eastern part of the island, with its highest hill (411 m (1348 ft)), is bare and arid; the western half is milder, with water from springs, and supports a modest terraced agriculture. With its poverty and lack of sheltered harbours, Folégandros was never an island of any importance. Its destinies were closely linked with those of Náxos. In Roman times it was a place of exile.

Situation and characteristics

From the landing-stage at Karavostáso on the east coast it is an hour's walk (3 km (2 miles); mules available) to the chief place on the island, Folégandros (Khóra), a village of typical Cycladic houses with a medieval Kástro. To the east is the hill of Palaiókastro, with scanty remains of the ancient town.

North-west of Khóra is the island's largest village, Ano Meriá. On the east coast are the caves of Khrysospiliá and Yeoryítsi (access difficult), with ancient graffiti.

Fourni Φούρνοι/Fúrni   D5

Region: Aegean Islands
Island group: Southern Sporades
Nomos: Sámos

Motor boats from and to Ikaría and Sámos.

Boat services

The Foúrni Islands are a group of rocky islets with much-indented coasts lying between Sámos, Ikaría and Pátmos. In addition to the main island of Foúrni (30 sq. km (11½ sq. miles); 0–486 m (0–1595 ft); pop. 1000), with the village of Foúrni on its west side, the group includes the smaller islands of Thimena (12 sq. km (4½ sq. miles); 0–483 m (0–1585 ft)) to the west and Ayios Minás (5 sq. km (2 sq. miles); 0–250 m (0–820 ft)) to the east, together with the rocks of Andro, Makronísi and Diapori. In the Middle Ages the islands were the haunt of pirates, who were able from commanding viewpoints on the hills to keep a look-out for shipping passing between Sámos and Ikaría. The inhabitants now live by farming and fishing.

Situation and characteristics

125

Hydra ΄ Ὕδρα/Ídra   D3

Region: Central Greece
Island group: Saronic Islands
Nomos: Attica
Area: 55 sq. km (21 sq. miles)
Altitude: 0–590 m (0–1936 ft)
Population: 2800
Chief place: Hýdra

Boat services

Several services daily from and to Athens (Piraeus; 3¼ hours). Hydrofoils from Athens (Zéa; 1¼ hours). Local connections with Spétses and Ermioni.

Situation and characteristics

The island of Hýdra (ancient Hydraea) is a bare monolithic ridge of limestone, 12 km (7½ miles) long by 5 km (3 miles) wide, lying off the south-east coast of the Argolid. Arid and infertile, it lives mainly from the tourist trade and the sale of craft products (jewellery, pottery, embroidery, hand-woven cloth, leather-work). A tempting local speciality is the almond cake called amygdalotá.

History

Hýdra was already settled in Mycenaean times, but was a place of no importance until the 18th c. In the 15th c. and again in 1770, after the revolt in the Morea, Albanian refugees made their home on the island, and as a result of their efforts – in trade and shipping, but also in piracy – it became prosperous and wealthy. During the War of Greek Independence the Hydriots converted their trading vessels into warships and met a large

The harbour and town of Hýdra

proportion of the cost of the war. The island has now reverted to its original unimportance.

Sights

The chief place on the island, the little town of Hýdra (pop. 2500), climbs picturesquely up the slopes of the hills round its sheltered harbour on the north coast of the island. It is now a favourite resort of artists, particularly painters, and intellectuals, who give the town its particular aspect and atmosphere. On the quay is the old Conventual Church of the Panayía (17th c.), with a beautiful cloister. On either side of the harbour are the imposing mansions of early 19th c. shipowners and merchants, including the houses of Admiral Iákovos Tombázis (now occupied by an outstation of the Athens Academy of Art) and Dimítrios Voúlgaris. One such mansion houses a training school for the merchant navy. The plain white and sometimes colour-washed houses of the town on the slopes above the harbour are rather Cycladic in type. Above the town to the west are the ruins of a medieval castle, and lower down are fortifications built during the War of Independence.

Hýdra town

'The town

West of Hýdra, at the fishing village of Vlykhós, can be seen the remains of ancient Chorisa. – 1·5 km (1 mile) south is Kaló Pigádi (view), with 18th c. country houses in the surrounding area. – Farther south, in a beautiful hill setting, is the 15th c. Monastery of Profítis Ilías (3 hours' walk; or by mule). – At the eastern tip of the island (3 hour's walk; or by mule) is Zoúrvas Monastery (16th c.). – There are a number of other monasteries, mostly abandoned.

Dokós

North-west of Hýdra is the little grazing island of Dokós (the ancient Aperopia), with the village of the same name in a sheltered bay on the north coast.

Ikaria Ἰχαρία/Ikaría   D5

Region: Aegean Islands
Island group: Southern Sporades
Nomos: Sámos
Area: 255 sq. km (98 sq. miles)
Altitude: 0–1037 ft (0–3402 ft)
Population: 7700
Chief place: Ayios Kýrikos

The regular service between Athens (Piraeus) and Rhodes, six times weekly in each direction, calls in at Ayios Kýrikos. Local connections with Sámos, Foúrni and Pátmos.

Boat services

Ikaría (Turkish Nikarya), a largely barren island 40 km (25 miles) long and up to 8 km (5 miles) wide, lies in the north-eastern Aegean some 18 km (11 miles) south-west of Sámos. The whole length of the island is occupied by the bare Athéras range (1037 m (3402 ft)), which falls steeply down to the sea on the south coast. The northern slopes of the hills, covered

Situation and characteristics

127

with a macchia of oak and spruce and cut by fertile valleys with an abundance of water, fall away more gently to the coast, on which there are a number of small unsheltered bays. The inhabitants, mostly concentrated on the north side of the island, live by farming and fishing. Ikaría has preserved much of its distinctive character unspoiled.

Myth and history

The island owes its name to Ikaros, son of Daidalos, the Attic sculptor and inventor of Minoan times, who flew too near the sun with the wings, of feathers bound together with wax, made for him by his father and plunged to his death in the sea in this area. Local legends tell a different tale – that he died when his ship, with great white sails, sank in a storm.

Ikaría was settled from Miletus in the 8th c. B.C., when the towns of Oinoe, Histoi, Therma and Drakanon were founded. In Byzantine times it was used as a place of exile. Later it was held by a series of Frankish and Genoese rulers; in 1481 it passed to the Knights of St John, and in 1567 it was captured by the Turks.

On 17 July 1912, after a successful rising against Turkish rule, the inhabitants proclaimed the free State of Ikaría, which soon afterwards joined the kingdom of Greece.

Sights

The island's chief town and port, Ayios Kýrikos (pop. 2000), lies near the east end of the south coast. There is an interesting little archaeological museum in the Gymnasion.

3 km (2 miles) north-east is the little spa of Thérma, with hot mineral springs (52·5 °C (126·5 °F); radioactive, sulphureous). Above the town is the ancient acropolis, which can be climbed from Katafíyi (3 km (2 miles) north-east) on a path lined by tombs of the 6th c. B.C.

7 km (4½ miles) south-west of Ayios Kýrikos is the Monastery of Lefkádos Evangelismós.

On Cape Fanári (1 hour by boat), at the northern tip of the island, where according to legend Dionysos was born, are the remains of the Hellenistic Fort of Drakanos.

Évdilos

Half-way along the north coast lies the picturesque village of Évdilos, once the chief place on the island. 2·5 km (1½ miles) west, at the village of Kámpos, can be found the remains of ancient Oinoe (small museum). In the neighbourhood of Kámpos are a number of beehive tombs (tholaria) and small medieval forts (kastrakia). – 5 km (3 miles) south of Évdilos, at Kosíkia, is the Byzantine stronghold of Koskinas.

At the north-west end of the island is the little port of Armenistís. 5 km (3 miles) south-west are the remains of a Temple of Artemis (probably 5th c. B.C.).

Ionian Islands   'Ιόνιαι Νῆσοι/Ióniaí Nísi   C1–D3

Situation and characteristics

The Ionian Islands, also known as the Eptánisos (Seven Islands), are strung out along the west coast of Greece from the Albanian frontier to the Peloponnese. In this westerly situation, with more rain than most other parts of Greece, the islands have a mild climate and a lush growth of vegetation, with the exception of Kýthira, which lies apart from the others off the southern tip of the Peloponnese.

The Ionian Sea, which was equated by ancient authors with the Adriatic and is now seen as its southern continuation, and the Ionian Islands owe their name, according to Aeschylus, to the wanderings of Io, and according to later sources to the Illyrian hero Ionios (spelt with omicron, the short *o*). They thus have no connection with the Ionian Greeks (derived from Ion with omega, the long *o*) who left Greece in the 11th and 10th c. B.C. and settled on the Anatolian coast, giving this eastern Greek territory its name of Ionia.

Evidence of settlement dating back to Mycenaean times has been found on the islands, but their first emergence into the light of history was in 734 B.C., when Corinth founded the city of Korkyra, later Kérkyra. In the 5th c. B.C. the islands came under Athenian influence, and in the 2nd c. B.C. all of them, including Kýthira, became Roman. Later they came under Byzantine rule, and in 1085 were conquered by the Normans; subsequently in 1203–04 the Fourth Crusade brought another change of masters. The islands now fell into the hands of Italian rulers, and then, one after another, came under Venetian control – Kýthira in 1363, Kérkyra (thereafter known as Corfu) in 1386, Zákynthos in 1479, Kefallinía in 1500 (after a 21-year period of Turkish rule) and finally Lefkás (which had been Turkish since 1467) in 1684.

Venetian rule lasted until the fall of the Republic of St Mark in 1797. During this period the islands provided a refuge for many Greeks fleeing from the Turks, including artists from Crete who founded a school of their own here, and throughout these centuries they enjoyed a richer cultural life than the rest of Greece.

After an interlude of French rule the young Republic of the Seven Islands became a British Protectorate in 1815; in 1864 Britain returned the islands to Greece.

For descriptions of the individual islands, consult the Index.

Myth and history

Ios ΄΄ Ιος/Ίος

D4

Region: Aegean Islands
Island group: Cyclades
Nomos: Cyclades
Area: 105 sq. km (40 sq. miles)
Altitude: 0–732 m (0–2402 ft)
Population: 1100 (in 19th c. 3500)
Chief place: Íos (Khóra)

Íos is served by boats sailing from Athens (Piraeus) to Páros, Íos, Santoríni and Iráklion.

Boat services

Íos is a hilly island, largely fringed by cliffs, roughly half-way between Páros or Náxos and Santoríni. Until quite recently its

Situation and characteristics

Ios: the harbour
　　　　　　　　　　　An island church

only source of income was agriculture on the terraced slopes of the Káto Kámpos Valley and its side valleys, but in the last few years it has been invaded by large numbers of backpackers and hippies who have destroyed – at any rate during the summer months – the peace and harmony of the island.

According to an ancient tradition Homer's mother Klymene was a native of Íos and he himself was buried on the island.

Sights

The little port of Órmos Íou, with the domed Church of Ayía Iríni (17th c.), lies in a sheltered bay on the west coast of the island. 1 km ($\frac{3}{4}$ mile) up the fertile Káto Kámpos Valley, conspicuously and picturesquely situated on the hillside, is the chief place on the island, Íos (Khóra; pop. 700). Its white Cycladic houses and 20 or so churches and chapels are enclosed within a dilapidated circuit of medieval walls. On the hill above the village stands a double row of windmills, 12 in all (now out of use).

°Windmills

There are some 150 other churches scattered over the island. In a cave on the north side of Mount Pýrgos (732 m (2402 ft)), near the Plakotó Monastery, are the remains of a sanctuary (probably Hellenistic), which is said to contain Homer's tomb. On the north side of the island can be seen a ruined Venetian castle.

Vathý Bay, Ithaca

Ithaca ῎Ιθάχη/Itháki C2

Region: Ionian Islands
Nomos: Kefallinía
Area: 93 sq. km (36 sq. miles)
Altitude: 0–808 m (0–2651 ft)
Population: 9000
Chief place: Vathý (Itháki)

Ferry from Pátras via Sámi (Kefallinía) several times weekly.

Boat services

Ithaca (Itháki, popularly Thiaki) is a rocky island separated from Kefallinía by the 4 km (2½ mile) wide Ithaca Channel and almost cut into two by the long Gulf of Mólos on its east side; the isthmus joining the two halves, at Mount Aetós (380 m (1247 ft)), is only 600 m (650 yd) wide. In the north of the island is the Ani range (Mount Neritos, 808 m (2651 ft)), in the south Mount Stefani (671 m (2202 ft)). Much of the island has been marked by karstic action, but agriculture is possible in the few fertile valleys.

Present-day Ithaca is generally accepted as being Odysseus' island of Ithaca, as described in the "Odyssey", though Wilhelm Dörpfeld located the Homeric Ithaca on the island of Lefkás (see entry).

Situation and characteristics

The earliest finds of pottery point to a first settlement of the island towards the end of the 3rd millennium B.C. A number of Mycenaean sites have been identified, though their poverty is

History

difficult to reconcile with the wealthy Homeric Ithaca, which is dated to the Mycenaean period. During the 1st millennium B.C., however, the island seems to have attained a degree of prosperity through an active trade with mainland Greece and Italy.

From Roman times Ithaca shared the destinies of the other Ionian Islands. During the Middle Ages the inhabitants were driven out by pirates, who established their base in what is now Vathý. In the 17th c. the island was resettled by peasants from Kefallinía.

After a long history of devastating raids and earthquakes (most recently in 1953) practically all Ithaca's older buildings have been destroyed.

Sights

Vathý

The chief place on the island is the sheltered port of Vathý or Itháki (pop. 2500), probably founded by the Romans, which is charmingly situated in a bay – generally accepted as being the Bay of Phorkys, in which the Phaeacians put the returning Odysseus ashore ("Odyssey", XIII, 96 ff.) – defended by two Venetian forts.

2 km (1¼ miles) west, on the slopes of Mount Ayios Nikólaos, is the Mármaro Spília, a stalactite cave and an ancient cult site

Cave of the Nymphs

which is said to be the Cave of the Nymphs ("Odyssey", XIII, 107–108). 5 km (3 miles) west of Vathý, on Mount Aetós, is the acropolis of an ancient city (7th c. B.C.; perhaps Strabo's Alalkomenai) which was excavated by Schliemann; it is popularly known as the Castle of Ulysses.

6 km (4 miles) south of Vathý on a difficult footpath is the Fountain of Arethusa, under the Ravens' Crag ("Odyssey", XIII, 408–409). Farther south lies the Plateau of Marathiá, planted with olive trees and affording far-ranging views. Eumaios' farmyard ("Odyssey", XIV, 6) is supposed to have been in this area.

3 km (2 miles) south of Vathý we come to the site of Palaiokhóra, the island's capital until the 16th c.

Stavrós

The numerous ancient finds made in the vicinity of the village of Stavrós, in the north-west of the island, have suggested this as the most likely site for the city and palace of Odysseus.

Pólis Bay

Below Stavrós, to the south-west, lies beautiful Pólis Bay, the only harbour of any size on the west coast of Ithaca. A cave on the west side of the bay was a Sanctuary of Athena and Hera in Mycenaean times. Off the bay, near the coast of Kefallinía, can be seen the tiny island of Daskalio, which is identified with the ancient Asteris ("Odyssey", XVI, 365).

1 km (¾ mile) north, on Mount Pelikata above Pólis Bay, are remains of a settlement dated between 2200 and 1500 B.C. 1 km (¾ mile) farther north stands the Chapel of Ayios Athanásios. West of Stavrós are the beautiful bays of Fríkes and Kióni.

Panayía Kathará Monastery

6 km (4 miles) south of Stavrós is the Monastery of Panayía Kathará (magnificent view; festival celebrated on 8 September).

Átokos

10 km (6 miles) north-east of Ithaca is the uninhabited rocky island of Átokos.

Kalamos   Κάλαμος/Kálamos   C2

Island group: Ionian Islands
Nomos: Kefallinía
Area: 24 sq. km (9 sq. miles)
Altitude: 0–740 m (0–2428 ft)
Population: 1500
Chief place: Kálamos

Connections with Astakós and Lefkás.   Boat services

Kálamos, lying off the coast of Acarnania, is a hilly island of   Situation and characteristics
karstic terrain and steep rocky coasts, with some agriculture.
The chief place, Kálamos, is on the south-east coast.
To the south of Kálamos lies the island of Kastós, inhabited by
a few fishermen.

Kalymnos   Κάλυμνος/Kálimnos   D5

Island group: Southern Sporades
Nomos: Dodecanese
Area: 109 sq. km (42 sq. miles)
Altitude: 0–678 m (0–2225 ft)
Population: 13,000
Chief place: Kálymnos (Póthia)

Kálymnos harbour

Kalymnos

Regular services several times weekly from and to Athens (Piraeus: 14–19 hours; cars carried). Local Dodecanese service: Rhodes – Sými – Tílos – Nísyros – Kos – Kálymnos – Léros – Lipsí – Pátmos – Arkí – Agathonísi – Sámos; also Rhodes – Kos – Kálymnos – Astypálaia.

Situation and characteristics

Kálymnos is a bare limestone island, slashed by numerous gorges, lying 12 km (7½ miles) north-west of Kos (see entry) and separated from Léros (see entry), to the north-west, by the narrow Diapori Channel. The coasts are mostly steep and rocky, with numerous coves and inlets.

The inhabitants live partly by farming in the few fertile valleys and depressions, but mainly – as they have for centuries – by fishing for sponges in the south-eastern Mediterranean and processing them for export to America. The departure (April–May) and return (September–October) of the sponge-fishing fleet are celebrated with lively festivities.

History

Finds in various caves round the coasts, particularly at Daskalió, near Vathý, and Ayía Varvára, show that Kálymnos has been continuously inhabited since the Neolithic period. The island never played a prominent part in history.

Sights

A limestone ridge rising to 678 m (2225 ft) separates the north of the island from the south, in which most of the population has been concentrated since ancient times. From the foot of the

The island of Télendos, seen from Kálymnos

hills a fertile plain extends south to the island's capital and port, Kálymnos (formerly called Póthia; pop. 9500; radioactive springs), its handsome houses, in the neo-classical style popular in the islands in the 19th c., rising above the harbour on the gentle slopes fringing the bay. There is a small museum containing Neolithic material and finds from the Sanctuary of Delian Apollo (see below).

Kálymnos

North-west of the town is the former capital of the island, Khorió (17th c.), with a Byzantine castle. Half-way between Kálymnos and Khorió, off the road to the west, stands the Frankish stronghold of Péra Kástro.

To the west of Khorió, in the valley above Linari Bay, is the ruined Church of Christ of Jerusalem, an Early Christian basilica built in the 6th c., reusing ancient stones, on the foundations of a Temple of Delian Apollo.

Church of Christ of Jerusalem

There are also many ancient remains round the sheltered Bay of Pánormos on the west coast, including fortifications at the little Cove of Aryinóntas (on the south side of the bay) at Xirókampos and Vriokástro and the ruined fort of Kástro (probably Carian) high above the Cove of Emporió on the north side of the bay.

Pánormos Bay

Télendos

Pánormos Bay is closed on the west by the rocky island of Télendos (458 m (1503 ft)). On Mount Ayios Konstantínos stands a medieval castle, and at the foot of the hill can be seen the ruined Monastery of Ayios Vasíleios.

Karpathos   Κα'ρπαδος/Kárpathos   E5

Region: Aegean Islands
Island group: Dodecanese
Nomos: Dodecanese
Area: 332 sq. km (128 sq. miles)
Altitude: 0–1220 m (0–4003 ft)
Population: 6000
Chief place: Kárpathos (Pygádia)

Airfield 16 km (10 miles) south of Kárpathos. One to three flights daily Kárpathos – Rhodes, daily flights Kárpathos – Kásos.

Air services

Regular weekly services from and to Athens (Piraeus; 26 hours); also from and to Crete. Local Dodecanese services: Rhodes – Khalkí – Kárpathos – Kásos.

Boat services

Kárpathos (Italian Scarpanto), a long narrow island in the Dodecanese extending for some 48 km (30 miles) from north to south, forms, together with its neighbouring island of Kásos, a transition between Rhodes and Crete. A rugged and infertile range of limestone hills, rising to 1220 m (4003 ft) in Kalí Límni, extends along the whole length of the island. The coasts mostly fall steeply down to the sea, with small sandy beaches edged by numerous caves at the south end, on the west coast round

Situation and characteristics

135

Ancient columns at Pygádia, Kárpathos

Arkása and on the east coast at Pygádia. The inhabitants' main sources of income are stock-farming, cabinet-making, wood-carving and the hand-woven cloth and embroidery produced by the women.

History

The island was originally occupied by settlers from Crete, followed by other settlers from Argos; thereafter it became subject to Rhodes. It had four ancient cities – Arkesia (of which there are scanty traces) at the south end of the west coast, Poseidion at the south end of the east coast, Thoantion on the west coast and Vrykos at the north end – and it gave its name to the sea between Crete and Rhodes.

Sights

Kárpathos

The chief place on the island and its principal port, Kárpathos (pop. 1200), founded only in the early 20th c., lies on the site of ancient Poseidion in a wide bay near the south end of the east coast. A rewarding trip from here (by bus or taxi) is to the typical old mountain village Ólympos (beautiful view; wind-mills, still functioning) in the northern half of the island; it can also be reached from Diafáni, near the north end of the east coast. The inhabitants of Ólympos still wear their richly embroidered traditional costumes, and the traditional wedding festivities, lasting three days, are famed throughout Greece. Another interesting village is Apérion, north-west of Kárpathos.

Sariá

Off the northern tip of Kárpathos, separated from it by a channel only 100 m (110 yd) wide, lies the island of Sariá (16 sq. km (6 sq. miles); 0–565 m (0–1854 ft)), the ancient Saros. On the south side are the ruins of a Byzantine city.

Kasos   Κάσος/Kásos   E5

Region: Aegean Islands
Island group: Dodecanese
Nomos: Dodecanese
Area: 65 sq. km (25 sq. miles)
Altitude: 0–583 m (0–1913 ft)
Population: 1500
Chief place: Fry

Airfield 1 km ($\frac{3}{4}$ mile) north-west of Fry. Daily service Rhodes – Kárpathos – Kásos.

Air services

Weekly services from and to Athens (Piraeus) and Rhodes. Local Dodecanese services: Rhodes – Khalkí – Kárpathos – Kásos; also connections with Crete (Sitía and Ayios Nikólaos).

Boat services

The island of Kásos (Italian Caso, Turkish Kasot), south-west of Kárpathos, is rocky (numerous caves), barren and without any sheltered harbours. Its inhabitants live by farming (in the north) and boat-building.

Situation and characteristics

Coastal scenery, Kásos

Throughout its history Kásos has shared the destinies of the neighbouring island of Kárpathos. After the War of Greek Independence Albanian sponge-fishers settled on the island. The chief place on Kásos, Fry, lies above the landing-stage, to the south, on the site of the ancient city.

Off the north coast of Kásos is the little island of Armáthia, now deserted, which has a sandy beach.

Kastellorizo   Καστελλόριζο/Kastellórizo   D6

Region: Aegean Islands
Island group: Dodecanese
Nomos: Dodecanese
Area: 9 sq. km (3½ sq. miles)
Altitude: 0–271 m (0–889 ft)
Population: 200
Chief place: Meyísti

Boat services

Regular service twice weekly from and to Rhodes. Excursions from Kaş (Turkey).

Situation and characteristics

Kastellórizo (from Italian Castelrosso, the Red Castle; Turkish Meis), also known as Meyísti (Largest or Greatest), is the most easterly outpost of Greece, lying only 2 km (1¼ miles) off the south coast of Asia Minor (Lycia). This rocky and infertile island has only 200 inhabitants, compared with the population

The harbour, Kastellórizo

of some 15,000 it is said to have had about 1900. There has been a rapid decline in numbers since then as a result of emigration, particularly to Australia.

Sights

Archaeological evidence shows that the island was already well populated in the Neolithic period. Its subsequent destinies were closely linked with Rhodes.

The chief place on the island, Meyísti, a village of brightly painted houses, many of them now abandoned, lies above its sheltered harbour (sponge-fishing) in the north-east of the island, dominated by a castle (13th–16th c.) of the Knights of St John, occupying the site of a fort of the 4th c. B.C. At the foot of the castle hill is a domed Lycian tomb (4th c. B.C.).
An excursion which should not be missed is to the Blue Grotto in the south-east of the island.

Meyísti

Ro and Strongylí

5 km (3 miles) west and 4 km (2½ miles) south-east of Kastellórizo are the islets of Ro and Strongylí, now uninhabited and used only for the grazing of stock.

Kea Κέα/Kéa

D4

Region: Aegean Islands
Island group: Cyclades
Nomos: Cyclades
Area: 131 sq. km (50 sq. miles)
Altitude: 0–560 m (1837 ft)
Population: 4000
Chief place: Kéa (Khóra)

Regular services several times weekly from and to Rafína and Lávrion (Attica). Local connections with Kýthnos and Kárystos (Euboea).

Boat services

Kéa, the most westerly of the larger Cyclades, lies some 20 km (12½ miles) south-east of Cape Soúnion. The island's agriculture and the traditional harvesting of acorns for use in tanning have declined as a result of emigration. There is a certain amount of tourist traffic from the Greek mainland.

Situation and characteristics

Originally settled by Dryopes from Euboea and later by Ionians, the island was known in antiquity as **Keos** and was a tetrapolis – a State comprising the four cities of Ioulis, Karthaia, Koressia and Poiessa.

History

Sights

The chief place on the island, Kéa (Khóra; pop. 1700), lies at the foot of Mount Profítis Ilías (560 m (1837 ft)), on the site of ancient Ioulis, of which there are some remains within

Kéa (Khóra)

The Lion of Kéa

the medieval Kástro (1210). Ioulis was the home of two notable poets, Simonides and his nephew Bakchylides (6th–5th c. B.C.).

Koríssia

4 km (2⅓ miles) north-west of Kéa, on the south side of the Bay of Ayios Nikólaos (in the 13th c. a pirate stronghold), is the little port of Koríssia (also known as Livádi), on the site of ancient Koressia. There are remains of the ancient town walls and a Sanctuary of Apollo. The Kouros (statue of a youth) of Kéa (530 B.C.) which was found here is now in the National Archaeological Museum in Athens.

1.5 km (1 mile north), at the seaside resort of Vourkári, stands the little Church of Ayía Iríni, amid the remains of a strongly fortified ancient city (3rd millennium B.C. to 3rd c. A.D.), including the oldest temple found in Greece (15th c. B.C.).

°Lion of Kéa

On a hillside 1.5 km (1 mile) north-east of Kéa can be seen a 9 m (30 ft) long lion carved from the native rock (6th c. B.C.).

Karthaia

At the south end of the east coast are the massive terrace walls of ancient Karthaia. On the lowest of the terraces are the foundations of a Doric Temple of Apollo; on a 6 m (20 ft) long block in the polygonal walls of the terrace above this is an ancient inscription and on a still higher terrace are the foundations of another temple. Higher still again are the walls of the upper town and remains of buildings.

Poiessa

Above Poísses Bay, on the west coast of the island, are scanty remains of ancient Poiessa. On the way back from here to Kéa is the abandoned Monastery of Ayía Marína, near which is a well-preserved tower of the 4th c. B.C.

On Cape Kefála, on the north coast, are remains of a Neolithic settlement (4000–2800 B.C.). East of this, at Otziás, are the Trypospilies (ancient mine workings).

In the north-east of the island is the Monastery of Panayía Kastrianí (18th c.), with beautiful views.

Kefallinia/Cefalonia Κεφαλληνία/Kefallinía   C2

Region: Ionian Islands
Island group: Ionian Islands
Nomos: Kefallinía
Area: 781 sq. km (301 sq. miles)
Altitude: 0–1628 m (0–5341 ft)
Population: 40,000
Chief place: Argostóli

Airport 9 km (5½ miles) from Argostóli. Daily services from and to Athens.

Air services

Regular daily service (cars carried) between Pátras and Sámi.

Boat services

Kefallinía (Italian Cefalonia), the largest of the Ionian Islands, is an island of bare limestone mountains rising to 1628 m (5341 ft) in Mount Aínos and slashed by fertile valleys with luxuriant subtropical vegetation. It is generally accepted as being the Homeric island of Same (but for Wilhelm Dörpfeld's divergent view see Lefkás). The island's main sources of income are agriculture and the tourist trade.

Situation and characteristics

In the "Odyssey" the two islands of Same and Doulichion are described as belonging to the kingdom of Ithaca but Odysseus' subjects are also called Cephallenians.

In the 6th and 5th c. B.C. the island, like Corfu, was under the influence of Corinth; then in 456 B.C. Tolmides compelled it to submit to Athens. At that time there were four city states on Kefallinía – Kranioi, Pale, Pronnoi and Same – which Thucydides refers to as a tetrapolis. The cities were members of the Aeolian League, and Cephallenian vessels fought against Philip V of Macedon (220–217 B.C.). They fought, too, against the Romans, but eventually the island fell into the power of Rome. Thereafter Kefallíní shared the destinies of the other Ionian Islands.

Myth and history

Sights

Kefallinía's chief town, Argostóli (pop. 10,000), lies on the east side of a peninsula projecting into Argostóli Bay (or Livádi Bay), which cuts deep into the south-west coast of the island. Once an attractive old town, it was almost completely destroyed by an earthquake in 1953 and has since been rebuilt. The Archaeological Museum contains Mycenaean and Roman material.

Argostóli

To the north of the town, at the tip of the peninsula, are the famous sea-mills, now partly buried as a result of the 1953 earthquake. The mills were driven by sea-water surging along

Sea-mills

Fiskárdo harbour, Kefallinía

a channel cut through the rock and then disappearing into hidden underground passages through the limestone, to emerge on the east side of the island at the Melissáni Cave.
6 km (4 miles) south-east of Argostóli are the remains of ancient Kranioi (Krane).

*Ayios Yeóryios Castle

9 km (6 miles) south-east of Argostóli at the village of Kástro, once the flourishing capital of the island, is the 13th c. Castle of Ayios Yeóryios (alt. 320 m (1050 ft; view). The 17th c. Monastery of Ayios Andréas has fine frescoes (12th c.) and icons. The site of ancient Kephallenia is believed to have been in this area. To the south, under Mount Ayios Yeóryios, extends the fertile upland region of Liváto. Byron stayed at Metaxáta in 1823. In the neighbourhood are three Mycenaean rock-cut tombs.

Sámi

24 km (15 miles) east of Argostóli is Sámi (pop. 1200), with the island's principal harbour. Ancient Same, the island's capital, which prospered particularly in the time of the Diadochoi, lay to the south of the modern town on the slopes of the double-topped hill which rises above it (remains of town walls; Roman villa of 2nd c. A.D.).

*Stalactitic caves

In the vicinity of Sámi are the stalactitic caves of Drongaráti (south-west) and Melissáni (north-west; underground lake). – Near the village of Ayía Effímia on the Erisso Peninsula, on the north side of the Gulf of Sámi, are remains of the walls of Same. At Assos is a ruined Venetian castle (1595; view). At the north-eastern tip of the peninsula is the port of Fiskárdo (ancient

Panormos), named after the Norman leader Robert Guiscard, who died here in 1085. Some of the old houses in the village have been converted for use as holiday homes.

North-west of Argostóli, on the Palikí Peninsula on the far side of the bay, lies the port of Lixoúri (pop. 6000; ferry and road to Argostóli), to the north of which are scanty remains of the ancient city of Pale.

Lixoúri

Kimolos   Κίμωλος/Kímolos   D4

Region: Aegean Islands
Island group: Cyclades
Nomos: Cyclades
Area: 35 sq. km (13½ sq. miles)
Altitude: 0–398 m (0–1306 ft)
Population: 1500
Chief place: Kímolos

Local connection with Melos.

Boat services

Kímolos is an arid and inhospitable island of volcanic origin lying to the north-east of Melos. It was known in antiquity for its terra kimolia (cimolith), used both as a detergent and in medicinal baths.

Situation and characteristics

The chief place on the island, Kímolos, lies near the shelterd port of Psáthi (beach), round the remains of the late medieval settlement of Kástro. On the island's highest point is the ruined medieval Castle of Palaiókastro.

Ayios Andréas

Off the south-west coast of Kímolos is the little islet of Ayios Andréas, which in ancient times was connected with the main island by a narrow strip of land. On it was the oldest organised settlement on Kímolos, Hellenikon (1000 B.C.; remains of walls in the sea).

Polyaigos

2 km (1¼ miles) east of Kímolos lies the uninhabited little island of Polyaigos.

Kos   Κώς/Kos   D5

Region: Aegean Islands
Island group: Southern Sporades
Nomos: Dodecanese
Area: 295 sq. km (114 sq. miles)
Altitude: 0–846 m (0–2776 ft)
Population: 16,000
Chief place: Kos

Kos

Air services	Airfield 27 km (17 miles) south-west at Antimákhia. Daily services Athens – Kos; weekly Rhodes – Kos.
Boat services	Regular services from and to Athens (Piraeus) 6 times a week (21 hours; cars carried). Local services in Dodecanese: Rhodes – Sými – Tílos – Nísyros – Kos – Kálymnos – Léros – Lipsí – Pátmos – Arkí – Agathonísi – Sámos; also Rhodes – Kos – Kálymnos – Astypálaia. Excursions from Bodrum (Turkey).
Situation and characteristics	Kos (Italian Coo, Turkish Istanköy) lies at the mouth of the Gulf of Kos (Turkish Gulf of Kerme), which cuts deep into the coast of Asia Minor. It was separated from the Bodrum (Halikarnassos) Peninsula, 5 km (3 miles north-east), by the collapse of a rift valley in the Pliocene period. It is the largest island in the Dodecanese after Rhodes.
	A range of limestone hills, rising to 846 m (2776 ft) in Mount Díkaios (ancient Oromedon), runs along the island for almost its entire length from west to east. Unlike most other Aegean islands, Kos has a population that is increasing in numbers. The island's main sources of income are agriculture and horticulture, the rearing of small livestock, fishing, crafts (particularly pottery and weaving) and, increasingly, the tourist trade.
History	Kos has been well populated since Neolithic times. About 700 B.C., together with the five other cities of the Hexapolis (Knidos, Halikarnassos, Líndos, Ialysos and Kamiros), Kos was an outpost of the Dorian League of cities on the Carian coast and the neighbouring islands. The earliest capital of the island, Astypalaia, was situated in the wide bay at the south-west end; another important place, Halasama, was half-way down the south coast. The island was celebrated for the oldest cult site of the healing god Asklepios and for a medical school of which the most famous representative was Hippokrates (5th c. B.C.). The Sanctuary of Asklepios was destroyed by an earthquake in A.D. 554 and on its ruins was built the Monastery of Panayía tou Alsoús (of the Grove – recalling the ancient sacred grove).

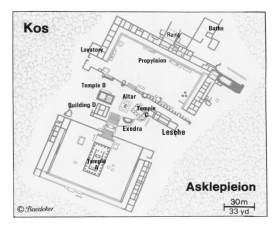

The Byzantines were succeeded as rulers of the island by the Knights of St John (1309–1523), who in the 14th c. established the main seat of their Order in the island's capital, Narangia (now the town of Kos).

Kos was captured by the Ottomans some years earlier than Rhodes. Occupied by Italy in 1912, during the Balkan War, it was returned to Greece in 1948.

Sights

The chief town, Kos (pop. 6000), rebuilt after an earthquake in 1933, lies in a deep bay, now silted up, on the north-east coast, at the east end of the plain which extends along the north coast – the only plain of any size on the island. On the east side of the sheltered harbour stands the Castle of the Knights (1450–80), with pieces of ancient sculpture and inscribed stones built into its walls. On the south side of the castle is Hippokrates' Plane Tree, under which Hippokrates is traditionally said to have taught his disciples. In fact, however, the mighty tree, with a girth of 12 m (40 ft), is only some 500 years old. To the south of the tree is the ancient Agora, on the west side of which are the charming 18th c. Defterdar Mosque (now disused), with Hellenistic and Byzantine columns, and the Archaeological Museum, which, among much else, displays the most recent finds from the Asklepieion.

South-west of the harbour are the remains of Hellenistic and Roman baths. To the south and south-west of the town can be seen remains of a Temple of Dionysos, the Gymnasion, the Stadion (Hellenistic), the Roman Odeion, the Theatre (Hellenistic and Roman) and a reconstructed Roman villa of the 3rd c. A.D., the Casa Romana, with fine mosaics.

8 km (5 miles) south-east of the town is the little spa of Ayios Fokás.

4 km (2½ miles) south-west of the town, magnificently situated 100 m (330 ft) above the sea, is the Asklepieion, the Sanctuary

Kos Town

**Hippokrates' Plane Tree

*Archaeological Museum

*Asklepieion

Remains of the Asklepieion

In the Asklepieion

The mountain village of Kéfalos

of Asklepios (Aesculapius), famous for its medical school. Laid
out on three terraces, it was built in the early 3rd c. B.C. on the
site of an earlier (5th c.) Temple of Apollo. On the lowest
terrace, to the north, extends a rectangular area some 90 m
(300 ft) long by 45 m (150 ft) wide surrounded on three sides
by Doric colonnades, to the rear of which were a series of
rooms. On the north side, to the left of the entrance, can be seen
the remains of three houses of the Roman or Late Hellenistic
period. At the north-east corner of the area a bath-house was
later inserted, subsequently converted into the Church of
Panayía tou Alsoús. Adjoining this is a small museum. Along
the south side of the terrace is the retaining wall of the next
terrace. To the left, between the second and third buttresses, is
the sacred spring. To the right, in front of a stretch of wall
without buttresses, is a naiskos (small temple) dedicated to
Nero, the "new Asklepios", by C. Stertinius Xenophon.
From here steps lead up to the second terrace, the oldest part of
the sanctuary. At the top of the steps stands an altar, which in
its present form is later than the small marble Temple of
Asklepios (c. 400 B.C.) to the west; of the earlier temple on this
site only scanty traces have survived. To the east of the altar is
an Ionic peripteral temple of 6 by 9 columns, possibly dedicated
to Apollo. To the south-west was a semicircular exedra
(recess), and facing this, behind the old temple, a Roman
building on earlier foundations.
Between these two buildings a monumental staircase 11 m
(36 ft) wide leads up to the third terrace, 12 m (40 ft) higher up,
with the later (2nd c. B.C.) Temple of Asklepios, a Doric
peripteral temple of 6 by 11 columns. The black marble sill-
stone has been preserved.
Higher up the hill (a $\frac{3}{4}$-hour climb) is the Vourinna Spring,
which supplied the ancient city with water.

From Kos town to the western tip of the island

The road first follows the northern slopes of the hills.
10 km (6 miles): Zipári, with the Early Christian Basilica of St
Paul, which has a fine baptistery and mosaics. 4 km (2½ miles)
south is the charming mountain village of Asfendíou, in a fertile
vegetable-growing area. From here Mount Díkaios (beautiful
panoramic views) can be climbed.
5 km (3 miles): side road (4 km (2½ miles) south) to Palaiá Pilí,
with a castle of the Knights of St John. In the deserted village
at the foot of the castle hill is a church with Byzantine frescoes.
13 km (8 miles): Antimákhia. 5 km (3 miles) south is another
castle of the Knights, prominently situated on a hill at Palaiá
Antimákhia, which was rebuilt after an earthquake in 1493
(coats of arms of knights). Within its walls can be found
another deserted village.
1 km (¾ mile): Kos Airport. 6 km (4 miles) south is the fishing
village of Kardámena (fruit-growing, particularly melons;
pottery).
17 km (10½ miles): Kéfalos, a mountain village perched high
above the sea, with an ancient theatre. It is the principal place
in the western part of the island. Important prehistoric remains
were found in the caves at the entrance to the village. Near by
is the ruined Early Christian Basilica of Ayios Stéfanos. In the
bay are the picturesque St Nicholas Rock, with a small chapel,
and the St Stephen Rock.

Psérimos

Off the north coast of Kos lies the island of Psérimos (17 sq. km/ $6\frac{1}{2}$ sq. miles; 0–268 m/0–879 ft; pop. 100), which has a beautiful sandy beach.

Kythira   Κύθηρα/Kíthira   D3

Region: Peloponnese
Island group: Ionian Islands
Nomos: Attica
Area: 285 sq. km (110 sq. miles)
Altitude: 0–506 m (0–1660 ft)
Population: 5000
Chief place: Kýthira (Khóra)

Air services

Airfield 10 km (6 miles) north-west of Kýthira. Daily services from Athens.

Boat services

Regular service between Athens (Piraeus) and Ayía Pelayía several times weekly (10 hours); Athens (Piraeus) – Kapsáli weekly (5 hours); Athens (Piraeus) – Antikýthira weekly (22 hours).
Local connections with Pórto Káyio, Gýthion, Néapoli, Monemvasia, Elafónisos, Antikýthira and Kísamos (Crete).

Situation and characteristics

Kýthira, the ancient Kythera (Cythera), lies some 15 km (9 miles) south of the eastern tip of Laconia. It is the most southerly of the Ionian Islands (Eptánisos), an island of rugged karstic hills and coasts falling steeply down to the sea. The island's unproductive agriculture has driven many young people to emigrate, mainly to Australia.

History

Kýthira's abundance of murex shells (producing a much-valued purple dye) led to an Early Phoenician settlement on the island. Later it belonged to Sparta, and the Phoenician cult of the goddess Astarte gave rise to the Greek cult of Aphrodite, who was said to have emerged from the sea in a large shell off the shores of Kýthira. As a military stronghold off the coast of Lacedaemon the island was of great strategic importance in ancient times.
Under Venetian rule (from 1207) Kýthira was known as Cerigo. Thereafter, as a late addition to the Eptánisos, it shared the destinies of the Ionian Islands.

Sights

*Kýthira (Khóra)

At the southern tip of the island, high above the bay and harbour of Kapsáli, is the charming village of Kýthira (Khóra: pop. 750), the chief place on the island. Above the village stands a massive Venetian castle (16th c.).

Palaiókhora

Magnificently situated above the north-east coast are the ruins of the island's former capital, Palaiókhora, with a medieval castle; the town was destroyed by the Turks in 1536. North of this, in a wide bay on the north-east coast, is the island's second port, Ayía Pelayía, used during the military dictatorship as a place of exile for opponents of the régime.

Ayía Pelayía

Kapsáli harbour, Kýthira

Above a bay on the west coast is the medieval Castle of Milopótamo. Near by is a stalactitic cave.

Milopótamo

10 km (6 miles) north-west of Kapsáli is the 17th c. Monastery of Panayía Myrtidiótissa, with an icon which is revered as wonder-working.

Panayía Myrtidiótissa

On the east coast is the Bay of Avlémona (or Ayios Nikólaos), where the yacht "Mentor", carrying some of the Elgin marbles from the Parthenon, sank in 1802; they were subsequently recovered and sent on to Britain.

Avlémona

There are numerous rocky islets off Kýthira – to the south Avgó, with the Blue Grotto, to the east the two Dragonéra Islands (with some cultivated land).

Antikýthira

South-east of Kýthira, roughly half-way to Crete, lies the little limestone island of Antikýthira (Italian Cerigotto; 22 sq. km (8½ sq. miles); 0–360 m (0–1180 ft)), the ancient Aigila or Aigilla. The inhabitants live mainly by farming and fishing. In the channel between the two islands the wreck of a Roman ship was discovered in 1900; its cargo of bronze and marble statues of the 5th to 2nd c. B.C., including the "Ephebe of Antikýthira", together with pottery, glass and an astronomical clock, is now in the National Archaeological Museum in Athens.

Kythnos   Κύδνος/Kíthnos   D4

Island group: Cyclades
Nomos: Cyclades
Area: 101 sq. km (39 sq. miles)
Altitude: 0–326 m (0–1070 ft)
Population: 1200
Chief place: Kýthnos (Khóra or Mesariá)

Boat services

Regular service from and to Athens (Piraeus) 5 times weekly (4 hours; cars carried). Local connections with Kéa and Sérifos.

Situation and characteristics

Kýthnos, a rocky and barren island of karstic limestone, lies south-east of Kéa. The coast is much indented and for the most part falls steeply down to the sea. The inhabitants live by farming and fishing. In antiquity iron was mined on the island.

History

The first settlers were Dryopes from Euboea, who were later driven out by Ionians. Kýthnos never played any important part in history.

Sights

Kýthnos (Khóra)

The chief place on the island, Kýthnos (Khóra, Mesariá), lies in the north-east of the island, 6 km (4 miles) south of the harbour of Ayía Iríni. On the north side of the bay are the hot mineral springs (40–55 °C (104–131 °F)) of Loutrá, which were already

Loutrá

The port of Mérikhas, Kýthnos

frequented in Roman times. During the period of Venetian rule
the island was known, after the springs, as Thermiá (Italian
Fermenia). The present bathing establishment was built in the
reign of Otto of Bavaria, first King of Greece.

Farther north, high above the sea, is the medieval Kástro Oriás.   Kástro Oriás

7 km (4½ miles) south-west of Kýthnos lies the island's principal   Mérikhas
port, Mérikhas. To the north, on a high crag (150 m (490 ft))
above the bays of Apókrousis and Episkopí, are the ruins of the
island's former capital, Vryókastro (Evraiokastro). On a rocky   Vryókastro
offshore islet, originally connected with the mainland, traces of
the agora and of a number of tombs in the surrounding area can
still be identified.

6 km (4 miles) south of Kýthnos, on both sides of a rocky gorge,   Dryopís
is the lively little village of Dryopís (also called Syllakas or
Khorió), which preserves the name of the original settlers on
the island. Round the village are numerous windmills and the
Katafaki Cave, which served in the past as a place of refuge.
In the south-east of the island is Kanála, with the Church of the
Panayía, which contains a miraculous icon.

Lefkas   Λευκάς/Lefkás   C2

Region: Ionian Islands
Island group: Ionian Islands
Nomos: Lefkás
Area: 302 sq. km (117 sq. miles)
Altitude: 0–1158 m (0–3799 ft)
Population: 25,000
Chief place: Lefkás

Airport at Aktion, 18 km (11 miles) north, on the mainland.   Air services
Regular daily service from Athens.

Regular bus service Athens–Lefkás several times daily.   Access by road

Lefkás (ancient Leukas; Italian Santa Maura) is a hilly island,   Situation and characteristics
marked by karstic action, lying off the Playiá Peninsula in
Acarnania, from which it is separated by a shallow lagoon
varying in width between 600 m (650 yd) and 5 km (3 miles).
It is now linked with the mainland by a causeway and a ferry
(shuttle service).
Most of the island is occupied by a range of hills rising to a
height of 1158 m (3799 ft) in Mount Stavrotás and running
south-west to end at Cape Doukáto or Lefkádas (72 m (236 ft);
lighthouse) at the tip of the Lefkás Peninsula. It was from this
Leucadian Rock of gleaming white limestone that Sappho was
supposed to have thrown herself for love of the handsome
Phaon. The main sources of income of the inhabitants are
farming on the island's thin soil, fishing, the recovery of salt
from the lagoon and various crafts, particularly lace and
knitwear.
Lefkás never had any permanent natural connection with the
mainland. The shingle spit at the northern tip of the island was
pierced in ancient times by the Corinthians to provide a channel
for shipping, and, like the spit to the south of Lefkás town

Lefkas

The entrance to Lefkás harbour

which came into being in the Middle Ages as a result of the establishment of salt-pans, allowed vessels of some size to pass through.

History and archaeology

The earliest evidence of human settlement on the island dates from the Neolithic period. In the 7th c. B.C. the town of Leukas was founded by settlers from Corinth, who closed off the south end of the lagoon, opposite the Castle of Ayios Yeóryios, by a 600 m (650 yd) long mole, remains of which are still visible under water. They cut a channel through the spit of shingle at the north end of the lagoon, opposite the Castle of Ayía Mávra – though by the time of the Peloponnesian War, in which Leukas was allied with Sparta, the channel had silted up. In the time of the Achaean League Leukas was the capital of Acarnania. It supported Philip II of Macedon against Rome, but was conquered in 197 B.C. by the Romans, who subsequently built a bridge from Leukas to the mainland.

In the Middle Ages the island belonged to the barons of Cefalonia and Zante and other Frankish dynasts. In 1479 it was taken by the Turks – the only one of the Ionian Islands to fall into their hands – but was recovered for Venice by Morosini in 1684. After a brief interlude of French rule during the Napoleonic period it was assigned in 1815 to Britain, which returned it to Greece, together with the other Ionian Islands, in 1864.

As a result of the vicissitudes of its history and of a series of earthquakes (the most recent in 1953) Lefkás has preserved very few old buildings.

Dörpfeld's theory

The German archaeologist Wilhelm Dörpfeld (1853–1940), who worked on Lefkás and made his home there, believed that this island, and not the one now called Ithaca, was the Homeric Ithaca, the home of Odysseus. He based his theory mainly on topographical similarities between Lefkás and the Ithaca described in the "Odyssey" but this was contested by other archaeologists, and Dörpfeld's excavations failed to produce convincing evidence in its support.

According to Dörpfeld Homer's Zakynthos was the present-day island of that name, Doulichion was present-day Kefallinía, Same present-day Ithaca and Ithaca the present-day island of Lefkás. He believed that Odysseus' city was in the western part of the Nídri Plain; and excavation at many points in this area did in fact yield house walls and sherds of pottery (monochrome, with scratched decoration) at depths of between 4 and 6 m (13 and 20 ft) which might be held to support Dörpfeld's theory.

In the south of the island are two inlets, Skýdi Bay to the south-west and the narrow Sýbota Bay to the south-east, with caves in the hillside along its shores. The latter, in Dörpfeld's view, was the Cove of Phorkys, the Old Man of the Sea, where Odysseus was put ashore by the Phaeacians and hid his treasures in the Cave of the Nymphs ("Odyssey", XIII, 345 ff.). From there he made his way up through the hills to the farm of the swineherd Eumaios, situated "far from the city" at the Spring of Arethusa, which Dörpfeld would identify as the spring at the village of Évyiros ("Odyssey", XIII, 404 ff.; XIV, 6, 399; XXIV, 150). Skýdi Bay would then be the place where Telemachos landed ("Odyssey", XV, 495). On his return voyage from Pylos, warned by Athena, he had escaped the ambush prepared for him by the suitors on the islet of Asteris – perhaps Arkoúdi (0–135 m (0–443 ft)), south of Lefkás.

Sea-cave on the island of Meganísi

Sights

Lefkás

At the north end of the island is its chief town, Lefkás (pop. 6500). The unusual structure of the houses, with supporting timber posts and beams and lightly built upper storeys, is designed for protection against earthquakes.

Santa Maura

3 km (2 miles) north of the town, on the shingle spit at the north end of the lagoon, is the Venetian Fort of Santa Maura (13th c.) – 3 km (2 miles) west is the Fanerómeni Monastery (fine view) – 3 km (2 miles) south, on a hill, are the remains of ancient Leukas, with the acropolis, an aqueduct, stretches of the town walls and a theatre.

Leukas

Nídri Bay

14 km (9 miles) south of Lefkás is Nídri Bay, reaching far inland. On Cape Kiriáki, opposite the little port of Nídri on the east side of the bay, are Dörpfeld's house and grave.

Off Nídri Bay, to the east, lie the picturesque little islands of Spárti (sea-caves), Madourí, home of the 19th c. poet Aristotelis Valaoritis, and Skorpiós, which belongs to the Onassis family.

Meganísi

Off the south-east coast of Lefkás is the beautiful unspoilt island of Meganísi (18 sq. km (7 sq. miles); 0–267 m (0–876 ft); pop. 2500), the ancient Thaphos, with sandy beaches and sea-caves. There is some farming land in the flatter western part of the island; the eastern part is occupied by a range of wooded hills (quarries). The chief place is the little port of Vathý (regular service from Lefkás). To the west is the harbour of the village of Spartokhóri.

Lemnos Λῆμγος/Límnos   B/C4

Region: Aegean Islands
Nomos: Lesbos
Area: 476 sq. km (183 sq. miles)
Altitude: 0–470 m (0–1542 ft)
Population: 17,000
Chief place: Mýrina

Air services

Airfield 25 km (15 miles) north-east of Mýrina. Several flights daily from Athens; daily from Salonica; several flights weekly from Mytilíni (Lésbos).

Boat services

Regular service Athens (Piraeus) – Lemnos – Samothrace – Alexandroúpolis.

Situation and characteristics

Lemnos is a hilly island in the northern Aegean, rising to 470 m (1542 ft) at its highest point. Fertile and almost treeless, it produces corn and, increasingly cotton. The coast is much indented, with two inlets, Pourniás Bay in the north and Moúdros Bay in the south, cutting so deep inland that the eastern and western parts of the island are joined by a strip of land only 4 km (2½ miles) wide. The volcanic rock in the east recalls the ancient tradition that after his fall from Olympus Hephaistos set up his smithy and married Aphrodite here. The people of Lemnos were notorious for their "wicked deeds", as reported by Herodotus, which provided the Athenian General Miltiades with a pretext for his conquest of the island.

The walled city of Poliochni dated back to the beginning of the 3rd millennium B.C. and belonged to the same pre-Greek culture as Troy and Thermoi (on Lésbos). The first Greeks came to Lemnos about 800 B.C., but a century later gave place to the Tyrseni from Asia Minor, whose language, on the evidence of inscriptions found at Kamínia, was related to the Etruscan. This provides some support for the theory, first put forward by Herodotus, that the Etruscans originally came from the region of Lydia in Asia Minor. The island was resettled by Greeks after the Athenian conquest at the end of the 6th c. B.C. It was celebrated for the cult of Hephaistos, centred on an "earth fire" near the city of Hephaisteia in the north of the island. In the 4th c. A.D. Hephaisteia became the see of a bishop, but the see was later transferred to Mýrina on the west coast.

After the Fourth Crusade the island was occupied by the Venetians. A hundred years later it was recovered by the Byzantines and was then granted to the Gattelusi family of Lésbos as a fief. It was held by the Turks from 1479 to 1912. During the Orlov Rising of 1770 it became a Russian naval base, and in the First World War Moúdros Bay was the Royal Navy's base during the Gallipoli campaign.

History

Sights

The island's chief town and principal harbour is Mýrina (pop. 3400), usually called Kástro, which occupies the site of ancient Mýrina on the west coast, under a crag crowned by a Venetian castle built on the ancient acropolis. The crag, from which there are views of the town and surrounding area and a prospect extending on a clear afternoon as far as Mount Athos, some 60 km (40 miles) away, separates two bays; the one to the south is the harbour, while the one to the north has a long and beautiful sandy beach. In the north bay is the well-arranged Museum, which contains material from the prehistoric settlement of Poliókhni, the site of Hephaisteia and the Sanctuary of the Kabeiroi at Khlói.

Mýrina

Museum

Kontiás, 10 km (6 miles) east of Mýrina, is beautifully situated in a bay with a sandy beach.

Kontiás

The island's second port, Moúdros (pop. 1200), lies on the east side of Moúdros Bay, 28 km (17 miles) east of Mýrina. From here a road runs via Kamínia, near which were found the Tyrsenian inscriptions mentioned above, to Poliókhni (34 km (21 miles)), where Italian archaeologists found the remains of a prehistoric settlement dating back to the 3rd and 4th millennia B.C. (town walls, houses and a gate approached by a ramp similar to that of Troy II).

Moúdros

In the north-east of the island, reached by way of Kontopoúli (30 km (19 miles); pop. 1100), are the site of ancient Hephaisteia, on Pourniás Bay (necropolis of 8th–6th c.; Hellenistic theatre), and the ancient port of Chloe (Khlói), where excavations by Italian archaeologists (not yet complete) have brought to light a Sanctuary of the Kabeiroi. The visible remains include two cult buildings of the 6th–5th and 4th c. B.C.

Hephaisteia

Leros Λέρος/Léros   D5

Island group: Southern Sporades
Nomos: Dodecanese
Area: 53 sq. km (20 sq. miles)
Altitude: 0–327 m (0–1073 ft)
Population: 6000
Chief place: Ayía Marína

Air services	Daily flights Athens – Léros; several times weekly Kos – Léros.
Boat services	Regular service from and to Athens (Piraeus) several times weekly (11–12 hours; cars carried). Local Dodecanese services: Rhodes – Sými – Tílos – Kos – Kálymnos – Léros – Lipsí – Pátmos – Arkí – Agathonísi – Sámos.
Situation and characteristics	Léros is a hilly and fertile island with an abundance of water and a much-indented coast. The inhabitants live by farming and fishing.
History	In antiquity Léros was dependant on Miletus. Although continuously inhabited since then, it has never played a part of any importance in history. In the 14th c. the Knights of St John established themselves on the island and held it against the Turks until the 16th c. During the Second World War it was a German naval base and subject to heavy attack.

Kástro, a castle of the Knights of St John above Ayí Marína

Sights

The chief place on the island, Ayía Marína (pop. 2500), lies on the south side of Alinda Bay, on the east coast. Above the little town, on the ridge of hills between Alinda Bay to the north and Plátanos Bay to the south, stands the Kástro, a castle of the Knights of St John, on the site of the ancient acropolis.

Ayía Marína

To the south of Ayía Marína, in a sheltered bay cutting deep into the west coast, is Lakkí (pop. 1500; British military cemetery). The village has a medieval Church of St John. In the plain south-east of Lakkí lies the village of Xerókambos, above which are the remains of ancient Palaiokastro, a fortress of the 4th c. B.C.
In the north of the island is Parthéni Bay (closed military area), closed to the north-west by the little island of Arkhángelos.

Lakkí

Palaiokastro

Lesbos   Λέσβος/Lésbos (Lésvos)   C4/5

Region: Aegean Islands
Nomos: Lésbos
Area: 1630 sq. km (629 sq. miles)
Altitude: 0–967 m (0–3173 ft)
Population: 97,000
Chief place: Mytilíni

Airport 8 km (5 miles) south-east of Mytilíni. Four flights daily from Athens; daily from Salonica; several times weekly from Lemnos.

Air services

Regular service from and to Athens (Piraeus) several times weekly (cars carried); from and to Salonica, Rhodes and Kými weekly. Ferry from Dikili (Turkey).

Boat services

Lésbos (popularly called Mytilíni; Turkish Midilli, Italian Metellino), the third largest of the Greek islands (after Crete and Euboea), lies in an angle formed by the Anatolian coast, which is only 10 km (6 miles) away on the north side of the island and 15 km (9 miles) away on the east side. An island of great scenic beauty, Lésbos is also one of the most fertile regions in Greece. It is broken up by the gulfs of Kalloní and léra, which cut deep inland on the south-west and south-east sides. The island's proximity to the mainland of Asia Minor was a major factor in the vicissitudes of its history.

Situation and characteristics

At Thermí, 12 km (7½ miles) north of Mytilíni, excavation has brought to light a pre-Greek settlement established about 2700 B.C. which belonged to a cultural group embracing also the Troad and the offshore islands as far away as Lemnos. About 1000 B.C. Aeolian Greeks from Thessaly arrived on the island and founded the cities of Mytilene and Methymna, ruled by aristocratic families which were constantly in a state of strife. About 600 B.C. the tyrant (sole ruler) Pittakos put an end to faction and arbitrary government, retired voluntarily after ten years and thereafter was accounted one of the Seven Sages. From 546 to 479 B.C. Lesbos was under Persian rule, and after its liberation became a member of the Attic maritime league. Throughout this period, however, and in Hellenistic and

History

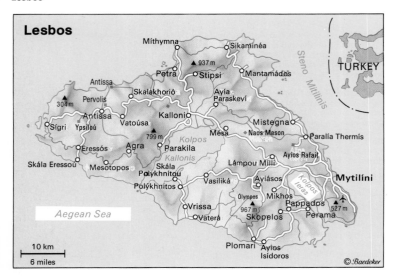

Sappho

Roman times it was able, like Chíos, to maintain its independence.

Lesbos was the home of the poet Terpandros (7th c. B.C.), who was credited with the invention of the seven-stringed lyre; about 600 B.C. the singer Arion was born in Methymna, the poet Alkaios was born in Mytilene and Sappho, the greatest Greek poetess, was born in Eressos. She instructed young girls in the arts – with no suggestion of the later meaning of "Lesbian". Another native of Lésbos was the philosopher Theophrastos (322–287 B.C.), who became head of Aristotle's Lyceum in Athens.

In 1355 a Genoese nobleman named Francesco Gattelusi married a daughter of the Byzantine Emperor, who received Lésbos as her dowry. Thereafter the Gattelusi ruled the island as a Byzantine fief until 1462, when Lésbos was capture by the Turks. During the period of Turkish rule, which lasted until 1913, many of the inhabitants moved to the mainland, particularly to the nearby town of Kydonia (now Ayvalık in Turkey). After the catastrophe of 1922–23 their descendants returned to the island, the economy of which was badly hit by the loss of its Anatolian hinterland.

Mytilíni

The chief town, Mytilíni (Khóra; pop. 26,000), lies in a bay on the east coast, on the site of ancient Mytilene. A breakwater, which is also a popular promenade, protects the harbour, on which the commercial activity of the town is centred. Above the tiled roofs of the low houses, some of them fronted by colonnades, rises the characteristic dome of the Church of Ayios Therapón, the architecture of which betrays Western

Mytilíni

influence. Between the present south harbour and the ancient harbour to the north is an area of low ground, once traversed by a canal, which separates the main part of the town from the massive Gattelusi Castle, built on a crag projecting eastward into the sea. A path runs up through a pine wood to the entrance, on the strongly fortified south-east side. Fragments of ancient masonry in the walls and towers are a reminder that the extensive castle ward occupies the area of the ancient acropolis. There are a number of mosques dating from the Turkish period. Over a side entrance in the north-west wall are the coats of Francesco I Gattelusi (1355–86) and his Byzantine Princess, with an inscription of 1377. From the north end of the castle there is a fine view of the ancient north harbour, with the remains of its breakwater.

To the west, above the north harbour, is the ancient theatre (3rd c. B.C.), which gave Pompey the idea of building the first stone theatre in Rome.

Ancient theatre

At the south end of the castle hill stands a monument to those who died during the fighting with the Turks between 1821 and 1923. Near by is a swimming-pool. The small Archaeological Museum contains, among other things, a number of capitals of the rare Aeolian type and mosaics dating from late antiquity.

Archaeological Museum

The north of the island (circuit, 125 km (78 miles))

12 km (7½ miles) north-west of Mytilíni is the little spa of Paralía Thermís, near which is the prehistoric settlement of Thermí,

159

dating back to 2700 B.C. The road continues via Mantamádos (38 km (24 miles)), which has a much-revered miraculous icon of the Mother of God (pilgrimage on 8 November), and Sikaminéa (50 km (31 miles)), birthplace of the contemporary writer Stratis Mirivillis, to Míthymna (63 km (39 miles); ancient Methymna; also known as Mólyvos; pop. 1800), a little port situated under a Gattelusi castle, from which there is a view extending to Asia Minor. As H. G. Buchholz explains in his monograph on Methymna, the first settlement here was established in the 3rd millennium B.C. in the area known as Palaiá Míthymna, to the east; in the latter part of the 2nd millennium it was moved to the present site, and in the 1st millennium the city developed extensive trading connections, reaching in the Hellenistic period as far afield as Egypt.

Kallóni

*Límonos Monastery

Continuing south from Míthymna, we pass the little port of Petrá (72 km (45 miles)), at the foot of a high crag, and come to Kallóni (87 km (54 miles); pop. 2000), 4 km (2½ miles) north of the Gulf of Kallóni, which reaches 21 km (13 miles) inland. Near here is the Monastery of Límonos, with a richly carved iconostasis and completely preserved wall-paintings in the principal church (admission for men only). The large monastic library, its archives and a museum are housed in new buildings.

Lámpou Mílli

The road now turns south-east, leaving the Gulf of Kallóni at Mésa (94 km (58 miles)). Near here are the remains of a temple, with a church which was later built into it. At Lámpou Mílli (also called Mória; 109 km (68 miles)) are remains of a Roman aqueduct. Then back to Mytilíni (125 km (78 miles)).

The west of the island (circuit, 177 km (110 miles))

Antissa

Going west from Mytilíni, we come to Shalakhorió (54 km (34 miles)), where a road goes off to the remains of ancient Antissa.
Beyond Vatoúsa (61 km (38 miles)), to the right of the road, is Perivólis Monastery (17th c. frescoes), and beyond the new village of Antissa (69 km (43 miles)) the Ypsiloú Monastery, on Mount Ordímnos (manuscripts; magnificent view).

Sígri

*Petrified forest

The road reaches the sea at Sígri (84 km (52 miles); pop. 550), a little holiday resort on the west coast. South-east of the village is a petrified forest of trees which were buried in volcanic ash at least 700,000 years ago.

Eressós

From Eressós (98 km (61 miles); museum) it is worth making a detour to Skála Eressoú (101 km (63 miles)), on the south coast, with a beautiful sandy beach. This is the site of ancient Eressos, birthplace of Sappho and Theophrastos. To the west, near the beach, are the ruins of an Early Christian basilica known as the Skholí Theofrástou, the School of Theophrastos. Returning to Eressós, we continue via Agra (118 km (73 miles)) and Kallóni (147 km (91 miles)) to Mytilíni (177 km (110 miles)).

The south of the island

Ayiásos

An interesting trip to the south of the island is to Ayiásos (30 km (19 miles); pop. 5000), on the northern slopes of Mount Ólympos (967 m (3173 ft)). Its central feature, the pilgrimage

Míthymna

Lámpou Mílli (Mória)

church (last restored in 1816), attracts thousands of pilgrims on the Feast of the Dormition (15 August). Fine pottery and homespun cloth.

From Ayiásos its is worth continuing to Polykhnitos (24 km (15 miles); pop. 5100), its port of Skála Polykhnítou and the Damándri Monastery (frescoes of 1580). Beyond Polykhnitos is Vaterá, with a good beach.

Polykhnitos

For another excursion to the south coast, leave Mytilíni on the road which runs along the north end of the Gulf of Iéra and then turns down its west side to reach the bathing beach of Ayios Isídoros and the town of Plomárion (42 km (26 miles); pop. 5200).

Plomárion

Lipsi Λειψοί/Lipsí D5

Region: Aegean Islands
Island group: Southern Sporades
Nomos: Lipsí
Area: 18 sq. km (7 sq. miles)
Altitude: 0–275 m (0–902 ft)
Population: 500
Chief place: Lipsí

Local connections with Pátmos and Léros.

Boat services

Makronisos

Situation and characteristics | Lipsí, formerly called Lepsia, is a small island in the Southern Sporades, 12 km (7½ miles) east of Pátmos, which was resettled in the 19th c. On the south coast is the modest little village of Lipsí which is the chief place on the island and its principal port. It was a naval base during the War of Greek Independence. The inhabitants live by farming and fishing.

Makronisos   Μακρόνησος/Makrónisos   D4

Island group: Cyclades
Nomos: Cyclades
Area: 18 sq. km (7 sq. miles)
Altitude: 0–281 m (0–922 ft)

Situation and characteristics | Makrónisos, the Long Island, lies 5 km (3 miles) off the coast of Attica to the east of Cape Soúnion. In antiquity it bore the name of Helen, who according to Pausanias rested here.
Archaeological evidence points to a modest degree of settlement from the Neolithic period onwards. In more recent times the island has frequently been used as an internment camp. It is now inhabited only by a few shepherds.

Melos/Milos   Μῆλος/Mílos   D4

Region: Aegean Islands
Island group: Cyclades
Nomos: Cyclades
Area: 147 sq. km (57 sq. miles)
Altitude: 0–751 m (0–2464 ft)
Population: 4500
Chief place: Mílos

Air services | Airport 5 km (3 miles) from Mílos. Daily flights Athens–Melos.

Boat services | Regular service from and to Athens (Piraeus) several times weekly. Local connections with neighbouring islands.

Situation and characteristics | The island of Melos or Mílos (from the Greek word for "apple"; Italian Milo), the most westerly of the larger Cyclades, owes its distinctive topography and the pattern of its economy to its origin as the caldera of a volcano of the Pliocene period, to which the sulphureous hot springs in the north-east and south-east of the island still bear witness. It has one of the best harbours in the Mediterranean, formed when the sea broke into the crater through a gap on its north-west side. The north-eastern half of the island is flatter and more fertile than the upland region in the south-west, which rises to 751 m (2464 ft) in Mount Profítis Ilías. The island's principal sources of income are its rich mineral resources, including pumice, alum, sulphur and clay. The tourist trade now also makes a contribution to the economy.

History | The island was already densely populated in the 3rd millennium B.C., when the inhabitants made implements and weapons from the large local deposits of obsidian and exported them all over the Aegean and as far afield as Asia Minor and Egypt. About 1200 B.C. Dorian incomers settled on the island and founded the city of Melos, defended by walls and towers, on a hill on the north side of Mílos Bay, on the site of present-day Kástro, with its harbour at what is now the hamlet of Klíma. They prospered through the export of sulphur, pumice, clay and alum, and also of oil, wine and honey.

In Roman and Early Christian times Melos was also a notable art centre. Its best-known work is the Aphrodite of Melos or Venus de Milo (2nd c. B.C.), now in the Louvre.

After the fall of the Roman Empire Melos became Byzantine; in the Middle Ages it belonged to the Venetian Duchy of Náxos; and after centuries of Turkish rule it became part of the newly established kingdom of Greece.

Venus de Milo

Sights

The port of Adámas (pop. 750) on the north side of Mílos Bay, is a typical little Cycladic town. 4 km (2½ miles) north-west is the chief place on the island, Mílos or Pláka (alt. 200 m (650 ft); pop. 900), which has an interesting little museum. On the way up to the Venetian fortress on the top of the hill stands a notable church, the Panayía Thalassítras.

Adámas

° Mílos (Pláka)

1 km (¾ mile) below Pláka is the village of Trypití (the name means "riddled with holes"), from which a concrete road leads to the Early Christian catacombs (2nd c.), with a Saint's tomb in the principal chamber and some 2000 tomb niches. The catacombs are unique in Greece.

° Catacombs

Adámas

Melos — A side road which branches off the concrete road leads to the remains of the ancient Dorian city of Melos. A signpost (on the left) marks the spot where the Aphrodite of Melos (Venus de Milo), a Hellenistic work of about 150 B.C., was found in 1820. A short distance away, beautifully situated on the hillside overlooking the bay, is a small Roman theatre.

Phylakopé — East of Trypití, above the precipitous north coast, is the site of Phylakopé (Fylakopí), with the foundations of houses of the 3rd and 2nd millennia B.C. and Mycenaean walls of about 1500 B.C.

Apollónia — Beyond this is the pretty little port of Apollónia (11 km (7 miles)), with a sandy beach.

Zefyriá
Palaiokhorá — South-east of Adámas are Zefyriá (6 km (4 miles)) and the ruins of Palaiokhorá, founded in the 8th c. and abandoned in 1793.

Antímilos

North-west of Melos lies the rocky island of Antímilos (8 sq. km (3 sq. miles); 0–643 m (0–2110 ft)), which is inhabited only by wild goats.

Glaronísia

Off the north coast of Melos are the Glaronísia (Seagull Islands), four bizarrely shaped basalt stacks (Sykia caves).

Mykonos Μύκονος/Míkonos D4

Region: Aegean Islands
Island group: Cyclades
Nomos: Cyclades
Area: 75 sq. km (29 sq. miles)
Altitude: 0–364 m (0–1194 ft)
Population: 4000
Chief place: Mýkonos (Khóra)

Air services — Airfield 3 km (2 miles) from Mýkonos town. Several flights daily from Athens.

Boat services — Regular service from and to Athens (Piraeus) several times daily (6–7 hours; cars carried). Local connections with Delos and other neighbouring islands depending on weather conditions.

Situation and characteristics — The bare rocky island of Mýkonos, the most easterly of the northern Cyclades, was once one of the most important trading centres in the western Aegean. Its arid and only moderately fertile soil permits only a modest development of agriculture, but its beautiful beaches have made it one of the most popular holiday islands in the Aegean. It has a flourishing craft industry. Mýkonos is also a good base from which to visit the neighbouring islands of Delos and Rínia.

Myth and history — According to legend Mýkonos was the rock with which Poseidon slew the giants. The island's history was closely

The town of Mýkonos

Paraportianí Church

bound up with that of Tínos. Unlike Tínos, however, it was occupied by the Turks, though it contrived to maintain a considerable degree of independence under Turkish rule.

Sights

˙ Mýkonos (Khóra)

The chief place on the island, Mýkonos or Khóra (pop. 2500), is a charming little town of cube-shaped whitewashed houses, with numerous churches and several windmills, extending in a semicircle round a bay on the west coast. It occupies the site of the ancient city of the same name. There is a small museum with archaeological material from Rínia and Delos. The most interesting of the churches is the Paraportianí Church, which is built on four levels.

The mascot of Mýkonos for more than 30 years was a tame pelican named Pétros. After his universally lamented death in December 1985 he was stuffed and can now be seen in the local museum.

10 km (6 miles) east of Mýkonos town, at the quiet little village of Ano Merá, is Tourlianí Monastery. A little way north, at Palaiokástro, can be found a ruined Venetian castle, built on the ruins of an ancient settlement.

From the two summits of Mount Profítis Ilías, to the north-west (364 m (1195 ft)) and east (351 m (1152 ft); closed military area), there are superb views.

Dragonísi

2 km (1¼ miles) east of Mýkonos lies the rocky island of Dragonísi, with sea-caves frequented by seals.

Naxos Νάξος/Náxos   D4

Region: Aegean Islands
Island group: Cyclades
Nomos: Cyclades
Area: 445 sq. km (172 sq. miles)
Altitude: 0–1003 m (0–3291 ft)
Population: 14,000
Chief place: Náxos

Boat services

Regular service from and to Athens (Piraeus) several times daily (8 hours; cars carried). Local connections with the larger neighbouring islands.

Situation and characteristics

Náxos, the largest and most beautiful of the Cyclades, is traversed from north to south by a range of hills which fall away steeply on the east but slope down gradually on the west into fertile rolling country and well-watered plains. The hills rise to a height of 1003 m (3291 ft) in Mount Zás (the ancient Mount Drios) and are cut by two passes. Since ancient times the economy of the island has depended on agriculture, marble-quarrying, emery-mining and the recovery of salt from the sea, occupations which have brought it a considerable degree of prosperity. In recent years the tourist trade has been an additional source of revenue.

With its limited hotel resources, the island is not equipped to cope with mass tourism, but it has much to offer visitors – an

A windmill on Mýkonos ▶

equable climate, a wide variety of scenery, from the sandy beaches of the west coast by way of the green fields of the interior to the austere landscape of the hills, and monuments of antiquity and the medieval period.

Myth and history

Náxos was a centre of the cult of Dionysos. Mythology tells us that it was here that Theseus abandoned Ariadne.

There is much archaeological evidence to show that the island was first settled by Carians and Cretans and developed a flourishing Cycladic culture in the 3rd and 2nd millennia B.C. In the 1st millennium B.C. these first settlers were followed by Ionian Greeks, who in the 6th c. B.C. extended their rule over Páros, Ándros and other neighbouring islands. During this period there was a celebrated school of sculptors on Náxos, notable for such works as the colossal statue of Apollo on Delos. A member of the first Attic maritime league, Náxos became subject to Athens after an unsuccessful rising and was compelled to accept the redistribution of land on the island to Athenian citizens. In spite of this it became a member of the second Attic maritime league. After being held by Macedon it passed under Egyptian rule, was briefly assigned to Rhodes by Mark Antony and thereafter became part of the Byzantine Empire.

In 1207 Náxos was occupied by a Venetian nobleman named Marco Sanudo, who made it the centre of the Duchy of the Twelve Islands in the Aegean (Duchy of Náxos), which continued in existence until 1566 and achieved a considerable degree of prosperity. It was taken by the Turks in 1579, and was under Russian rule from 1770 to 1774, but, like the other Cyclades, retained a measure of independence. In 1830 it joined the newly established kingdom of Greece.

Náxos town

The island's capital, Náxos (pop. 2500), in a fertile district growing vines, fruit and vegetables, is picturesquely situated on the slopes of a rocky hill crowned by the ruins of a Venetian castle, the Kástro (1260; panoramic views), which now houses a school run by Ursuline nuns. Features of interest in the town are a number of dilapidated Venetian palaces (particularly the Barozzi and Sommaripa palaces), the Catholic Church of St Mary (13th c.) and the 15th c. St Anthony's Chapel on the waterfront.

*Museum

There is an interesting museum with archaeological material from all periods of the island's history, including a fine collection of stone vessels and Cycladic idols of the 3rd millennium B.C., pottery of the Geometric, Archaic and later periods, statues and capitals. In the courtyard are stones carved with Venetian coats of arms and a large mosaic of Europa and the bull.

Náxos occupies the site of the ancient capital of the island, the main visible relics of which are a 6 m (20 ft) high marble gateway and the foundations of an unfinished Temple of Apollo or Dionysos (6th c. B.C.) on the rocky islet of Sto Paláti, which is connected with the main island by a stone causeway.

*Marble gateway

North-east of the town stands the old fortified Monastery of St John Chrysostom. 10 km (6 miles) north-east is the whitewashed Faneroméni Monastery, with a church of 1603.

Náxos town　　　　　　　*Rim of crater, Nísyros*

Excursion to the marble quarries

Above Apollónia Bay, to the south-east of Cape Stávros, the northernmost tip of the island (40 km (25 miles) from Náxos town), are a number of ancient quarries of the Naxian marble which was used in sculpture and architecture and also as a roof-cladding. In the Ston Apollona Quarry is the 10·40 m (34 ft) long figure of a kouros (youth), left unfinished because of a defect in the marble. Above the quarry is the Venetian Castle of Kalóyero. The characteristic coarse-grained Naxian marble also outcrops between Mélanes and Potamiá, farther south, where there are other unfinished kouroi and a door-jamb which was presumably destined for the Sto Paláti Temple.
On the slopes of the Vóthri Valley can be seen large emery-mines which were already being worked in ancient times.

*Ston Apollona

Other features of interest

Below the south-east side of Mount Zás is the Hellenistic marble Tower of Kimáro and on the west side of the hill the Cave of Zeus, an ancient cult site.

Kimáro Tower

Also worth visiting are the Venetian castles of Ápano Kástro (2 km (1¼ miles) from Khalkí; 13th c.), Áno Potamiá (south-east of Náxos town; guide needed), Apaliros (in the south-west of the island) and Cape Panerimos (south-east of the island).

Venetian castles

Characteristic of the Venetian and Turkish periods on Náxos are the fortified tower houses (pyryi) to be seen, for example, at

Tower houses

169

Khalkí (15 m (9 miles) east of Náxos town) and in the Drimália Valley.

Churches

Many churches on the island have Byzantine wall-paintings, including the churches of Ayios Kýriakos at Apíranthos and Ayios Artemios at Sangrí (frescoes of 9th c. A.D.).

***

Nisyros Nίσυρος/Nísiros   D5

Region: Aegean Islands
Island group: Southern Sporades
Nomos: Dodecanese
Area: 41 sq. km (16 sq. miles)
Altitude: 0–698 m (0–2290 ft)
Population: 2000
Chief place: Mandráki

Boat services

Regular weekly service from and to Athens (Piraeus) and Rhodes. Local connections in Dodecanese: Rhodes – Sými – Tílos – Nísyros – Kos – Kálymnos – Léros – Lipsí – Pátmos – Arkí – Agathonísi – Sámos.

Situation and characteristics

Nísyros, lying half-way between Kos and Tílos, 18 km (11 miles) south-west of the Reşadiye (Knidos) Peninsula in Asia Minor, is an extinct volcano, Mount Diabates, which was still occasionally active in the Middle Ages and erupted in 1522 but now manifests itself only in the form of solfataras (venting of sulphurous fumes). It is a green and well-watered island, with fertile soil which is cultivated on laboriously constructed terraces on the outward-facing slopes. Pumice is exported.

History

Nísyros was originally settled by Dorians from Kos and Kámiros. In 1312 it was occupied by the Knights of St John, and later became a fief of the Assanti family. It was taken by the Turks in 1533.

Sights

Mandráki

The island's capital and principal port, Mandráki (pop. 1200; thermal springs), lies on the west coast. Above it, to the west, stands the castle of the Knights of St John, now a monastery. Within the precincts of the castle is the Late Byzantine cave Church of the Panayía Spilianí, and to the south is the Palaiokástro, with impressive and well-preserved remains of walls and flights of steps belonging to the Hellenistic city (4th–3rd c. B.C.).

Páli

Emporió

Nikiá

3 km (2 miles) east of Mandráki is the port of Páli or Thérma, with hot sulphureous springs (remains of ancient baths). From here it is an hour's climb to the hilltop village of Emporió, with a medieval castle (fine views), and a further hour's walk along the rim of the crater (alt. 410–570 m (1345–1870 ft); diameter 2700–3800 m (3000–4000 yd)) to Nikiá.

Caldera

In the caldera (139 m (456 ft)) of the volcano is the little Plain of Lakkí, the northern part of which is cultivated, while the southern half is covered with bubbling hot springs and mud pools, brightly coloured concretions and steaming fumaroles.

Palaiokastro, Nísyros

On the west side is a small crater which is the highest point on the island (698 m (2290 ft)).
An hour's walk south of the crater lies the beautifully situated hilltop village of Nikiá, with a medieval castle.
Other medieval castles are Sto Stavró in the south of the island and Parkettiá in the south-east.

Yialí

Off the north coast of Nísyros in the direction of Kos is the little obsidian island of Yialí (Gyalí; 6 sq. km (2¼ sq. miles); 0–177 m (0–581 ft); pumice quarry). To the west are the islets of Pasikiá and Peroúsa, both with ancient watch-towers, and Kande-lioúsa (2 sq. km (¾ sq. mile); 0–103 m (338 ft); lighthouse).

Oinousai Islands   Οἰνοῦσαι Νῆσοι/Inoúsai Nísi   D2

Region: Peloponnese
Nomos: Messenia

The Oinousai (Inousai) Islands, notoriously subject to storms, lie off the south coast of Messenia at the south-western tip of the Peloponnese. The group consists of the two larger islands of Sapientsa (0–226 m (0–742 ft)), off Methóni Bay (sheltered anchorage by the lighthouse), and Schiza (or Cabrera; 0–196 m (0–643 ft)), together with a number of rocky islets and isolated rocks. There are several ancient wrecks on

Sapientsa
Schiza

the sea bed round the islands, and they offer excellent opportunities for underwater diving – though here, as elsewhere in Greek waters, the use of breathing apparatus is not permitted.

Othonian Islands   C1

Region: Ionian Islands
Nomos: Corfu

The Othonian Islands are an archipelago north-west of Corfu in the northern Ionian Sea, consisting of the islands – either totally uninhabited or only temporarily inhabited – of Othoni (Italian Faro; lighthouse). Erikoúsa (Italian Merlera), Mathráki and Diaplo. One of these is supposed to have been the island of Calypso.

Paros Πάρος/Páros   D4

Region: Aegean Islands
Island group: Cyclades
Nomos: Cyclades
Area: 186 sq. km (72 sq. miles)
Altitude: 0–771 m (0–2530 ft)
Population: 8000
Chief place: Páros (Parikía)

Air services   Several flights daily from Athens.

View of Sapientsa from Methóni

Erikoúsa, one of the Othonian Islands

Fishing-boats in Páros harbour

Regular service from and to Athens (Piraeus) several times daily (cars carried). Local connections daily with the neighbouring islands of Náxos, Ios, Santoríni, Sýros and Antíparos.

Boat services

Páros, lying some 8 km (5 miles) west of Náxos, is occupied by a range of hills of gently rounded contours, rising to 771 m (2530 ft) in Mount Profítis Ilías (rewarding climb, with guide; magnificent panoramic views). Three bays cut deep inland – in the west the sheltered Parikía Bay, with the island's capital; in the north the bay, even better sheltered, containing the little town of Náousa (pop. 1400), which in Roman times was the island's main port for the shipment of Lychnites marble; and in the east the flat Mármare Bay. The whole island is covered with a layer of coarse-grained crystalline limestone, in which lie rich beds of pure white marble.

Situation and characteristics

The island's considerable prosperity has depended since ancient times on agriculture, favoured by fertile soil and an abundance of water, and on the working of marble, which is still quarried on a small scale. In recent years the rapid development of the tourist trade has brought changes in the landscape, the island's economy and its social structure.

Excavations on the islet of Saliangos, which was once joined to Páros, have yielded evidence of settlement in the Late Neolithic period (5th–4th millennium B.C.). The island, which has preserved its ancient name, was already well populated in the age of the Cycladic culture (3rd millennium B.C.). In the 1st millennium B.C. Ionian Greeks settled on Páros and made it a considerable sea-power, minting its own coins; in the 7th c. B.C. Páros founded colonies on Thásos and in Thrace. In

History

the 6th and 5th c. Páros was celebrated for its school of sculptors. It was a member of the first Attic maritime league, and its unusually large contributions to the league (30 talents in 425 B.C.) are evidence of the islands wealth in the 5th c. B.C. In Hellenistic, Roman and Byzantine times Páros was of no importance. In the 9th c. A.D. it was depopulated as a result of raids by Arab pirates, plundering and burning. From 1207 to 1389 it belonged to the Duchy of Náxos, and thereafter was ruled by various dynasts until its capture by the Turks in 1537. It was reunited with Greece in the 19th c., after the foundation of the new Greek kingdom.

Sights

Páros town (Parikía)

The chief town, Páros or Parikía (pop. 3000), occupies the site of the ancient capital on the west coast. The central feature of the city was a 15 m (50 ft) high gneiss crag on the south-east side of the bay, now occupied by the Kástro, a ruined Frankish castle of about 1260, with stonework from an ancient Ionic temple, the Hekatompedon (Hundred foot long), built into its walls. The tower incorporates a circular building of the 4th c. B.C., walled in during the Frankish period, part of which serves as the apse of the castle chapel. To the west, on the highest point of Kástro, are the foundations of an unfinished temple of about 530 B.C., below which are remains of prehistoric houses (3rd millennium B.C.). The marble wall of the temple was used as the outer wall of the Church of Ayios Konstantínos on its south side.

In ancient times there was another harbour to the east of the hill, some remains of which can be seen under water.

Cathedral

At the west end of the modern lower town stands the Cathedral, the Church of Ekatontapylianí (Hundred-gated), which was built in three stages between the 5th and 7th c. Its proper name is Katapolianí (Situated in the lower town). The principal church (built in the second phase, about 600, reusing ancient stones) is a two-storey domed cruciform church with a barrel-vaulted gallery for women (the oldest part, belonging to a 5th c. basilica). The High Altar is borne on two Doric column drums and has an egg and dart moulding of the 6th c. B.C. In the semicircular apse are three tiers of stone benches for the clergy, with the bishop's throne in the middle. To the right is the baptistery (a domed basilica of the 7th c.), with a cruciform font set into the floor.

Páros
Katapolianí Church
(Cathedral)

A Principal church
B Church of St Nicholas
C Church of Anaryiri
  (diakonikon/sacristy)
D Baptistery

20 m

22 yd

© Baedeker

To the left of the church are a number of Hellenistic sarcophagi, reused in Byzantine times.

Adjoining the church is the Archaeological Museum, with inscriptions (including one referring to the poet Archilochos, who lived on Páros in the 7th c. B.C.), funerary reliefs, small works of sculpture, Cycladic idols and a fragment (relating to the years 336–299 B.C.) of the "Marmor Parium", a record of events in Greek history, which was found here in 1627. The major part of it is in the Ashmolean Museum in Oxford.

ˑ Archaeological Museum

To the east, beyond the rear wall of the Cathedral, can be seen a well-preserved Hellenistic tomb.
On the hills outside the ancient city, which covered a larger area than the modern town (some sections of walls brought to light by excavation), were a number of other temples.

North-west of the town, near the sea, on a terrace below the hill with the windmills, is the Doric Asklepieion (4th c. B.C.), with some remains of walls and a fountain basin (6th c. B.C.). A building laid out round a square courtyard, with a central altar, dates from a later period. Beyond this is the new fountain basin. On the terrace above the Asklepieion stood the Python, the Sanctuary of Apollo Pythios and of Asklepios, who was associated with him. The square building on the lower level was used for the treatment of those who came to seek healing at this sanctuary.

Asklepieion

On Mount Kounados, to the east of the town, was the sacred precinct of Aphrodite, with a rock-cut altar in the centre of the precinct. 40 m (130 ft) lower down, on the south side of the hill, is the Cave of Eileithyia, which contains a spring.
On the highest point (the south-westerly peak; view of the semicircle of the Cyclades) of Mount Taxiarkhis, beyond Parikía Bay in the north-west of the island (about 45 minutes from Páros town), was the Delion, the sanctuary of the three Delian divinities Apollo, Leto and Artemis.
At Tris Ekklisiés, 1·5 km (1 mile) east of Parikía, on the site of the Heroon of Archilochos, the foundations of an aisled basilica of the 7th c. A.D. have been brought to light.

Sanctuary of Aphrodite

A little way north of the Monastery of Ayios Minás in the Maráthi Valley (1 hour north-east of Parikía) are the quarries which produced the famous Parian marble, worked from the time of the Cycladic culture (3rd–2nd millennium B.C.; vessels, idols) to the 15th c. A.D. The marble, called Lychnites (lamp-lit) because it was hewn in underground shafts, was purer and more translucent (up to a thickness of 3·5 mm, or just under one-seventh of an inch) and was highly prized in antiquity, being used on Delos, at Epidauros and Delphi and in Imperial Rome. The old shafts have been preserved. On the west side is the so-called Cave of Pan, one of the entrances to the quarry face, with a figure of a nymph carved from the rock.

ˑ Marble quarries

Antíparos

South-west of Páros, separated from it by a channel varying in width between 1 km (¾ mile) and 8 km (5 miles), is the island of Antíparos (46 sq. km (18 sq. miles); 0–299 m (0–981 ft); pop. 600), the ancient Oliaros. The chief place, also called Antíparos, clusters round a Venetian castle. There is a beautiful stalactitic cave on the island.

Off the northern tip of Antíparos can be seen two islets of volcanic origin, Diplo and Kavoura.

Some 500 m (550 yd) south-west of Antíparos is the small island of Despotiki (8 sq. km (3 sq. miles)), with a sheltered harbour. Still farther south-west is the islet of Strongylí.

Patmos   Πάτμος/Pátmos   D5

Region: Aegean Island
Island group: Southern Sporades
Nomos: Dodecanese
Area: 34 sq. km (13 sq. miles)
Altitude: 0–269 m (0–883 ft)
Population: 2500
Chief place: Pátmos (Khóra)

Boat services

Regular service from and to Athens (Piraeus) several times weekly (10 hours; cars carried); from and to Salonica and Rhodes weekly. Local connections in Dodecanese and with Ikaría and Arkí.

Situation and characteristics

Pátmos lies in the eastern Aegean south of Sámos and south-east of Ikaría. The most northerly of the Dodecanese, it is a rugged island of volcanic origin – perhaps the rim of the crater of an extinct volcano – with a much-indented coast. It has been celebrated since the Middle Ages as the island of St John the Divine, who is said to have written the Book of Revelation while living in exile on Pátmos.

History

Pátmos was originally settled by Dorians and later by Ionians, and had a Sanctuary of Artemis. The early history of the island – a place of no political or economic importance – is unknown. Like its barren neighbouring islands, Pátmos was used as a place of exile in Roman times. During the early Middle Ages it seems to have been abandoned and desolate.

The island was given a new lease of life as an intellectual and religious centre when Abbot Christodoulos fled from Asia Minor and transferred his monastery from Mount Latmos, near Miletus, to Pátmos in 1088. The monastic island, receiving rich donations and granted extensive privileges, grew wealthy and influential. Living under its own strict Rule (Typikon), it survived 250 years of Turkish rule unscathed, subject only to the annual payment of tribute.

Since 1946 the whole island has been under statutory protection as an ancient monument. The acquisition of land by foreigners and the export of antiquities are prohibited save in exceptional circumstances.

Sights

Pátmos town (Khóra)

The island consists of three parts joined by narrow isthmuses. At the head of the longest inlet on the east side is the busy little port of Skála. From here it is an hour's climb (3 km (2 miles) bus service) to the quiet little town of Pátmos or Khóra (alt. 130 m (427 ft); pop. 1000) with its whitewashed houses and its monasteries, churches and chapels. The most notable of these is the Monastery of St John the Theologian (St John the

The fortified Monastery of St John

Divine; Ayios Ioánnis Theológos), towering above the town within its massive 15th c. walls topped by 17th c. battlements.

A ramp leads up through the entrance gateway into a courtyard surrounded by loggias. On the left is the principal church (Katholikón), with an open exonarthex containing four ancient columns and some mediocre 18th and 19th c. paintings. The church itself was decorated and furnished in the 19th c. at the expense of the Tsars of Russia (iconostasis of 1820 with rich carving). The paintings include many representations of St John and his apocalyptic visions. In the first chapel on the right is the silver-plated sarcophagus of the founder, Osios (Blessed) Christodoulos. In the second chapel, dedicated to the Panayía, are frescoes of 1745, under which older paintings were discovered, including the Mother of God enthroned, Abraham entertaining the three angels and the Woman of Samaria (12th c.). Frescoes of the 14th c. have been preserved in the trápeza (refectory).

Monastery of St John

The Treasury contains mitres, vestments, chalices, crosses, etc., as well as a number of valuable icons. There is a rich Library, with 890 manuscript codices and 35 parchment rolls, 2000 early printed books and the monastic archives, containing over 13,000 documents. Some of the finest items are displayed, including the Charter of 1088 (1·42 m (5 ft) long) granting Pátmos to Christodoulos, 33 pages of a 6th c. manuscript of St Mark's Gospel, an 8th c. manuscript of the Book of Job with 42 miniatures and a manuscript of 941 containing a book of sermons by St Gregory of Nazianzus. Of the rich collection of ancient literature once possessed by the monastery there

Treasury Library

remains a manuscript of the "History" of Diodorus Siculus. Together, the Treasury and the Library constitute what is surely the richest collection of its kind outside the monasteries of Athos.

From the roof terraces of the monastery (now unfortunately closed to visitors) there are superb views of Pátmos and the surrounding islands.

Monastery of the Apocalypse

° Iconostasis

Half-way up the road from the port of Skála to Pátmos town, on the left, is the Monastery of the Apocalypse (Moní Apokalýpseos), with the cave in which according to tradition John wrote the Book of Revelation. The iconostasis in the right-hand chapel, which is built into the cave, depicts John's visions, and on the floor and on the wall are marked the places where he rested, where he heard "a great voice, as of a trumpet", and where he wrote down his visions. Immediately above the monastery can be seen the ruins of the 18th c. Patmiás School, and above this again the terraced buildings of the modern Theological College which continues the tradition.

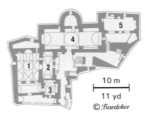

Patmos
St John's Monastery

1 Katholikón
2 Chapel of Panayía
3 Chapel of Christodoulos
4 Refectory
5 Kitchen

10 m
11 yd
© *Baedeker*

Paxi Παξοί/Paxí   C2

Region: Ionian Islands
Island group: Ionian Islands
Nomos: Corfu
Area: 19 sq. km (7½ sq. miles)
Altitude: 0–247 m (0–810 ft)
Population: 3000
Chief place: Paxí (Gáios)

Boat services

Regular weekly service from and to Pátras (cars carried); several times daily from and to Corfu town (2½ hours).

Situation and characteristics

Paxí is an attractive little island south of Corfu covered with subtropical vegetation, with beautiful bathing beaches and good diving grounds. The inhabitants live mainly by farming (the local olive oil is highly esteemed) and fishing. On islets lying off the principal port, Paxí or Gáios (pop. 500), are a Venetian fort and the former Monastery of the Panayía (pilgrimage on 15 August).

On the south coast the Ypapantí sea-cave (seals) is worth visiting. Off the south-east coast of Paxí lie the islets of Mongonísi (causeway) and Kaltsonísi.

Mother of God Eleousa

Christodoulos

Gáios (Paxí)

Antípaxi

South-east of Paxí is its rocky little sister island of Antípaxi (6 sq. km (2¼ sq. miles); 0–107 m (0–351 ft)), which has beautiful lonely beaches. The 100 or so inhabitants live by sheep-farming and fishing.

There is a boat service from Paxí to Antípaxi in summer; but the island has no accommodation for visitors.

Piraeus Πειραιεύς/Piraiéfs   D3

Region: Central Greece
Nomos: Attica
Altitude: 0–15 m (0–50 ft)
Population: 200,000

Piraeus (modern Greek Pireás), now part of the Athens conurbation, is the largest port in Greece, with shipping lines sailing to ports in Europe and the Near East. It is also the home port of most of the Greek domestic shipping services.

From 482 B.C. onwards Piraeus was developed by Themistokles into a commercial harbour and naval base for Athens. It was connected with Athens by the Long Walls and laid out in the time of Perikles on a rectangular street pattern according to the system evolved by Hippodamos of Miletus. The town was destroyed by Sulla in 86 B.C. and thereafter was a place of no importance. In the Middle Ages it was known as Porto Leone after an ancient marble lion which stood at the entrance to the harbour; the lion was carried off to Venice in 1682 and now stands outside the Arsenal there. Piraeus recovered its importance after the liberation of Greece in the 19th c., when the modern town was laid out on a rectangular plan (by the German architect Schaubert) as the ancient one had been.

The port

In addition to the principal harbour, Kántharos, the two smaller ancient harbours on the east side of the town are still in use – Pasalimáni (ancient Zéa) and, more recently, Mikrolímano (ancient Mounychia). New port installations to relieve the pressure on Piraeus are under construction at Fáliron, which was the original harbour of Athens before the development of Piraeus.

The most characteristic parts of the modern town, combining the atmosphere of a large port with the amenities of a city, are round the principal harbour, round Mikrolímano with its tavernas and in Kórais Square, on the higher ground between them.

Ancient remains

The remains of ancient boat-sheds can be seen under water in the harbours on the east side of the town. Near the Archaeological Museum is the Hellenistic Theatre of Zéa (2nd c. B.C.). There are remains of the walls built by Konon (394–391 B.C.) at the south-west end of the town.

*Shipping Museum

At the south end of Pasalimáni harbour, at the new Marina of Zéa, is a semicircular building housing the interesting Shipping Museum, which covers the history of Greek shipping from antiquity to modern times.

Map labels:

Anastasis Cemetery · Perama · Athens
Kypru · Kanelopulu · Foka · Sparlis · Akti · Kondyli · Station (N. Greece) · Konon · Station (Athens and Peloponnese) · Alipedu · Athens, Soúnion
Asty Gate · Distomu · Karaïskaki-Stadion
Gunari · Pilis · Evangelistrias · Venizelu · Bíti Karaoli · Neon Faliron Station
Landing-stage · Miaulis · Pl. Theatre · Koraïs · Tzavéla · Neórion · Leondu · Pavlu
Mittel-hafen · Akti · Ancient Theatre
Alkimos-Spitze · Ajios Nikolaos · Archäol. Museum · Town Hall · Mounychia (Kastella)
Vorhafen · Akti · Alkimon · Sachturi · Jacht-hafen · Sirangiu · Vas. · Mikrolimano
Public · Asklepieíon
Gardens · Hatzikiriaku · Theatre of Zéa · Alexandra-Spitze · Stalis
Karaïskos · Theochari · Favieru · Saronic Gulf
Kazanova · Hatzikiriaku · Shipping Museum · Zea
Ajia Marina · Ajios Vasileos
Ajia Paraskevi

© Baedeker

Piraeus
(Pireéfs)

500 m
550 yd

– – – – – Line of ancient walls

Piraeus: the new marina of Zéa

181

Poros Πόρος/Póros

Region: Central Greece
Island group: Saronic Islands
Nomos: Attica
Altitude: 0–345 m (0–1132 ft)
Population: 4500
Chief place: Póros

Boat services

Regular service from and to Athens (Piraeus) 6–10 times daily (2½ hours). Hydrofoil from Athens (Zéa) several times daily (65 minutes). Regular shuttle service to Galatás, on the mainland. Local connections with Hýdra/Spétsai, Aegina and the Methana Peninsula.

Situation and characteristics

Póros, the ancient Kalaureia, lies south-west of the Methana Peninsula (Peloponnese), separated from the north coast of the Argolid by a strait between 250 m (275 yd) and 1000 m (1100 yd) wide, 1·5 km (1 mile) long and up to 4 m (13 ft) deep. Most of the island is covered with thin woodland and macchia. The inhabitants, many of whom are of Albanian descent, live by farming the fertile coastal areas on the mainland which belong to Póros and, increasingly, by the tourist trade.

History

There was a settlement in Mycenaean times on the site later occupied by the Sanctuary of Poseidon. The ancient city was abandoned after the Roman period, and the modern town was established only in the late Middle Ages.

Póros town

Sights

The island's capital, Póros (pop. 4300; naval training school), is beautifully situated on ancient Sphairia, a promontory of volcanic origin on the south side of the island linked with it by the narrow Bísti Isthmus. In the 18th and 19th c. this was the principal naval harbour on the south-east coast of Greece.

Póros

5 km (3 miles) north-east of the town are scanty remains of the Sanctuary of Poseidon (5th c. B.C.), the centre of the Kalaurian amphictyony (religious league) of the maritime cities on the Saronic and Argolic Gulfs. It was here that Demosthenes, fleeing from the henchmen of the Macedonian Governor Antipatros, poisoned himself in 322 B.C. The numerous remains of buildings in the surrounding area suggest that this was the site of ancient Kalaureia.

4 km (2½ miles) east of Póros is the 18th c. Monastery of Zoodókhos Piyí.

Monastery of Zoodókhos Piyí

On the mainland opposite the island lies the huge lemon grove of Lemonodásos (30,000 trees), which belongs to Póros. 10 km (6 miles) west, at the village of Damalás, are the scanty remains of ancient Troizen, the setting of the legend of Hippolytos and Phaidra.

* Lemon grove

Psara Ψαρά/Psará   C4

Region: Aegean Islands
Nomos: Chíos
Area: 40 sq. km (15 sq. miles)
Altitude: 0–564 m (0–1850 ft)
Population: 500
Chief place: Psará

Local connections with Chíos.

Boat services

The bare rocky island of Psará, the ancient Psyra (Mycenaean tombs found), lies 18 km (11 miles) north-west of Chíos. The chief place, also called Psará, lies on the south coast, below a medieval castle. To the north-east is the Monastery of the Dormition (Kimísis Theotókou).

Situation and characteristics

Now poor and depopulated, the island had a period of considerable prosperity in the 18th c., when the descendants of the Albanians who had settled on the island in the 16th and 17th c. made it the third naval power in the Aegean, after Hydra and Spétsai. The island's dilapidated old mansions and the stumps of windmills on the hills bear witness to this period, when Psará had a population of some 20,000. Then, in reprisal for the islanders' stubborn resistance to the Turks, a Turkish force landed on the island and slaughtered the inhabitants. After Psará became part of the new kingdom of Greece in the 19th c. it was resettled from Chíos. The population lives by farming and seafaring.

South-west of Psará is the smaller island of Antipsara.

Antipsara

183

Psará harbour

Rhodes Ρόδος/Ródos   D/E5/6

Region: Aegean Islands
Nomos: Dodecanese
Area: 1398 sq. km (540 sq. miles)
Altitude: 0–1215 m (0–3986 ft)
Population: 60,000
Chief town: Rhodes (Ródos)

Air services

Airport 16 km (10 miles) south-west of Rhodes town. Several
flights daily from and to Athens (55 minutes); twice weekly
from and to Salonica (70 minutes); several times weekly from
and to Crete (Iráklion and Sitía; 40 minutes); twice daily from
and to Kárpathos (45 minutes); daily from and to Kásos (80
minutes); several times weekly from and to Kos (30 minutes).

Boat services

Regular service from and to Athens (Piraeus) several times
daily (16–22 hours; cars carried); also from Venice or Ancona
via Brindisi (less frequently Dubrovnik), Corfu, Pátras (less
frequently) and Athens (Piraeus). Local connections in
the Dodecanese: Rhodes – Sými – Tílos – Nísyros – Kos –
Kálymnos – Léros – Lipsí – Pátmos – Arkí – Agathonísi – Sámos;
Rhodes – Kos – Kálymnos – Astypálaia; Rhodes Kastellórizo;
Rhodes – Khálki – Diáfani – Kárpathos – Kásos.

Situation and characteristics

Rhodes, the Island of Roses (actually of hibiscus), the largest
of the Dodecanese and the fourth largest Greek island (after
Crete, Euboea and Lésbos), is one element in the island bridge

which extends from the Peloponnese by way of Crete and Kárpathos to Asia Minor, from which it is only 18 km (11 miles) distant. 78 km (48 miles) long and up to 30 km (19 miles) wide,

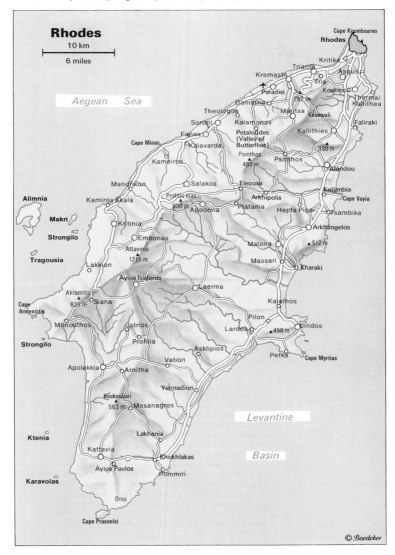

Rhodes

10 km

6 miles

Aegean Sea

Cape Koumbourno
Rhodes
Kritika
Trianta
Kremasti
Tris
Koskinou
Thermai
Kallithea
Paradisi
262 m
Damatria
Maritsa
Theologos
Koskouli
Faliraki
Soroni
Kalamonas
Petaloudes
(Valley of
Butterflies)
Kallithies
Fanes
Cape Minas
Kalavarda
Psinthos
480 m
Psinthos
330 m
Kameiros
Afándou
Mandrikon
Salakos
Eleousa
Kolýmbia
Alimnia
Kamiros-Skala
Profitis Ilias
900 m
Arkhipolis
Cape Vayia
Makri
Apollona
Platania
Hepta Pigai
Tsambika
Strongilo
Kritinia
Arkhángelos
Tragousia
Embonas
Attaviros
1215 m
Malona
512 m
Lakkion
Massari
Kharaki
Ayios Isidoros
Cape
Armenistis
Akramitis
825 m
Siana
Laerma
Kalathos
Monolithos
Istrios
Pilon
Strongilo
Profilia
Lardos
458 m
Lindos
Asklipios
Pefka
Cape Myrtias
Apolakkia
Arnitha
Vation
Yennadion
Koukouliari
563 m
Mesanagros
Levantine
Ktenia
Lakhania
Basin
Kattavia
Khokhlakas
Ayios Pavlos
Plimmiri
Karavolas
Oros
Cape Prasonisi

© Baedeker

Rhodes

Colossus of Rhodes

The stag and the hind

Rhodes is traversed from end to end by a long mountain ridge rising to 1215 m (3986 ft) in Mount Atáviros. The land falls away gradually towards the coasts, well watered and well wooded, affording good soil for agricultural use, particularly near the coast.

With its beautiful scenery, its excellent beaches and its fine old buildings erected by the Knights of St John, now well restored, Rhodes holds a wealth of attraction for visitors and has long been a major tourist centre. In and around Rhodes town is one of the largest concentrations of hotels in Greece, but the island is still relatively unspoiled, particularly in the south.

History

The island of Rhodes was already occupied in the Neolithic period, but its great cultural flowering came only with its settlement by Dorian Greeks. Their three cities of Lindos, Ialysos and Kameiros were members of the Hexapolis, the league of six Dorian cities, which became subject to the Persians in the 6th c. B.C. In the 5th c. B.C. Rhodes became a member of the Confederacy of Delos. About 408 B.C. the new capital city of Rhodes was laid out on a regular plan by the famous Greek town-planner Hippodamos of Miletus, and in the 4th c. it overshadowed Athens itself in commercial importance. Its great landmark, one of the Seven Wonders of the World, was the celebrated Colossus of Rhodes, a 32 m (105 ft) high bronze statue of the sun god Helios standing on a stone base 10 m (35 ft) high. Cast between 304 and 292 B.C. by Chares of Lindos, it stood at the entrance to the harbour and probably served as a lighthouse. It collapsed in an earthquake about 225 B.C.

With the extension of Roman control in the East the island's

Colossus of Rhodes

trade declined, but the city remained an important cultural centre, with a well-known school of rhetoric which was attended by Cicero and Caesar and a major school of sculptors which produced the famous Laokoön group (c. 50 B.C.) now in the Vatican Museum.

During the Middle Ages Rhodes was a bone of contention between the Arabs, the Byzantines, the Venetians and the Genoese. In 1309 it was occupied by the Knights of St John, who developed the town into a powerful stronghold and in the 15th c. defended it and the rest of the island against Egyptian and Turkish attack, but were compelled to surrender it to Süleiman the Magnificent in 1522. After almost 400 years of Turkish rule the island was occupied by Italy in 1912. In 1947, after the Second World War, it was returned to Greece.

Rhodes town

The town of Rhodes (Ródos: pop. 33,000), situated at the northern tip of the island, has been the capital of the island since its foundation in 408 B.C., and is now the administrative centre of the nomos of the Dodecanese. Laid out on a rectangular grid in accordance with the principles of Hippodamos of Miletus, the ancient city extended from the acropolis hill in the west to the east coast of the island. Some of the streets in the considerably smaller medieval town (Street of the Knights, Homer Street, Hippodamos Street and Pythagoras Street) still follow the ancient grid. The Knights' town, the Collachium, occupied the northern part of the walled town, with its streets running roughly at right angles. The larger southern part was occupied by the Greeks, while the west part became the Turkish quarter and the smaller east part the Jewish quarter, which existed until the Second World War.

The old town, within which no Christian was allowed to live during the Turkish period (1523–1912), is surrounded by the magnificent 4 km (2½ mile) long circuit of the 15th and 16th c. town walls, with towers, bastions and a moat – one of the finest examples of the medieval art of fortification. Particularly impressive are the Amboise Gate (with gardens and a deer-park adjoining), built by Grand Master Aimeri d'Amboise in 1512, to the north-west, and the Marine Gate (1468; relief of the Virgin) to the north-east, by the Commercial Harbour. | **Town walls**

Amboise Gate

Marine Gate

Visitors can take a fascinating walk round the old town on the walls, starting from the square in front of the Grand Master's Palace (entrance at Artillery Gate). A walk round the town outside the walls is also full of interest.

The Commercial Harbour (Emborikó Limáni), the town's principal harbour, used by the ships sailing to and from Piraeus, and the old Mandráki Harbour, in continuous existence since 408 B.C. and now mainly used by pleasure-craft (yacht marina) and excursion boats, are protected by long breakwaters. On the Mandráki breakwater stand three disused windmills, and at its northern tip are Fort St Nicholas, built by the Knights about 1400 and strengthened in 1460, and a lighthouse. Flanking the entrance to the harbour are stone columns topped by figures of a stag and a hind, the town's heraldic animals. (Accordingly red deer are a protected species on Rhodes, and surplus animals are given away to zoos throughout the world.) | **Commercial Harbour**

Mandráki Harbour

Stag and hind

Rhodes

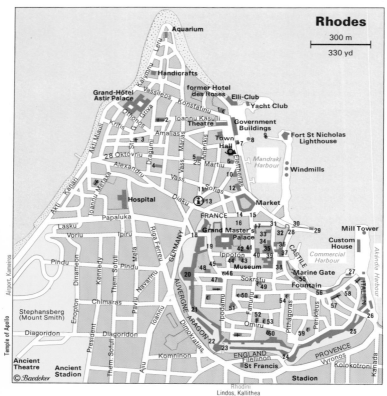

Rhodes

300 m

330 yd

Aquarium

Handicrafts

Grand-Hôtel Astir Palace

former Hotel des Roses

Elli-Club

Yacht Club

Ioannu Kasulli Theatre

Government Buildings

Fort St Nicholas Lighthouse

Town Hall

Mandraki Harbour

Windmills

Hospital

Market

FRANCE

Grand Master's Palace

Mill Tower

Custom House

Commercial Harbour

Ippotón

Museum

Marine Gate

Fountain

Stephansberg (Mount Smith)

Diagoridon

AUVERGNE ARAGON

Sokrátu

Ancient Theatre

Ancient Stadion

Komninón

ENGLAND
Filellinon
St Francis

PROVENCE
Vyronos
Kolokotroni

Stadion

© Baedeker

Rhodini
Lindos, Kallithea

Temple of Apollo

Airport, Kameiros

Akandia Harbour

1 Murad Reis Mosque	22 St Mary's Tower	41 Inn of France
2 Church of Our Lady (RC)	23 St Athanasius' Gate	42 Inn of Provence
3 Church of Assumption	24 Koskinou (St John's) Tower	43 Inn of Spain
4 German Consulate	25 Tower of Italy	44 Loggia (Turkish school)
5 Telephone and Telegraph Office	26 Gate of Italy	45 Clock-Tower
6 Harbour Office	27 St Catherine's Gate	46 Süleiman Mosque
7 Evangelismós Church	28 Arsenal Gate	47 Turkish Library
8 Stag	29 Naillac (Arab) Tower	48 Medresse Mosque
9 Hind	30 St Paul's Gate	49 Aga Mosque
10 Law Courts	31 Freedom Gate	50 Sultan Mustapha Mosque
11 National Bank of Greece	**OLD TOWN**	51 Süleiman Baths
12 Bank of Greece	32 Temple of Aphrodite	52 Church of Ayios Fanoúrios
13 EOT, Tourist Police	33 Municipal Picture Gallery	53 Redjeb Pasha Mosque
14 Bus Station	34 Archaeological Institute	54 Ibrahim Pasha Mosque
15 Taxi stance	35 Museum of Decorative Art	55 Commercial Tribunal
16 Son et Lumière	36 Inn of Auvergne	56 Archbishop's Palace
17 St Peter's Tower	37 Church of the Order of St John (museum)	57 Church of Our Lady of the City
18 Amboise Gate	38 Inn of England	58 Hospice of St Catherine
19 Artillery Gate	39 Inn of Italy	59 Dolapli Mosque
20 St George's Tower	40 Palace of Villiers de l'Isle-Adam	60 Bourouzan Mosque
21 Tower of Spain		

A doorway in the . . .   *. . . Street of the Knights*

On the east side of the old town is the Akándia Harbour, with a boatyard.

The Freedom Gate, at the south end of the Mandráki breakwater, leads into the busy old town with its labyrinth of narrow streets and lanes, its domes and minarets set amid palms and plane trees. In Sými Square are the remains of a Temple of Aphrodite (3rd c. B.C.) and the Municipal Art Gallery (modern art). Immediately south of this lies picturesque Aryirokástro Square, in the centre of which is a small fountain constructed from fragments of a Byzantine baptistery. On the west side of the square is the former Arsenal (14th c.), now housing the Archaeological Institute and the Museum of Decorative Art. A passage leads through to the former Church of the Order of St John (on the left), now a Museum of Early Christian and Byzantine Art.

Diagonally opposite the church stands the massive Hospital of the Knights (15th c.; restored), now occupied by the Archaeological Museum.

*Hospital of the Knights (Archaeological Museum)

From the inner courtyard a flight of steps leads up to the Infirmary on the upper floor (small chapel in a recess opposite the entrance; gravestones of Knights). A passage on the right leads to the rooms displaying finds from Ialysos, Kameiros and other sites, including two Archaic kouroi (6th c. B.C.) and, in the same room, the funerary stela of Krito and Tamariste (end of 5th c. B.C.). In another room are a life-size figure of Aphrodite and an expressive Hellenistic head of Helios, and in another the small crouching figure of Aphrodite known as the Venus of Rhodes (1st c. B.C.). Also of interest is the rich collection of vases in the rooms opening off the gallery encircling the

Grand Master's Palace: courtyard . . .   *. . . and towers*

courtyard, which covers all periods from Mycenaean times onwards and includes some particularly fine examples of Rhodian work.

° Street of the Knights

From the north side of the hospital the Street of the Knights (Odós Ippotón) runs west. In this street, which still conveys an excellent impression of a street of the 15th and 16th c., were most of the Inns of the various nations in the Order of St John. The finest of these is the Inn of France (on the right), built between 1492 and 1503. At the west end of the street, on the highest point in the town (to the right), stands the Grand Master's Palace, a massive stronghold which was defended by a triple circuit of walls. It suffered heavy destruction during the Turkish siege, and was almost completely destroyed by an explosion in 1856, but during the period of Italian occupation (1912–43) was rebuilt on the basis of old plans (commemorative tablet at entrance). The interior arrangement does not, however, follow the original pattern. Notable features of the interior are the many pebble mosaic pavements from the island of Kos.

° Grand Master's Palace

On the north-east side of the palace are beautiful gardens (entrance in Papagos Street; *son et lumière* shows in summer). At its south-west corner is the Artillery Gate (St Anthony's Gate), which gives access to the town walls.

Süleiman Mosque

To the south of the Grand Master's Palace can be seen a striking 19th c. Clock-Tower. Still farther south is the Süleiman Mosque (beautiful Renaissance doorway), the largest mosque on the island, and facing this, to the south, the Turkish Library (1794), with valuable manuscripts of the Koran.

From here lively Sokrates Street (Odós Sokrátous), flanked by bazaars, leads south through the centre of the old town towards the Commercial Harbour. South-east of the Marine Gate are the Commercial Tribunal (1507) and the Archbishop's Palace (15th c.), on the north side of Archbishop's Square, with the beautiful Seahorse Fountain.

To the south of Sokrates Street stretches a picturesque maze of lanes round Fanoúrios Street, Homer Street (Odós Omírou), both spanned by flying buttresses, and Pythagoras Street, with numerous mosques, including the Ibrahim Pasha Mosque, the oldest in the town (1531), and, opposite the magnificent Süleiman Baths with their many domes (open to visitors as well as bathers), the Sultan Mustapha Mosque (1765). In Fanoúrios Street is the little Orthodox Church of Ayios Fanoúrios, partly underground (founded 1335; converted into a mosque during the Turkish period).

On the west side of the old town, near St George's Tower, stands the Hurmale Medrese, originally the Byzantine Church of the Redeemer, with a picturesque inner courtyard.

The new town, with Government offices and many hotels and restaurants, extends to the north of the old town, reaching almost to the sandy northernmost tip of the island. At Mandráki Harbour is the massive New Market (Néa Agorá), with a large inner courtyard. From here Freedom Avenue (Eleftherías) runs north, past the Law Courts and the Post Office, to the Evangelismós Church (originally Roman Catholic, now Orthodox), a reproduction (1925) of the old Monastic Church of St John, which originally stood beside the Grand Master's Palace and was destroyed in the 1856 explosion. Farther north are the Venetian-style Government Buildings (Nomarkhia), the Town Hall and the Theatre. Beyond these we come to the charming Murat Reis Mosque, surrounded by the old Turkish cemetery, with the tombs and mausoleums of Muslim dignitaries who died in exile here.

New town

At the northern tip of the old town, which is edged by beaches, is an Aquarium, with a small museum of natural history. 500 m (550 yd) south is the Casino.

2 km (1¼ miles) south of the old town, on the road to Kallithéa, are a large Orthodox cemetery as well as a Roman Catholic, a Jewish and a new Turkish cemetery.

Farther south lies the beautiful Rodíni Valley, with a park, a small zoo, a folk theatre and various attractive footpaths.

3 km (2 miles) south of the new town, on Mount Ayios Stéfanos (Mount Smith; 111 m (364 ft); view), can be seen remains of the ancient acropolis, with fragments of temples. On the slopes of the hill are a stadium and a theatre (restored).

15 km (9 miles) south-west of Rhodes town (bus service) rises Mount Filérimos (267 m (876 ft); view), with the remains of the acropolis of Ialysos, one of the three ancient cities on the island. The hill was occupied by a series of strongholds from Mycenaean times (c. 1400 B.C.) onwards. In 1308 it served as a base for the Knights of St John during their siege of Rhodes, and in 1522 it was occupied by the Turks. The ancient acropolis was approached by a handsome wide stepped road. On the plateau can be seen the foundations of a Temple of Athena, built in the 3rd c. B.C. on the site of an earlier temple and replaced in Early Christian times by a church (cruciform font set into the ground). There are also a small chapel with 15th c.

Ialysos

frescoes and the church and cloister (rebuilt during the Italian occupation) of the Filérimos Monastery. Lower down the hill, reached by a flight of steps in poor condition, is a Doric fountain-house of the 4th c. B.C.

Rhodes via Kámeiros to Líndos (111 km (69 miles) or 131 km (81 miles))

Kameiros

The road runs south-west along the coast. In 16 km (10 miles), beyond the airport, a road (7 km (4½ miles)) branches off on the left and runs via Kalamónas to the Valley of Butterflies (Petaloúdes), which in the height of summer is the haunt of thousands of reddish-brown butterflies. – 12 km (7½ miles): minor road to Embonas, offering an attractive alternative route. – 4 km (2½ miles): side road (1·5 km (1 mile)) to the site, partly excavated, of ancient Kameiros (6th c. B.C.–6th c. A.D.). The remains include the temple precinct, agora, cisterns, baths and houses. – The route continues on a beautiful panoramic road above the coast to Monólithos (32 km (20 miles); alt. 280 m (919 ft)), with an imposing Castle of the Knights of St John south-west of the village. – From Monólithos it is another 47 km (29 miles) eastward across the island to Líndos (below).

The road to Embonas mentioned above comes in 16 km (10 miles) to a side road on the left leading to Mount Profítis Ilías (798 m (2618 ft)), from which there are superb panoramic views.

Rhodes via Arkhángelos to Líndos (62 km (39 miles))

The road runs south, at some distance from the east coast for most of the way. – 7 km (4½ miles): road on left (3 km (2 miles)) to the seaside resort and former spa of Kallithéa, beautifully situated amid magnificent gardens. The thermal springs, known and frequented since ancient times, have quite recently dried up. The handsome bath-houses and spa establishments, now abandoned and dilapidated, were built by the Italians in the 1930s. – 2 km (1¼ miles): Koskinoú, picturesquely situated on a hill, with colour-washed houses which are regularly repainted at Christmas or Easter. 7 km (4½ miles): road on left (3 km (2 miles)) to Faliráki (beautiful sandy beach; ceramic factory). – 9 km (6 miles): Afándou (sandy beach; large carpet factory). – 6 km (4 miles): Kolýmbia (beautiful cove; bathing). – 6 km (4 miles): Arkhángelos, a picturesque place with a ruined castle on a hill to the south. – 7 km (4½ miles): Malóna, a modest little village surrounded by beautiful orange and lemon groves. – 18 km (11 miles): Líndos.

**Líndos

Líndos is one of the three ancient cities on the island (the others being Ialysos and Kámeiros) and, with its magnificent situation between two bays, its combination of sandy beaches and bizarrely shaped limestone crags, its whitewashed houses, its medieval castle and its ancient acropolis, the most striking and impressive of the three.
Remains of the Neolithic period and finds in Mycenaean necropolises bear witness to the occupation of this site, on the only natural harbour on the island, since the earliest times. During the Dorian period Lindos – a city mentioned in Homer – held more than half the island. About 700 B.C. it founded a colony at Gela in Sicily. Its heyday was in the 7th and 6th c.

Lindos: the acropolis

Entrance to the citadel

under the tyrant (sole ruler) Kleoboulos, one of the Seven Sages, who built a temple to the goddess of Lindos on the acropolis. Important historical sources found here were the "Temple chronicle of Lindos" and a list of priests for the years 375–327 B.C. The city continued to be occupied and developed during the Hellenistic period and into Late Roman times. A Byzantine castle was constructed on the acropolis, and in the 15th c. the Knights of St John built this up into a mighty stronghold. During the 15th, 16th and 17th c. the shipowners and sea-captains of Lindos grew wealthy leaving handsome mansions to bear witness to their prosperity.

Just before Líndos the road from Rhodes traverses a low pass, beyond which there is a fascinating view of the bay, the town and the acropolis. Cars must park at the entrance to the town, which is closed to all but pedestrian or donkey-borne traffic. Walking throught the narrow lanes of the town, visitors will see – in addition to the innumerable shops and stalls selling needle-work and pottery – the typical cube-shaped whitewashed houses of the inhabitants and some of the handsome mansions of wealthy sea-captains, built in stone with characteristic relief decoration. To the left of the road up to the acropolis, in a courtyard behind high walls, stands the beautiful Church of the Panayía, built for the Orthodox population by Pierre d'Aubusson, Grand Master of the Order of St John from 1476 to 1503. It has a richly decorated iconostasis and one of the pebble mosaic pavements which were much favoured in Líndos. On the barrel-vaulted roof and the dome are paintings of 1779. Below the town lies the sheltered harbour, now lined with tavernas and bathing-huts.

° Church of the Panayía

193

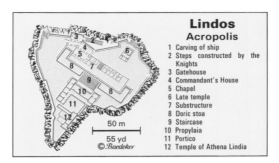

Lindos
Acropolis

1 Carving of ship
2 Steps constructed by the Knights
3 Gatehouse
4 Commandant's House
5 Chapel
6 Late temple
7 Substructure
8 Doric stoa
9 Staircase
10 Propylaia
11 Portico
12 Temple of Athena Lindia

50 m
55 yd
© Baedeker

Tomb of Kleoboulos

On the way up to the acropolis (on foot or donkey-back) there is a fine view of the harbour and the large circular tomb (6th c. B.C.) known as the Tomb of Kleoboulos.

*Acropolis

Within the acropolis there are both ancient and medieval buildings. Beyond the outer entrance is a small square (underground cisterns), below a sheer rock face with a carving of a ship, commemorating a Rhodian naval victory in 180 B.C. A steep flight of steps leads up to the gatehouse, which together with the adjoining buildings (the Commandant's House and the castle chapel) was built by the Knights of St John and was left undisturbed by the excavators of the ancient site.

Lindos: bay below the acropolis

At the top of the steps is a large terrace, dominated by an 80 m (260 ft) long stoa with projecting wings (partly re-erected), built about 200 B.C. in front of the 4th c. structures on the acropolis – a monumental staircase 21 m (70 ft) wide, the propylaia (with five openings, like the propylaia on the Acropolis in Athens) and the temple terrace. This highest terrace was surrounded on all four sides by colonnades, the foundations of which have survived. At the far left-hand corner of the terrace stands the Temple of Athena Lindia, a small shrine in a grandiose setting, built after 300 B.C. on the site of the 6th c. Temple of Kleoboulos. It is 23 m (75 ft) long by 8 m (25 ft) wide, with four Doric columns at the east end (the type technically known as prostyle tetrastyle). The unusual situation of the temple, on the very edge of the precipitous crag, suggests that the goddess was originally worshipped in the cave under the temple.

*Temple of Athena Lindia

From the farthest tip of the crag, beyond the temple, there are views of this cave (which can also be seen from the east end of the large stoa) and of the small and almost exactly circular harbour, the only natural harbour on the island of Rhodes. In antiquity it was the base of the Lindian fleet, and according to local tradition the Apostle Paul sought shelter from a storm here during his voyage from Ephesus to Syria in A.D. 51. There is a small chapel dedicated to St Paul.

From the acropolis there is also a view of a Hellenistic tomb in the rock face beyond the town.

Alimniá and Khalkí

To the west of Rhodes, at distances of up to 65 km (40 miles), are the islands of Alimniá (pop. 25), with a ruined Genoese castle, and Khalkí (pop. 3000; chief place Nimborió), a rocky island with a medieval castle and the remains of a Temple of Apollo.

Salamis Σαλαμίς/Salamís   D3

Region: Central Greece
Island group: Saronic Islands
Nomos: Attica
Area: 93 sq. km (36 sq. miles)
Altitude: 0–365 m (0–1198 ft)
Population: 18,000
Chief place: Salamína (Kouloúri)

Ferry (cars carried) from Pérama (5 km (3 miles) west of Piraeus) or Megálo Péfko (Mégara).

Boat services

Salamis (modern Greek Salamína), the largest island in the Saronic Gulf, with a much-indented coast, lies at the mouth of the Bay of Eleusis. Its limestone hills, much eroded by karstic action, bear a scanty growth of trees; but the island's modest agriculture, combined with some tourist trade, particularly in the south-east and north-west, is no longer sufficient to support the population (mostly descended from Albanian immigrants), who now find employment in the industrial enterprises (refineries, shipyards) which have been established

Situation and characteristics

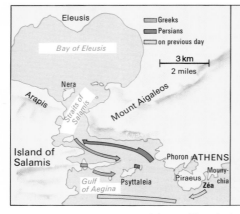

Battle of Salamís

27–28 September 480 B.C.

With only 378 triremes against a Persian force of over 1200 vessels, the Athenian fleet was able to inflict a decisive defeat on the Persians thanks to the manœuvrability of their ships, the local knowledge of their commanders and their skill in fighting at close quarters and to the Persian warships' inability to navigate in these narrow waters. The battle was watched by the Persian King Xerxes, seated on a golden throne on a hill near the coast. Cf. the account given by Aeschylus, who had himself taken part in the battle, in his drama "The Persians" (472 B.C.).

round the naval base in the north-east of the island and on the east side of the Bay of Eleusis.

History

The island owes its name (from shalâm, "rest, peace") to Phoenician settlers from Cyprus. For long disputed between Athens and Megara, it was finally won for Athens by Solon and Peisistratos in 598 B.C. The ancient capital lay on a tongue of land between the bays of Kamateró and Ambeláki on the east coast; then in the 6th c. B.C. it was moved south-west to Ambeláki (remains of acropolis and harbour, visible under water).

Salamis is celebrated as the scene of the great naval battle in 480 B.C., when the Athenians, their resources depleted by war, inflicted a devastating defeat on a much superior Persian fleet with their force of 378 triremes and thus finally destroyed Xerxes' plans to expand westward into Europe. The battle – which Aeschylus, an eye-witness, took as the theme of his tragedy "The Persians" – was fought in the waters to the East of Salamis between the island of Ayios Yeóryios to the north and the island of Psyttaleia and the Kynosoura (Dog's Tail) Peninsula to the south. Xerxes is said to have watched the battle from Mount Aigaleos, above Pérama.

Sights

Salamíba

The island's capital, Salamína or Kouloúri (pop. 17,000; local museum), lies on the north side of Salamína Bay. 3 km (2 miles) east is the principal port, Paloúkia (shipyards).

Faneroméni Monastery

6 km (4 miles) west of Salamína on a beautiful road stands Faneroméni Monastery (fine frescoes), which is revered as the scene of various apparitions of the Mother of God (the Virgin). The monastery was founded in 1661 on the site of an ancient sanctuary, reusing architectural elements from the older buildings. To the south are the remains of the small Fort of Boudorón (6th c. B.C.). At the foot of the hill on which the monastery stands is the landing-stage used by the ferry to Megálo Péfko (Megára).

6 km (4 miles) south-west of Salamína is the village of Enántio or Moúliki, with two churches of the 12th and 13th c. Farther south-west we reach the 18th c. Monastery of Ayios Nikólaos. There are scanty remains of Mycenaean settlements at many places on the island.

Salonica Θεσσαλονίχη/Thessaloníki B3

Region: Macedonia
Nomos: Salonica
Altitude: 0–15 m (0–50 ft)
Population: 700,000

Salonica, capital of Macedonia and Greece's second largest city, a university town and the see of a metropolitan, lies at the north end of the Thermaic Gulf, the most north-westerly gulf on the Aegean, below the foothills of the Khortiatis range. It is an important port and commercial city, noted for its international trade fair, and is also of great historical and artistic interest with its many Byzantine churches.

Situation and characteristics

The town was founded by Kassandros in 315 B.C. on the site of the old settlement of Thermai and named after his wife Thessalonike, a sister of Alexander the Great. In the Middle Ages it was the second city of the Byzantine Empire, but it suffered heavy blows when it was taken by the Normans (1185) and the Turks (1430), who expelled the Greek

History

Arch of Galerius and Rotunda

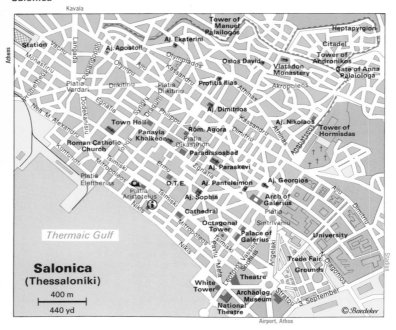

population. About 1600 there was a large influx of Spanish Jews, whose descendants were exterminated during the German occupation in the Second World War. In the 18th c. Greeks returned to the city, which was reunited with Greece in 1912. Thereafter the resettlement of the Turkish inhabitants and the great influx of Greek refugees from Asia Minor gave the city its present population pattern. After a disastrous fire in 1917, following a period of Allied occupation, the central area of the city was rebuilt in modern style.

*Arch of Galerius

In Egnatia Street is the Arch of Galerius, with carvings depicting the Emperor's campaigns against the Persians (A.D. 297). It originally consisted of two rows of four piers, with the four central piers supporting a dome. To the south were the Imperial Palace and the Hippodrome (the scene of a great massacre in A.D. 391 for which the Emperor Theodosius was taken to task by Ambrose, Bishop of Milan.

Rotunda

From the Arch of Galerius a colonnaded street ran north for 100 m (110 yd) to the Rotunda, built as a mausoleum for Galerius. About A.D. 400 it was converted into a Christian church dedicated to St George, with mosaic decoration; during the Turkish period it became a mosque and it is now a museum. The building, 24 m (80 ft) in diameter, still preserves the remains of fine mosaics in the dome and the recesses in the walls. The mosaic in the centre of the dome is missing, but below it can be seen the figures of angels, and below these again architectural façades on a gold ground.

South-east of the Arch of Galerius, set in gardens, is the Archaeological Museum, with a large and varied collection of material from Salonica itself, Macedonia and Thrace. Among items of particular interest are an arch from the Octagon of Galerius and statues and portraits of Roman emperors. A particular attraction since 1978 has been the collection of material from the Macedonian royal tombs at Véryina.

*Archaeological Museum

Some 500 m (550 yd) west, at the south-east end of the seafront promenade (Leofóros Vasileos Konstantínou), stands Salonica's great landmark, the White Tower – a 16th c. Turkish watch-tower once known as the Tower of Blood.

White Tower

From the White Tower Pávlou Méla Street leads to the Church of Ayía Sofía, an early form of domed cruciform church (8th c.) which in the 9th c., after the end of the conflict over the worship of icons, was decorated with new figural mosaics. Among them are a figure of the Mother of God Platytéra in the apse, replacing an earlier cross, and a magnificent representation of the Ascension in the dome.

Ayía Sofía

To the north of this church, on the far side of Egnatia Street, is the Early Christian Basilica of Ayía Paraskeví (5th c.), occupying the site of an earlier Roman villa, from which a mosaic pavement can be seen in the north aisle.

Ayía Paraskeví

Seafront promenade and White Tower

199

Panayía Khalkéon

Farther west along Egnatia Street is the Church of the Panayía Khalkéon (1028; restored some years ago), the Mother of God of the Coppersmiths, in the old coppersmiths' quarter.

˚Ayios Dimítrios

Some 500 m (550 yd) farther north-west we come to Salonica's principal church, Ayios Dimítrios, a five-aisled basilica built over a Roman bath-house, remains of which are visible to the north of the church, and a stretch of Roman road which can be seen from the crypt. The church was known until the 9th c. as the Church by the Stadium (which lay close by). Investigations from 1917 onwards confirmed the tradition that the Emperor Galerius caused an officer named Demetrius to be confined in the baths and subsequently killed (306). The martyred St Demetrius soon became the town's principal saint and patron. The basilica was originally built in the 5th c., and the general plan of this first church was preserved in a 7th c. rebuilding after a fire and in the reconstruction carried out from 1917 onwards.

At the south-east corner of the church is the aisled Chapel of St Euthymius, added in 1303, with wall-paintings of that period.

Upper town

There are other churches in the picturesque maze of narrow streets and alleys in the upper town, which also contains the birthplace of Atatürk. Among them are Ayía Ekateríni (13th c.), Profítis Ilías (14th c.), the small square domed Church of Osios Davíd (5th c.) with a mosaic of Ezekiel's vision and Vlatádon Monastery, immediately adjoining the Citadel (views of the city and the Thermaic Gulf).

The Citadel is an imposing stronghold, with seven towers and walls 10·50 m (35 ft) high. The highest tower, in the centre, was built by the Turks in 1431, a year after their capture of the town.

Considerable stretches of the town walls, which abut the Citadel on both sides, have been preserved, and a walk along the walls will take the visitor into some interesting old quarters of the town.

"Railway cemetery"

An attraction of a rather different nature is the large "Railway cemetery" in the old railway depot (much overgrown: beware of snakes!) on the western outskirts of the city, with numbers of old and rusting engines from many European countries (the oldest dating from 1887). It can be visited only with special permission from the railway authorities.

Salonica is a good base from which to visit the Chalcidice (Khalkidikí) Peninsula, with its beautiful beaches, or the Monastic Republic of Athos (men only; special authority required; advice from British or American consulate in Salonica).

Samos Σάμος/Sámos   D5

Region: Aegean Islands
Nomos: Sámos
Area: 476 sq. km (184 sq. miles)
Altitude: 0–1440 m (0–4725 ft)
Population: 33,000
Chief place: Sámos

Air services

Airfield 5 km (3 miles) south-west of Sámos town. Two flights daily from and to Athens.

Samós

Karlóvasi
Áyios Konstantínos
Avlákia
Zoodókhos Piyí
Kastanea
Profítis Ilías
Vourliótes
Vurliotes
Kokkári
Samos
Karvouni
Vati
Vigla
1433 m
Maratho-
kambos
Stavros
1153 m
Khóra
Míli
Pythagórion
Spatharei
Heraion
Pagondas
TURKEY
Aegean Sea
Foúrni
10 km
Samiopoula
© Baedeker
6 miles

Regular services from Athens (Piraeus) and Rhodes several times weekly (cars carried). Ferry from Kuşadası (Turkey). — Boat services

The island of Sámos (Turkish Sisam) has other attractions as well as the wine for which it is famed. It is a green, well-wooded island which has only recently become a target for mass tourism, with the site of one of the most important sanctuaries and cultural centres of the Ancient World, the Heraion. — Situation and characteristics

Geographically an outpost of Asia Minor, from which it is separated by a strait only 1.9 km (1 mile) wide, it rises in the centre to 1140 m (3740 ft; Mount Ampelos) and in the west to 1440 m (4725 ft; Mount Kérkis). The island's main sources of income from time immemorial have been farming, boat-building and fishing.

The first inhabitants of Sámos, probably Carians, were displaced at an early stage by Ionians, who used the island as a base for the conquest and colonization of the nearby coast of Asia Minor. In the second half of the 6th c. B.C., under the tyrant (sole ruler) Polykrates, the island grew rich and powerful. Like other tyrants of the period, Polykrates erected magnificent buildings and fostered the arts. Although allied with Persia, he was executed by the Satrap Oroites about 522 B.C. and succeeded by his brother Syloson, ruling subject to Persian overlordship, and other tyrants. The island took part in the Ionian Rebellion, achieved independence and became a privileged member of the first Attic maritime league. After a rising in 440 B.C. Sámos was conquered by Perikles, and until the end of the Peloponnesian War became a base for the Athenian fleet. Thereafter it was alternately under Spartan, Athenian and Persian influence. It did not join the second Attic maritime league. Its history in the perid after Alexander the Great is obscure, though it seems to have belonged to the empire of the Ptolemies in the 3rd c. B.C. Hostile to Rome but forced to submit to it, the island achieved independence in the reign of Tiberius (A.D. 17). — History

In subsequent centuries Sámos was held by Byzantines, Arabs (from A.D. 824), Venetians and Genoese. After being plundered by the Turks at the end of the 15th c. the island – then depopulated and devastated – came under Turkish rule in 1509. In 1562 it was resettled, and thereafter was granted considerable privileges. During the War of Greek Independence, in 1821, the islanders held out against the Turks, and under the London Protocol of 1832 Sámos was declared a principality required to pay tribute to the Ottoman Empire, under a prince who was appointed by the Sultan but must be a Christian. Its flag bore the Greek cross.

During the Tripolitanian War of 1912 Italian troops drove out the Turkish occupying forces, and after further military action the island was reunited with Greece later in that year.

Sámos was the home of the Greek mathematician and philosopher Pythagoras.

Sights

Sámos town

Since 1832 the capital of the island has been the little town of Sámos (pop. 8000), which was founded in that year. It lies in a semicircle round the sheltered inner harbour of Vathý, climbing picturesquely up the hill with its vineyards and olive groves to the upper town of Apáno Vathý. It has an attractive square and picturesque little streets and alleys.

*Museum

The Museum contains material recovered in the German excavations of the Heraion from 1910 onwards.

The main hall of the museum had to be specially enlarged in order to display the most sensational find made in the Heraion, the colossal marble figure, 5 m (16 ft) high, of an Archaic kouros (c. 580–570 B.C.), possibly a votive statue from the Sacred Way. The torso was found in 1980 and the head (70 cm (27½ in) high) in 1984 in a vineyard near the Heraion; the knee had been found 70 years earlier, in 1912. Another notable exhibit is an Archaic over-life-size female figure (c. 570 B.C.) excavated in 1984, a counterpart to the Hera of Cheramyes, found in the Heraion in 1879, which is now one of the treasures of the Louvre.

Mountain village on Sámos

In the room to the left are the base and three of the original six statues of a group by Geneleos, a sculptor of the Archaic period (*c.* 560 B.C.). The room to the right on the ground floor houses Hellenistic and Roman sculpture. The rooms on the upper floor contains prehistoric material, pottery, ivories and bronzes.

The friendly little port of Pythagórion or Tigáni, 11 km (7 miles) south-west of Sámos town on the south coast of the island, occupies the site of the ancient city of Samos. There are remains of town walls (4th c. B.C.) and the foundations of a breakwater. On the acropolis hill, near the cemetery, are the Church of the Metamórfosis (Transfiguration) and a castle built by Lykoúrgos Logothétis (1822–24). Near by is the site of a Hellenistic villa, over which a Christian basilica was built in the 5th c. No structures belonging to the ancient acropolis have been found. In the eastern part of the site of the ancient city is the Monastery of the Panayía Spilianí, below which, reached on a signposted path, can be seen a depression marking the site of a theatre.

Pythagórion (Tigáni)

Farther west is the entrance to an underground aqueduct 1 km (¾ mile) long constructed by Eupalinos in the 6th c. B.C. it is 1·75 m (6 ft) high and wide, and has been made passable for visitors. 425 m (465 yd) from the entrance can be seen the spot where the two shafts, one driven from each side, met one another, making an almost perfect join.

*Aqueduct

To the west (8 km (5 miles) from Pythagórion, 19 km (12 miles) from Sámos) is the Heraion. Here, at the mouth of the River Imbrasos, according to an ancient tradition, the Ionian settlers led by Prokles found a wooden image caught in the branches of a willow tree. Recognising it as a cult image of the goddess Hera, they erected an altar beside the tree, and this was followed by others. The seventh was the Altar of Rhoikos (*c.* 550 B.C.; partly rebuilt), which in size and magnificence was to be surpassed only by the Great Altar of Zeus at Pergamon.

*Heraion

*Altar of Rhoikos

To the west of the altar is the Temple of Hera. The modest wooden Temple I (first half of 8th c. B.C.) and Temple II (after 670 B.C.) were succeeded by a colossal stone structure, Temple III, built by Rhoikos and Theodoros in 570–550 B.C. This covered an area of 105 m (345 ft) by 52·5 m (172 ft) and had a double peristyle of Ionic columns 18 m (60 ft) high, 104 in all. Soon afterwards this temple was destroyed, and Polykrates thereupon commissioned a replacement, Temple IV. Covering an area of 112·20 m (368 ft) by 55·16 m (181 ft), this was the largest temple ever designed by Greek architects, but – like other gigantic Ionic temples – it remained unfinished. Nothing of this temple now survives but its massive foundations and a single column. Finally a small peripteral temple of 4 by 6 columns (Temple V) was built close to the altar to house the cult image.

Temple of Hera

The high water-table made excavation difficult, but the work of E. Buschor and his successors has made it possible to follow the development of the sanctuary in detail. In 1963 the excavators even brought to light the remains of the ancient willow tree. Near the site of the temples is the apse of an Early Christian church. To see some of the other remains in the area, however – such as the basin in which the image of Hera was annually bathed – it is necessary to have either a knowledgeable guide or a good plan of the site.

The return to Sámos is either via Pythagórion or by way of the medieval capital of Khóra (7·5 km (4½ miles) from the Heraion) and Mytilíni (10·5 km (6½ miles); pop. 5000).

Circuit of the island

The road from Sámos town along the north coast, which is mostly fringed by cliffs, comes in 10·5 km (6½ miles) to the little port of Kokkári. About half-way there, near a Chapel of Ayía Paraskeví on the right of the road, is a modest Early Christian baptistery. Beyond Avlákia (20 km (12½ miles)) a road goes off on the left to Vourliótes (3 km (2 miles)), from which it is 2 km (1¼ miles) to the Vrontianí Monastery (founded 1566), on the northern slopes of Mount Ampelos.

The coast road continues to Ayios Konstantínos (26 km (16 miles)) and Karlóvasi (32 km (20 miles)), a port at which the regular boats call (as well as at Vathý). From here there is an attractive return route to Sámos through the beautiful hilly country in the interior of the island, passing through Pýrgos, Koumaradéi and Khóra.

There are a number of other monasteries on the island, including Zoodókhos Piyí (founded 1756; extensive views), 8 km (5 miles) east of Sámos, Profítis Ilías (founded 1625), 4 km (2½ miles) south of Karlóvasi, and Stavrós (founded 1586), 3 km (2 miles) east of Khóra.

Samothrace Σαμοθράκη/Samothráki   B4

Region: Aegean Islands
Nomos: Evros
Area: 178 sq. km (69 sq. miles)
Altitude: 0–1640 m (0–5381 ft)
Population: 3000
Chief place: Samothráki (Khóra)

Boat services

Samothrace is on the shipping route from Athens (Piraeus) to Lemnos, Samothrace and Alexandroúpolis. Daily ferry service from and to Alexandroúpolis.

Situation and characteristics

Samothrace, lying 40 km (25 miles) off the Thracian coast, is the most north-easterly outpost of the Greek island world. From its highest peak, Mount Fengári (1640 m (5381 ft)), according to Homer, Poseidon watched the fighting at Troy. Lying by itself in a sea without any neighbouring islands, it is an island of great scenic beauty with a regular coastline and no sheltering bays to provide safe anchorages. The inhabitants live by arable farming, growing fruit and vegetables (particularly onions).

History

As its name (Thracian Samos) indicates, Samothrace was originally populated by Thracians, who founded the Sanctuary of the Great Gods here. About 700 B.C. the first Greeks arrived on the island, and thereafter the sanctuary grew and developed; until the 1st c. B.C., however, Thracian remained the cult language. In the 4th c. B.C. Philip II of Macedon was iniatiated into the mysteries, and it is said that he met his wife Olympias here. From the early 3rd c., when Ptolemy II and his sister

Arsinoe erected splendid new buildings in the sanctuary, the cult spread widely through the Hellenistic World. Under the Romans (from 168 B.C.) the cult of Kybele, which had originated in Asia Minor, became associated with that of the Great Gods. Only the spread of Christianity put an end to the cult, about A.D. 400, but the town of Palaiopolis, immediately west of the sanctuary, was inhabited until the 15th c.

Excavations by French and Austrian archaeologists in the 19th c. and more recent American excavations (Karl and Phyllis Lehmann, 1939 and 1948 onwards) have thoroughly explored the site and have thrown some light on the mysteries practised there, but our knowledge of the cult remains imperfect, partly because of the secrecy maintained by the adepts and partly because the remains have been overlaid by the deposits of many subsequent centuries.

The Kabeiroi, formerly thought to be the deities to whom the sanctuary was dedicated, were not the only objects of worship there. A central position among the Great Gods who are referred to in inscriptions was occupied by the Thracian mother goddess Axieros as mistress of nature. Associated with her were Axiersos and Axiersa, two divinities of the Underworld who were identified by the Greeks with Pluto and Persephone, the youthful vegetation god Kadmilos and the two Kabeiroi. They were revered as the protectors of nature, and later increasingly as the patrons of seafarers and rescuers of those in peril on the sea. Initiation into the mysteries, which took place in two stages, was open to both Greeks and non-Greeks, men and women, free men and slaves – a factor which no doubt promoted the later spread of the cult.

After the fall of the Roman Empire Samothrace alternated between Byzantine, Venetian and Genoese rule until it fell to the Turks in 1457. It was reunited with Greece in 1912 after the Balkan War. During the Second World War it was occupied by Bulgarians.

Sights

The chief place on the island, the picturesque little medieval village of Samothráki (Khóra; pop. 1500), lies in the hills 3 km (2 miles) east of the tiny port of Kamariótissa (ruined castle).

Samothráki (Khóra)

6 km (4 miles) north-east, above the site of ancient Palaiopolis, are the remains of the Sanctuary of the Great Gods or of the Kabeiroi, which have only recently been completely exposed. A chapel dedicated to Ayía Paraskeví and the ruins of a castle of the Gattelusi family on the slopes of the hill mark the site of the ancient harbour (shingle beach). In spite of repeated destruction by pirates, wars and earthquakes the sanctuary continued in existence until the 4th c. A.D. During the Middle Ages the ruins of the ancient buildings served as a quarry of dressed stone for the construction of fortifications.

*Sanctuary of Kabeiroi

The excavations lie 500 m (550 yd) inland. From the museum (behind the Xenia hotel and restaurant) a signposted path runs south-east, passes through an iron gate, crosses the middle one of three streams which traverse the hilly terrain and, after passing a viewpoint, reaches the first large structure on the site, the Anaktoron (House of the Masters or House of the Gods; c. 550 B.C.), in which the worshippers underwent the first degree of initiation (myesis). The northern part of the building, the holy of holies, was closed off; in the south-east corner is a

Anaktoron

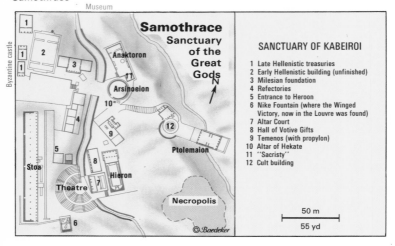

Museum

Samothrace
Sanctuary
of the
Great
Gods

SANCTUARY OF KABEIROI

1 Late Hellenistic treasuries
2 Early Hellenistic building (unfinished)
3 Milesian foundation
4 Refectories
5 Entrance to Heroon
6 Nike Fountain (where the Winged Victory, now in the Louvre was found)
7 Altar Court
8 Hall of Votive Gifts
9 Temenos (with propylon)
10 Altar of Hekate
11 "Sacristy"
12 Cult building

50 m
55 yd

©Baedeker

libation pit. Immediately south, on a higher level, is the "Sacristy", in which registers of the initiate were maintained.

Arsinoeion

Beyond this stood the Arsinoeion, the largest roofed rotunda of Greek antiquity (diameter over 20 m (65 ft)), built by Arsinoe (later Queen Arsinoe II of Egypt) between 289 and 281 B.C. It occupies the site of an earlier cult building, now represented by walls and a rock-cut altar brought to light by the excavators within the Arsinoeion.

On the hillside above the Arsinoeion are remains of an ancient road and a circular building. Other altars dating from the early period of the cult lie between the Arsinoeion and the next

Temenos

building to the south, the Temenos. Built between 350 and 340 B.C., this was the first marble building on the site, with an Ionic propylon which had a frieze of female dancers in Archaicising style (fragments in museum).

Hieron

Going along the middle terrace past an Archaic altar, we come to the re-erected façade of the Hieron, built in the late 4th c. B.C., with a portico added in the 2nd c. At the south end is an apse (under which a crypt was constructed in Roman times), giving the building a plan reminiscent of a Christian church. Here the adepts were admitted to the second degree of initiation (epopteia), probably after they had confessed their sins at two blocks of marble outside the east side of the building (Lehmann). Parallel to the Hieron are the Hall of Votive Gifts (6th c. B.C.) and the Altar Court, the colonnade of which probably served as the stage wall of the (badly ruined) Theatre built about 200 B.C.

°Archaeological Museum

South-east of the sanctuary are an ancient necropolis (7th–2nd c. B.C.) and the Archaeological Museum.

Palaiópolis

North-east of the sacred precinct is the site of ancient Palaiópolis, founded by Aeolian Greeks in the 7th c. B.C. The massive town walls (6th c. B.C.) extend high up the hillside.

Ancient columns on Samothrace

Little is left within the walls. On the hill once occupied by the ancient acropolis are the ruins of a castle (1431–44) of the Genoese Gattelusi family.

At Therma, to the east of Palaiopolis, a hot spring (55 °C (131 °F)) emerges from a 10 m (35 ft) high cone of silica deposits.

Mount Fengári (Fengan: 1640 m (5381 ft)), the island's highest peak, offers a rewarding climb. The ascent takes 6 hours; it is advisable to take a guide.

Mount Fengári

Santorini/Santorin Σαντορίνη/Santoríni   D4

Region: Aegean Islands
Island group: Cyclades
Nomos: Cyclades
Area: 73 sq. km (28 sq. miles)
Altitude: 0–584 m (0–1916 ft)
Population: 6000
Chief place: Thíra (Firá)

Airfield 6 km (4 miles) south-east of Firá. Daily flights from and to Athens (1½ hours).

Air services

Regular service from and to Athens (Piraeus; 12 hours; cars carried) and Crete (7 hours) several times weekly.

Boat services

Santoríni or Thíra (Thera, the Wild island; Italian Santorino or Santoríni, after the island's patron saint, Santa Irene), the most

Situation and characteristics

207

Santoríni
Thíra

Aegean Sea

Thirasía

1 Koloumbos
2 Profítis Ilías Monastery
3 Thera
4 Akrotíri
5 Elefsina

Khristiana Askania

3 km

2 miles

© Baedeker

southerly of the larger Cyclades, and the smaller islands of Thirasía (9 sq. km (3½ sq. miles); 0–295 m (0–968 ft)) and Aspronísi (2 sq. km (¾ sq. mile); 0–71 m (0–233 ft)) are part of the crater of a volcano which has been engulfed by the sea. The rim of the caldera emerges from the sea in a ring, open to the north-west and south-west, enclosing a basin up to 400 m (1300 ft) deep, in the centre of which are the Kaiméni islands, the peaks of a later volcano which came into being in historical times. Hot springs and emissions of gas bear witness to continuing volcanic activity (last eruption 1956).

The dense volcanic deposits lie on top of a massif of argillaceous schists and greywacke overlaid by semi-crystalline limestones. The highest points on the island are Mount Profítis Ilías (584 m (1916 ft)) in the south-east, Megálo Vounó in the north and Monólithos in the east. The inner wall of the crater falls down to the sea in sheer cliffs, ranging in height between 200 m (650 ft) and 400 m (1300 ft), of greyish-black lava with bands of white pumice and reddish tufa. On the outside the land falls away gradually to the sea, its fertile slopes covered with vineyards. Due to lack of water the island is treeless. The inhabitants achieve a modest degree of prosperity through the export of wine, pulses, pistachios and tomato purée, and also Santorin earth (pozzolana), a natural hydraulic cement used in structures exposed to water (harbour works, the Suez Canal). In recent years large numbers of visitors have been attracted to the island by its extraordinary natural structure and its excavation sites, which are among the most important in Greece, and the tourist trade has made an increasing contribution to the economy. But this is not an island for an ordinary seaside holiday, particularly with children.

In antiquity Thera was known as Kalliste (the Fairest island) or Strongyle (the Round island).

Thera was inhabited in the 3rd millennium B.C. (Cycladic culture), probably by Carians. Achaean Greeks settled on the island about 1900 B.C., but were later driven out by Phoenicians. The excavations at Akrotíri have shown that Santorin was a flourishing and prosperous place in the first half of the 2nd millennium B.C. It was in contact with Minoan Crete but had developed a distinctive culture of its own. It can be supposed that at least the city of Akrotíri was not ruled by some central authority but by a plutocracy of merchants and shipowners who had trading links reaching as far afield as Libya. This trade, and perhaps also an ethnic connection with North Africa, can be deduced from the wall-paintings, of astonishingly high artistic quality, which are now in the National Archaeological Museum in Athens.

The Golden Age ended with the eruption of the volcano, which seems to have taken place in the mid 15th c. B.C., after premonitory activity in the 16th c. It must have been many times more violent than the Krakatoa eruption of 1883. A number of archaeologists, in particular Spyridon Marinatos, believe that it explains the sudden end of the Minoan cities on Crete. It has been speculated also that the legend of the disappearance of the island kingdom of Atlantis under the sea might be associated with the eruption.

After the eruption the island remained uninhabited for 500 years, until the beginning of the 1st millennium B.C., when it was resettled by Dorian (Minoan) incomers from Crete, who established themselves on a limestone ridge south-east of Mount Profítis Ilías. In 630 B.C. their King, Grinos, founded a colony at Kyrene – the largest Greek colony in North Africa. Allied with Sparta at the beginning of the Peloponnesian War, the island was required to pay tribute to Athens from 427/426 B.C. onwards. It enjoyed a measure of prosperity under the Ptolemies, when an Egyptian garrison was stationed on the island. Thereafter it came under Roman rule.

In 1207, after the Fourth Crusade, Santoríni was conquered by Marco Sanudo, Duke of Náxos, and thereafter remained in Italian hands for three centuries. In 1539 it was taken by the Turks; in 1830 it was reunited with Greece.

The volcanic force which originally built up the island round the older limestone cone of Mount Profítis Ilías and then destroyed it shortly after 1500 B.C. continued to manifest itself in later centuries. The last violent volcanic phenomena, combined with earth tremors which caused considerable damage, took place in 1956.

Sights

Although many visitors now fly in to Santoríni, the approach by sea, entering the crater from the north-west, is an experience which it is a pity to miss. After passing the gentle green slopes on the outside of the island the boat enters the huge central basin, almost totally enclosed by steep rock walls. At the northern tip of the main island, clinging to the rim of the crater, is Ia (Oia), a trim little town of whitewashed houses which until the Second World War was the island's economic and commercial centre. Steep paths zigzag up the wall of the crater to the town from Ammoúdi Bay, to the west, and the little

*Approach by sea

*Ia

209

The new harbour, Santorini

harbour of Ayios Nikólaos, to the south. As the boat sails on the basin is closed off by the island of Thirasía (on the right) and the south-western tip of Thíra, visible in the distance beyond the Kaiméni islands. High up on the edge of the crater, beyond a projecting spur of rock can be seen Firá, the chief place on the island.

*Firá

Firá (or Thíra; pop. 1500) is reached from the landing-place in the little port of Skála either by walking or riding (on mule- or donkey-back) up the steep and winding stepped path (587 steps) or by taking the new cableway. Large passenger ships now regularly put in at the new port of Athiniós, to the south, from which there is a road (17 km (10½ miles)) to Firá.

With its whitewashed houses, some of them built into the rim of the crater, its winding lanes and little squares, continually opening up new views, and the turquoise-blue domes of its churches and chapels, Firá is a charming little town. The Archaeological Museum in the north of the town contains material of the Cycladic and Minoan periods (before the eruption of the volcano) and also later material of Dorian, Hellenistic and Roman date. It is planned to build a new museum beside the modern Mitrópolis Church (1956) to house the finds from Akrotíri.

*Profítis Ilías Monastery

From Firá a road runs south by way of the village of Pyrgos (6 km (4 miles)) to the summit of Mount Profítis Ilías (584 m (1916 ft)), the highest point on the island, from which there are far-ranging views. Just below the summit stands the interesting Monastery of Profítis Ilías (the Prophet Elijah). The principal church has a richly carved iconostasis and a Cretan

Ia, perched on the rim of the crater

Crown of Elijah (15th c.). In the museum are the mitre and crozier of Patriarch Gregorios V, hanged in Constantinople in 1821. Also of interest are the library, the monastic archives and the kitchen. The monastery ran one of the many "secret schools" which operated during the Turkish period.

From Mount Profítis Ilías a road leads east to the Sellála (a saddle between two hills), on either side of which are the necropolises of ancient Thera. From here a road on the left descends to Kamári, on the east coast, on the site of ancient Oia, and a road on the right runs south to Veríssa. Straight ahead the road winds its way up to Mount Mésa Vounó, passing the Church of Ayios Stéfanos, built on the site of a 5th c. basilica and incorporating ancient architectural elements, and continuing to the Evangelismós Chapel (alt. 297 m (974 ft)), adjoining which is a heroon of the 2nd c. B.C.

The remains of Thera, the ancient capital of the island, extend from the Sellála over the rocky ridge of Mésa Vounó, which falls down steeply on three sides. The town, which continued in existence into Byzantine times, has preserved its original Hellenistic layout. *Thera

From the Evangelismós Chapel a path winds its way southwards up the hillside to the retaining wall of a terrace on which are the remains of the Temple of Apollo Karneios (6th c. B.C.). The temple has a pronaos, naos and two rooms built against the south-west wall of the naos. The terrace to the south of the temple (also 6th c.), built up to make it larger, was used for ceremonies in honour of the god. Between the temple and the corner of the wall are the foundations of a rectangular building, within which, cut in the rock, are the names of various gods (north-west side; some dating from 8th c. B.C.) and of citizens of Thera (south-east side).

At the south-east end of the ridge can be seen the Gymnasion of the Ephebes (2nd c. B.C.). On the north-east side of a large courtyard is the Grotto of Hermes and Herakles; at the east end are a rectangular hall and a round building. Above are rock-cut inscriptions, some of them erotic in content.

Flanking the main street are the foundations of a number of Hellenistic houses with ground-plans of Delian type and the Theatre, with a Roman stage building, under which are traces of the Ptolemaic proscenium. At the entrance to the theatre a side street branches off the main street and goes up to the rock sanctuary of the Egyptian deities Isis, Serapis and Anubis.

Farther along the main street is a colonnade with shops, and beyond this are Roman baths. Then comes the Agora (market square), a long irregularly shaped area with a number of streets opening off it. On its south-east side is the Stoa Basilike (Royal Portico; 1st c. B.C.), with two inscriptions in the name of Kleitosthenes opposite the entrance. The inner hall is divided into two aisles by a row of Doric columns. The pilasters along the walls and the building at the north end (a tribunal?) were later additions.

Farther left, above the north end of the Agora, is a terrace with a Temple of Dionysos, converted in the 2nd c. B.C. to the cult of the Ptolemies and in the Roman Imperial period to the cult of the Emperors. Opposite it is a temple of the goddess Tyche (Fortune).

The main street continues north beyond the Agora. A side road runs west up the hill to the barracks (to the south) and the Gymnasion of the Ptolemaic garrison, on the highest point of Mésa Vounó.

At the lower end of the main street, near the Selláda, is the Temple of Artemidoros (3rd c. B.C.), with rock-cut reliefs.

From the Selláda it takes half an hour to reach the picturesque 19th c. Church of Períssa. South-west of the church, to the right of the courtyard, are the foundations of a round building of the Early Roman Empire, with inscriptions relating to the ownership of land (2nd–4th c. A.D.).

From Períssa the return to Firá is by way of Emborió and the Temple of Thea Basileia (1st c. B.C.), excellently preserved, with the ancient roof, a handsome door-frame and a niche in the interior, as a result of its conversion into the Church of Ayios Nikólaos Marmarítis.

** Akrotíri

Near the village of Akrotíri, 12 km (7½ miles) south-west of Firá, the Greek archaeologist Spyridon Marinatos excavated between 1967 and his death in 1974 considerable areas of a large city destroyed in the great eruption. The buildings date from the 16th c. B.C. and show evidence of the earthquake damage which preceded the final catastrophe, for example bulging walls which were held in place by the pumice sand deposited by the erupting volcano. Combined with the fact that some of the buildings were of two or three storeys, this created problems of excavations and conservation. Indeed Marinatos himself was killed during the excavation work and is buried in a building opposite the spot where the accident occurred.

Entering the site (which is roofed over for protection from the weather) on the south side, we pass between houses which have been preserved to first- and second-floor level. Going north along Odós Telkhinon, we come to a triangular space on

The steep ascent from Skála to Firá

the far side of which is the West House. This contained many frescoes (now in the National Archaeological Museum in Athens), including the representation of a naval expedition and well-preserved painting of a naked youth carrying bunches of fish. In the northernmost house are a number of jars for the storage of food. Returning south, we pass a house with a staircase leading up to the first floor, with steps broken by an earth tremor, and a large complex with a small room (No. 2) in which the Spring Fresco was found.

The principal buildings in this second Pompeii, which is 1600 years older than the Italian Pompeii and will keep the archaeologists busy for years to come, have plans and explanations for the benefit of visitors.

Similar settlements were found on the south coast of Thirasía.

The Kaiméni islands (reached by boat from Skála) are the cone – still active – of the volcano. A visit to the islands is fairly strenuous and not particularly spectacular.

Kaiméni islands

There are records of the emergence and disappearance of small islands in this area in 197 B.C. and between A.D. 19 and 46; volcanic changes took place in the year 726, probably on Palaiá Kaiméni (to the south-west) and in 1457 there was a non-volcanic rock-fall. Mikrá Kaiméni (to the north-east) came into being in 1570–73; in 1650 there was an eruption north-east of Thera (Koloumbos Bank); in 1707–11 Néa Kaiméni emerged from the sea, and between 1866 and 1870 there were further violent eruptions, when the island of Afroéssa, south-west of Néa Kaiméni (and later joined to it), was formed by masses of boiling lava. The George Crater (128 m (420 ft)) on the south-

A typical island church

Youth with bunches of fish

Excavations, Akrotiri

east coast of Néa Kaiméni, named after King George I of Greece, which still occasionally emits sulphureous vapours (most recently in 1956), can be climbed on its north side in half an hour from the bay between Néa and Mikrá Kaiméni.

Boat-owners like to put in at Néa Kaiméni for a day or two in order to expose the hull of their boat to the warm sulphureous water and thus cleanse it of seaweed and marine creatures.

Some 18 km (11 miles) south-west of Santorin are the islets of Khristiana (0–279 m (0–915 ft) and Askania (0–143 m (0–469 ft)), the most southerly of the Cyclades.

Saronic Islands Σαρωνικαί Νῆσοι/Saronikaí Nísi   D3

The collective name of Saronic Islands covers all the islands in the Saronic Gulf – Salamis, Póros, (see entries) and Angístri, together with numerous other islets and isolated rocks. The Argolic Islands (see entry) are also included in this general designation.

Serifos Σέριφος/Sérifos   D4

Region: Aegean Islands
Island group: Cyclades
Nomos: Cyclades
Area: 66 sq. km (25 sq. miles)
Altitude: 0–486 m (0–1595 ft)
Population: 1800
Chief place: Sérifos (Khóra)

Regular daily service from and to Athens (Piraeus; 5–6 hours; cars carried).

Boat services

Sérifos, north-west of Sífnos, is a bare and rocky island, its hills slashed by gorges; its highest point is Mount Toúrlos (486 m (1595 ft)). The island's main sources of income are its modest agriculture and its open-cast iron-mines, which have been worked since ancient times. The ore is shipped from Koutalás, on the south coast.

Situation and characteristics

Originally settled by Ionian Greeks, the island shared the fortunes of the other Cyclades. In Greek mythology it was the island where Danaë and the young Perseus were washed ashore.

History

Sights

In the island's capital Sérifos, above the sheltered harbour of Livádi, are the ruins of a Venetian castle (view).

Sérifos (Khóra)

In the north of the island is the Monastery of the Taxiarchs (Archangels; 1600), with a fine library. North-west of the monastery lies the pretty village of Panayía, with the Church of Xiló Panayía (950).

Monastery of the Taxiarchs

*Panayía Church

Sérifos (Khóra)

Sfaktiria/Sphakteria Σφακτηρία/Sfaktiría D2

Region: Peloponnese
Nomos: Messenia
Area: 5 sq. km (2 sq. miles)
Altitude: 0–137 m (0–449 ft)

Situation and characteristics

Sfaktiría, the ancient Sphagia, is a cliff-fringed island lying off the south-western Peloponnese, separated from it by the narrow Sikiá Channel (200 m (220 yd) wide). 4·6 km (2¾ miles) long and between 500 m (550 yd) and 1000 m (1100 yd) wide, it forms a protective barrier on the west side of Navarino Bay (Pylos Bay), in which on October 1827 a Turkish fleet of 82 warships suffered an annihilating defeat at the hands of a numerically inferior Russian and French fleet. The sea bed is still littered with wrecks.

On the saddle between the two highest points on the island is a spring, to the east of which are the Panagoula Chapel (annual consecration festival) and a monument to Russian sailors who fell in the battle.

On the east coast, on the south side of Panagoula Bay, are the Tsamados Cave and the Tomb of the Piedmontese General and phjlhellene Count Santa Rosa, who fell here in 1825, together with a Greek captain named Tsamados, in a fight with Ibrahim Pasha's Egyptian forces.

On the southern hill can be seen the Tomb of Prince Paul-Marie Bonaparte, killed off Spétsai in 1825. Opposite, on the mainland, stands the Venetian and Turkish fort of Néo Kástro (1573). Off Cape Kypri, on the south coast, is the islet of Pylos

(lighthouse), with a monument to French sailors killed in the Battle of Navarino.
In the north-east of Navarino Bay, on the flat rocky islet of Khelonáki (Marathonísi), is a memorial to British sailors.

Sifnos/Siphnos Σίφνος/Sífnos   D4

Region: Aegean Islands
Island group: Cyclades
Nomos: Cyclades
Area: 73 sq. km (28 sq. miles)
Altitude: 0–680 m (0–2231 ft)
Population: 2000
Chief place: Apollonía

Regular service from and to Athens (Piraeus) several times daily (5½ hours; cars carried). Local connections with Sérifos, Kímolos and other neighbouring islands.

Boat services

The island of Sífnos, one of the southern Cyclades, lies approximately in the middle of the triangle formed by Mílos, Sérifos and Páros. The north and north-west of the island are occupied by barren ranges of hills, the east and south by gentler uplands. The coast is much indented and lined by cliffs for much of its length. Agriculture (particularly onion-growing) on the island's fertile soil, the manufacture of pottery of traditional type and weaving bring the inhabitants a modest degree of prosperity.

Situation and characteristics

Sifnos

Sikinos

History

Already well populated in the period of the Cycladic culture (3rd and 2nd millennia B.C.), the island grew so wealthy in classical times from the produce of its silver-mines that the Siphnians built a treasury in the Sanctuary of Apollo at Delphi. When the flooding of the mines made it impossible to work the silver the island declined into insignificance. Entrances to the silver workings can be seen in the sea at Ayios Sóstis and Ayios Minás.

Sights

Kamáres

Apollonía

From the principal port, Kamáres (beach; pottery workshops), on the west coast, a road leads up to the island's capital, Apollonía. The Church of Ayios Sóson has beautiful wall-paintings, as have the Church of the Panayía Gourniá in Artemón (to the north) and the Church of the Panayía in Katavatí (to the south).

Kástro

5 km (3 miles) east, above a sheltered bay is the picturesque village of Kástro, with remnants of its medieval walls. According to Herodotus this was the site of the island's ancient capital; there are still some remains of walls (4th c. B.C.).
On the coasts are numerous Hellenistic, Roman and medieval watch-towers.
On the hill of Ayios Andréas, south-west of Apollonía, are the remains of a pre-Greek settlement. There are tombs of the same period at Vathý and Mávro Khorió.

Monasteries

There are a number of interesting monasteries on Sífnos, some of which have accommodation for visitors, including in particular the fortified monastery on Mount Profítis Ilías (680 m (2231 ft); pilgrimages), Khrysóstomos (lilac tree and palm of 1653); Panayía tis Vrysis (library), at the south-eastern tip of the island, the Taxiarchs (Archangels), above Vathý Bay, Panayía tou Vounoú (view), and Panayía Khrysopiyí, on the south coast, with a wonder-working icon (17th c.).
All over the island, particularly in the east, are Venetian dovecots.

Kitrianí

To the south-east of Cape Kontoú, the southern tip of Sífnos, lies the little marble island of Kitrianí, with a chapel.

Sikinos Σίκινος/Síkinos   D4

Region: Aegean Islands
Island group: Cyclades
Nomos: Cyclades
Area: 41 sq. km (16 sq. miles)
Altitude: 0–600 m (0–1970 ft)
Population: 350
Chief place: Síkinos

Boat services

Regular service from and to Athens (Piraeus) twice weekly (10 hours). Local connections with Íos and other neighbouring islands.

Situation and characteristics

Síkinos, 6 km (4 miles) south-west of Íos, is a bare rocky island fringed by sheer cliffs, with rugged hills in the north and north-west and gentler country in the south-east (terraced cultivation).

With its inhospitable soil and lack of sheltered anchorages, Síkinos was never of any political or cultural importance in antiquity. In Roman times it was used as a place of exile.

History

Sights

From the harbour of Aloprónia (sandy bay) it is an hour's climb (2·5 km (1½ miles); mules available) to the chief place on the island, Síkinos (pop. 350), in a wooded gorge. It is a typical little Cycladic village, with the picturesque Kástro quarter within its medieval walls. On the hillside above this lies the main village, Khorió. Higher up are the ruins of the Nunnery of Zoodókhos Piyí.

Síkinos

1½ hours' walk west is the chapel of the Panayía, which belonged to the Episkopí Monastery (5th–7th c.), built on the site of an ancient sanctuary of the 2nd c. B.C.

On the steep hill beside the little Church of Ayía Marína are scanty remains of the ancient city.

Skiathos Σχίαθος/Skíathos C3

Region: Thessaly
Island group: Northern Sporades
Nomos: Magnesia
Area: 48 sq. km (10 sq. miles)
Altitude: 0–438 m (0–1437 ft)
Population: 3900
Chief place: Skíathos

Airport 4 km (2½ miles) north-east of Skíathos. Daily flights from and to Athens in summer (55 minutes).

Air services

Regular service from Ayios Konstantínos daily, from Vólos twice daily (3–3½ hours); from Kými (Euboea) three times weekly (5 hours). Connections with neighbouring islands.

Boat services

Skíathos, a gently rolling wooded island in the Northern Sporades, lies 4 km (2½ miles) east of the Peninsula of Magnesia. With its equable climate and beautiful sandy bays it is a popular holiday island, particularly favoured by Greeks. The island's main source of income apart from the tourist trade is its 600,000 olive trees.

Situation and characteristics

Skíathos was never a place of any importance in ancient times. Herodotus mentions the island in connection with the naval battle off Cape Artemísion (480 B.C.), reporting that the men of Skíathos conveyed information about Persian naval movements by means of fire signals.

History

Sights

The chief place, and indeed the only town on the island, is Skíathos (pop. 3000), on the south-east coast. Founded in 1830, it occupies the site of the ancient city, on two low hill

Skíathos town

ridges flanking a small sheltered bay. From the Church of Ayios Fanoúrios, to the north-west of the town, there is a fine view. Skíathos was the home of the short-story writer A. Papadiamántis (1851–1911; museum in his house).

2½ hours' walk north of the town (also accessible by boat), on an impregnable crag, are the ruins of the island's medieval capital, Kástro (view) – stretches of the town walls, with a drawbridge, Turkish baths and three of the 22 churches the town once possessed, including the Church of Christós sto Kástro (17th c.; frescoes).

Half-way between Skíathos and Kástro is the Evangelístria Monastery (18th c.; Byzantine chapel), which was a refuge for Greek rebels during the War of Independence.

Monasteries

There are pleasant walks from Skíathos to the abandoned monasteries of Kharalámbos (8 km (5 miles) north), Kekhriá (7 km (4¼ miles) north-west; 18th c. frescoes), Panayía Kounístria (9 km (5½ miles) west; 17th c.) and Ayía Sofía at Toúrlos.

Koukinariés

9 km (5½ miles) west of Skíathos (bus, motor boat) is the beautiful sandy Bay of Koukinariés, one of the finest bathing beaches in the Aegean, with a fringe of umbrella pines to give shade. There are also interesting sea-caves.

Tsoúngrias

South-east of Skíathos are nine smaller islands, the largest of which is Tsoúngrias (6 sq. km (2¼ sq. miles); some land under cultivation). Off the harbour bay are the islets of Tsoungriáki, Daskalonísi (lighthouse), Myrmingonísi (Ant Island) and Marangós; farther north, off the east coast, are the isolated rocks of Répi, Arkí and Aspronísi; to the south is Prasonísi (lighthouse).

Skiathos harbour

Skopelos Σχόπελος/Skópelos   C3

Island group: Northern Sporades
Nomos: Magnesia
Area: 96 sq. km (37 sq. miles)
Altitude: 0–680 m (0–2231 ft)
Population: 4500
Chief place: Skópelos

Regular service from Ayios Konstantínos and from Vólos three times daily (4½ hours); from Kými (Euboea) three times weekly (3½ hours).

Boat services

Skópelos, known in antiquity and until the 3rd c. A.D. as Peparethos, is a hilly and well-wooded island in the Northern Sporades. The steep north-east coast is unwelcoming, and, apart from the wide Bay of Skópelos near the east end, without inlets or irregularities of any consequence, and the gentler south-east coast is also relatively featureless. The fertile areas on the island are mainly devoted to the growing of almonds and fruit (particularly plums; dried-fruit-packing station in Skópelos town). There are many convents in which the nuns make woven goods and other craft products. The tourist trade also makes a contribution to the economy.

Situation and characteristics

The oldest traces of human settlement date from the Neolithic period. The ancient city of Peparethos was said to have been founded by the Cretan hero Staphylos, son of Dionysos and Ariadne. In the so-called Tomb of Staphylos gold jewellery, idols, a variety of implements and utensils and Minoan double axes were found; they are now in the Vólos Museum. The archaeological evidence indicates, however, that from an early stage the inhabitants of the island were influenced by Mycenaean rather than Minoan culture.

Myth and history

After the 7th c. B.C. Skópelos prospered, and the tribute it paid as a member of the first Attic maritime league was substantial. The Peloponesian War, however, quickly and finally put an end to its prosperity. Thereafter it had a series of different masters – Macedonians, Romans, Byzantines, Venetians and finally Turks – who allowed this remote and economically un-important island a considerable measure of autonomy. In 1830 it became part of the new Greek kingdom.

Sights

The chief place on the island, Skópelos (pop. 3000), occupies the site of the ancient and Byzantine capital in a wide unsheltered bay. Its narrow lanes and whitewashed slate-roofed houses climb the slopes of the hill above the harbour, on which are the ruins of a Venetian castle and the foundations of a Temple of Asklepios (5th–4th c. B.C.). The flanks of the hill are covered with beautiful olive groves. The town is said to have some 120 churches and chapels, some of them dating from Byzantine times. The most notable are the Church of St Athanasius (9th–11th c.), built on the foundations of a temple, and the Church of St Michael, with fine carved woodwork, icons and ancient gravestones.

Skópelos town

There are scanty remains of settlements at Pánormos on the

A bay on Skópelos

Skópelos town and harbour

south coast and round Glóssa, the site of ancient Selinous, on the north-west coast.

There are some 360 churches, chapels and monasteries on the island. The most interesting are the Monastery of Evangelístrias (1712; view), above Skópelos town to the west, which has a 10th c. icon of the Mother of God framed in silver, the Metamorfósis Monastery, south-east of Skópelos, the oldest on the island (16th c.), the Monastery of Ayios Taxiárkhos, with an Early Christian church (672) in the forecourt, the Monastery of the Panayía Livadiótissa (17th c.), in the east of the island, with an icon of 1671 by the Cretan painter A. Agorastos, the Prodrómos Monastery (1721), also in the east of the island, the abandoned Monastery of Ayía Varvára (1648), the ruined Monastery of Episkopí, south-west of Skópelos, with a church of 1078, the Church of St Reyínos, the island's first Bishop and patron saint, to the south of the town (mid 4th c.), and the Church of the Zoodókhos Piyí, with a wonder-working icon said to have been painted by St Luke himself.

*Churches and monasteries on Skópelos

Round the north-western tip of the island are four old watch-towers.

In Agnóntas Bay, on the south coast, is the Trypití sea-cave.

Skyros/Skiros   Σκῦρος/Skíros   C4

Region:Central Greece
Island group: Northern Sporades
Nomos: Euboea
Area: 209 sq. km (81 sq. miles)
Altitude: 0–814 m (0–2671 ft)
Population: 2900
Chief place: Skýros (Khóra)

Several flights weekly from Athens (50 minutes).

Air services

Regular service from and to Kými (Euboea) four times weekly (2 hours); from and to Vólos twice weekly (12 hours).

Boat services

Skýros, the largest and most easterly of the Northern Sporades, is a rugged island, partly covered by a sparse growth of trees, with a much-indented coastline. It is divided into two distinct parts by a narrow neck of sandy low-lying land between Kalamítsa Bay on the west and Akhílli Bay on the east. The south-eastern half of the island is occupied by the steep and arid massif of Mount Kókhilas, rising to 814 m (2671 ft). In this area are the quarries of the coarse-grained variegated marble which was much prized in Roman times. The north-western half, rising to 403 m (1322 ft) in Mount Ólympos, is an area of gentler contours, with more water and a fertile soil. Here are the Mármara Quarries, which have been worked from ancient times down to our own day. The coasts of the island are steep and inhospitable, but there are beautiful sandy bays at the foot of the cliffs.

Situation and characteristics

In recent years the traditional terraced agriculture, practised since ancient times, has given place to the rearing of goats. The small pony-like horses which used to live wild on the island, particularly in the barren south-east, are now much reduced in numbers. The island's main sources of income are farming, a certain amount of tourism and the sale of its high-quality craft products (embroidery, carved furniture, pottery, copperware).

Myth and history

Homer tells us that Thetis disguised her son Achilles as a girl on Skyros in an attempt to prevent him from fighting in the Trojan War.

Traces of Neolithic occupation (5th millennium B.C.) have been found north-east of the Venetian Kástro. In the 2nd millennium B.C. Carian and Pelasgian farmers and seafarers settled on the island, then known as Pelasgia. In the 1st millennium B.C. they were displaced by Dolopians (a Dorian people), who made the island, now called Dolopia, a base for plundering raids in the Aegean. In 469 B.C. Athens drove out the pirates and settled farmers from Attica on the land. In Roman times the islanders achieved a modest prosperity through the export of their much-sought-after variegated marble, but their remote island remained of no political importance.

Skýros was reunited with Greece after 1821.

Sights

Skýros (Khóra)

The chief place on the island, Skýros (Khóra; pop. 2400), lies on the east coast. This little town of whitewashed cube-shaped houses of Cycladic type, finely decorated and furnished, nestles on the slopes of a hill the rocky summit of which was occupied by the ancient acropolis (4th c. B.C.; remains of walls) and is now crowned by a Venetian castle (originally Byzantine), the Kástro (view). From this crag, it was said, Theseus was cast down to his death; according to the legend his remains were later found here and deposited in the Theseion in Athens. In the Kástro stands the former Monastic Church of Ayios Yeóryios (museum).

In Platía Kýprou can be seen a monument to the poet Rupert Brooke, who died on his way to the Dardanelles in 1915 and is buried in the Bay of Tris Boúkes (below).

Linariá

10 km (6 miles) south of Skýros town, in the more westerly of the two inlets opening off Linariá Bay, which is sheltered on the north-west by the island of Baláxa, is Linariá, the principal port of Skýros.

At the south end of the west coast lies the sheltered Bay of Tris Boúkes, almost completely shut off from the open sea by the islands of Platý and Sarakíniko.

Off the west coast of Skýros are the uninhabited islets of Rínia and Skýropoula.

Spetsai Σπέτσαι/Spétsai   D3

Region: Central Greece
Island group: Saronic Islands
Nomos: Attica
Area: 22 sq. km (8½ sq. miles)
Altitude: 0–244 m (0–801 ft)
Population: 3500
Chief place: Spétses

Boats in Spétses harbour

Regular service from and to Athens (Piraeus) several times daily (4½ hours). Hydrofoils from Piraeus and Zéa (1½ hours). Local connection with Kósta (20 minutes).

Boat services

Spétsai or Spétses (Italian Spezzia), the ancient Pityousa (Island of Pines), is a hilly and well-wooded island off the south-west coast of the Argolid. The income of the inhabitants, who are mostly of Albanian descent, comes from farming and now, to an even greater extent, from the tourist trade, for the island's mild climate attracts large numbers of holiday-makers. No motor vehicles are allowed on Spétsai apart from public service vehicles.

Situation and characteristics

In antiquity Spétsai was an island of no importance. After the Orlov Rising, a rebellion against the Turks supported by Catherine the Great of Russia, the population was expelled from the island in 1770 and Spétses town was laid waste. The inhabitants soon returned to their island, however, and their trading and seafaring activities brought them prosperity. In 1821 Spétsai was the first island to take part in the War of Independence: an event commemorated every year by ceremonies in the Madonna Armada Chapel in Ayía Marína.

History

Spétses town

The island's capital, Spétses (pop. 3000), is built on the gentle slopes above the wide bay containing its harbour. The present town, with a number of handsome mansions and three interesting churches in Kastélli, the upper town, dates from the 19th c. There is a local museum in a late 19th c. mansion.

* Circuit of the island

The circuit of the island (12 km (7½ miles)) is a pleasant day's walk, or it can be done in a horse-drawn carriage. From Spétses the route runs south-west by way of the Monastery of Ayios Nikólaos (19th c.) to Ayía Marína, where there are scanty traces of a prehistoric settlement. Off Cape Bísti, at the south-east end of the island, is the islet of Spetsopoúla, which is owned by the shipowner Stavros Niarchos. Then westward to Cape Kouzouna, with the remains of an Early Christian basilica (5th c.), where the route turns north. In Anáryiri Bay (good bathing) is the Bekíri Cave, with remains of rock-cut sculpture.

From here it is possible to return direct to Spétses, or alternatively to continue round the island by way of Ayii Paraskeví (pilgrimage church) to Breloú, in a wooded region Then either over the highest point on the island, Mount Profítis Ilías (244 m (801 ft)) and the Monastery of Ayii Pantés to Ayía Marína, or on the beautiful coast road back to Spétses.

Sporades Σποράδες/Sporádes

Northern Sporades

In antiquity all the islands lying round the Cyclades were known as the Sporades (the Scattered Islands). Nowadays a distinction is made between the Northern Sporades or Magnesian Islands, lying north-east of Euboea, including Skópelos, Skíathos, Alónnisos, Skýros (see entries) and some

Southern Sporades

75 smaller islands and islets, and the Southern Sporades, off the south-west coast of Asia Minor, including Pátmos, Lipsí, Léros, Kálymnos, Kos, Nísyros, Tílos, Sými, Foúrni, Ikaría (see entries) and Khalkí. The islands of Lésbos, Chíos and Sámos (see entries) are sometimes also regarded as belonging to the Southern Sporades.

Symi/Simi Σύμη/Sími D5

Region: Aegean Islands
Island group: Southern Sporades
Nomos: Dodecanese
Area: 64 sq. km (25 sq. miles)
Altitude: 0–616 m (0–2021 ft)
Population: 2500
Chief place: Sými (Yialós)

Boat services

Regular service from and to Athens (Piraeus) twice weekly (27 hours). Local connections with Rhodes and Tílos.

Situation and characteristics

The island of Sými (Italian Simi, Turkish Sömbeki) lies 44 km (27 miles) north-west of Rhodes at the mouth of Sými Bay (Sömbeki Körfezi), which is bounded on the north by the Reşadiye (Knidos) Peninsula and on the south by the Daraçya Peninsula. It has a much-indented coast; according to Homer it possessed eight good harbours. The inhabitants live, as they have lived since ancient times, by sponge-fishing and boat-building. There is an experimental plant for the desalination of sea-water.

Sými

From ancient times the fortunes of Sými were closely linked with those of Rhodes. The island was occupied by the Turks in 1523, and after the Balkan War (1912) was held by Italy. It was reunited with Greece in 1947.

History

Sights

The island's capital, Sými or Yialós (pop. 2200), with its handsome 18th and 19th c. mansions, lies on the north coast, in a bay sheltered by the little island of Nimos (0–360 m (0–1180 ft)). This was also the site of ancient Syme, the acropolis of which was on the jagged crag now occupied by the medieval Kástro, which is reached on a flight of more than 500 steps. From the top there is an extensive view over Pédi Bay to the south.
1 km (¾ mile) east is a massive ancient tumulus.

Sými (Yialós)

On a long inlet in the south of the island stand the massive buildings of the Panormítis Monastery, dedicated to the Archangel Michael, with a charming bell-tower and a beautiful 12th c. church (pilgrimage centre).

Panormítis Monastery

North-west of Sými, in Nimborió Bay, can be seen the remains of an Early Christian basilica with beautiful mosaic pavements. To the south of the church are catacombs, said to have housed a school of icon-painters and sculptors in the 5th c. A.D.
There are more than a hundred churches, chapels and monasteries on Sými, as well as numerous windmills, mostly dismantled.
Off the southern tip of the island lies the islet of Sesklia (lighthouse).

Nimborió

Syros/Siros   Σῦρος/Síros   D4

Region: Aegean Islands
Island group: Cyclades
Nomos: Cyclades
Area: 82 sq. km (32 sq. miles)
Altitude: 0–415 m (0–1362 ft)
Population: 30,000
Chief place: Ermoúpolis (Néa Sýros)

Boat services

Regular service from and to Athens (Piraeus) several times daily (4½ hours; cars carried). Local connections with neighbouring islands in the Cyclades.

Situation and characteristics

The hilly island of Sýros lies half-way between Kýthnos and Mýkonos. Its central situation makes it the principal centre of administration, commerce and fisheries in the Cyclades and a focal point of the shipping routes in the Central Aegean. Agriculture makes a major contribution to the island's economy, supplemented in recent years by a rapidly developing tourist trade.

History

From the time of the Fourth Crusade at the beginning of the 13th c. until 1568 Sýros belonged to the Duchy of Náxos, and since that time it has had a substantial Roman Catholic minority, which during the Turkish period was under the protection of France. During the War of Greek Independence the island remained neutral, and those who had escaped the massacres of Chíos and Psará were able to find refuge here. Close to the town of Ano Sýros, which was founded in the 13th c. and had remained predominantly Catholic, these new settlers established the town of Ermoúpolis (City of Hermes) by the harbour, and this developed during the 19th c. into the largest Greek port, before being overtaken by Piraeus.

Sights

Ermoúpolis

The island's capital, Ermoúpolis or Néa Sýros (pop. 14,000), named after Hermes, the Greek god of trade, occupies the site of an ancient settlement of which no trace remains. It is the seat of the Prefect of the Cyclades, a Roman Catholic bishop and an Orthodox archbishop. The town owes its present extent to Greek refugees from Chíos, Psará, Crete, Hýdra and other islands, who settled here in 1821, after the War of Liberation, and built the town up into a major port on the sea routes between Asia Minor and western Europe. At the end of the 19th c., however, the economy of the town suffered from the competition of Piraeus.

The town extends, with its handsome houses in neo-classical style, from the harbour quarter of Ermoúpolis, the administrative and business centre, with the Town Hall (local museum) and Theatre (a copy of La Scala, Milan), up the slopes of two hills. On the south hill, Vrontado, is the Orthodox Greek quarter (built from 1834 onwards), dominated by the domed Church of Ayios Nikólaos (19th c.). On the hill to the north lies the Roman Catholic town of Ano Sýros, established during the Venetian period (13th c.), with a number of monasteries. On the summit of the hill stands the Roman Catholic Cathedral of St George (19th c.; panoramic views).

Ermoúpolis (Sýros)

Thásos

From Ano Sýros Mount Pýrgos, the island's highest peak (415 m (1362 ft)), to the north-west, can be climbed. From the summit there are beautiful views in all directions.

Mount Pýrgos

15 km (9 miles) south-west of Ermoúpolis is the popular seaside resort of Posidonía, formerly known as Santa Maria della Grazia. Near the town can be seen an ancient necropolis.

Posidonía

12 km (7½ miles) north of Ermoúpolis, at the village of Khalandrianí, is the fortified Cycladic settlement of Kastrí (c. 1800 B.C.). To the west lies Grammatá Bay, in earlier times a welcome harbour of refuge, with Roman and medieval inscriptions (expressions of thanks, prayers).

Kastrí

Grammatá Bay

Thasos Θάσος/Thásos B4

Region: Macedonia
Nomos: Kavála
Area: 379 sq. km (146 sq. miles)
Altitude: 0–1203 m (0–3947 ft)
Population: 16,000
Chief place: Thásos (Liménas)

Ferry services Kavála – Thásos, 15 times daily (30 minutes); Keramotí – Thásos, 12 times daily (40 minutes).

Boat services

Thásos, an attractive and fertile island, well watered in the north and east, lies just off the eastern Macedonian coast in the

Situation and characteristics

northern Aegean, here called the Sea of Thrace. It is occupied by a range of wooded hills rising to 1203 m (3947 ft) in Mount Ypsári and slashed by deep valleys. The northern and eastern slopes fall steeply down to the sea; on the south and west sides the hills slope down more gradually, forming numerous deep sandy bays along the coasts. The island's income comes from farming, mining (copper, zinc) and increasingly from the tourist trade.

History

The earliest traces of human settlement date from the Late Neolithic era. About the middle of the 2nd millennium B.C. Phoenicians settled on the island, later displaced by Thracians. In the 7th c. B.C. Ionian Greeks from Páros captured Thásos from the Thracians and thereafter grew prosperous through gold- and silver-mining and trade. Between 464 and 404 B.C. the island was occupied, after fierce resistance, by Athens, and later became subject to Philip II of Macedon.

After periods of Roman, Byzantine, Venetian and Bulgarian rule Thásos was occupied by the Turks in 1455. Between 1841 and 1902 it was an apanage (perquisite) of the Khedive of Egypt, granted by Sultan Mahmud. It was occupied by Greek forces in 1912, during the Balkan War.

Thásos (Liménas)

The island's capital and port, Thásos or Liménas (pop. 2000), occupies the western half of ancient Thásos, the greatness of which is evidenced by the imposing walls round the ancient naval harbour (now the fishing harbour), stretches of the town walls (7th–5th c. B.C.), originally 3515 m (3845 yd) long, and the foundations of houses and temples, which extend in a semicircle, rising south-eastward from the shore up the slopes of the ancient acropolis, now crowned by a ruined medieval castle, the Kástro (1431). At the south-western end of the castle can be seen an ancient relief of a funeral banquet.

Kástro

By the north gate, south-east of the ancient naval harbour, are the Museum, with a fine collection of Greek and Roman finds, and the Agora (4th c. B.C.), with a stoa. At its east corner is the Thereon, the residence of the city's chief dignitary, and to the south-east is the Sanctuary of Artemis Polo (6th c. B.C.).

* Museum
Agora

Odeion

At the south corner of the Agora are the Odeion (2nd c. A.D.) and, beyond the Roman road, a paved courtyard. Farther south-west we come to the remains of a triumphal arch erected in honour of the Emperors Caracalla and Septimius Severus in A.D. 213–217 and a Temple of Herakles (6th c. B.C.).

Temples

In the northern part of the ancient city are temples of Poseidon and Dionysos (both 4th c. B.C.), the theatre (3rd–2nd c. B.C.), a sanctuary dedicated to foreign divinities and, at the northern tip, a Sanctuary of the Patrooi Theoi (6th c. B.C.). Farther north, in the sea, can be seen remains of the breakwater of the ancient commercial harbour. On a hill south-west of the Kástro are the foundations of a Temple of Athena (5th c. B.C.; extensive views), and on the rocky slopes of a third hill a niche belonging to a Sanctuary of Pan.

Circuit of the island

There is an attractive drive (92 km (57 miles)) round the island on a good road which keeps close to the coast all the way. The road runs south from Thásos town to Panayía (9 km (5½ miles)) and Potamiá (12 km (7½ miles)), on the eastern slopes of Mount Ypsári, with beautiful views over the wooded valley to the sea and the 4 km (2½ mile) long beach of Khrysoammoúdio, on which is Potamiá Skála with its tavernas (14 km (8½ miles)).

The road continues via Kínyra (23 km (14 miles)) and the Alykí Peninsula (ancient marble quarries, remains of a Sanctuary of the Dioskouroi, two Early Christian basilicas) to Potós (45 km (28 miles)), where a road goes off on the right and traverses a romantic valley to the mountain village of Theológos (8 km (5 miles); 240 m (785 ft)).

Then on to the little mining town of Limenariá (50 km (31 miles); pop. 2000), with an office building above the harbour which belonged to the German firm of Krupp, and via Prínos (78 km (48 miles)) and Rakhóni (82 km (51 miles)) back to Thásos (92 km (57 miles)).

Tilos/Telos Tῆλος/Tílos   D5

Region: Aegean Islands
Island group: Southern Sporades
Nomos: Dodecanese
Area: 60 sq. km (23 sq. miles)
Altitude: 0–651 m (0–2136 ft)
Population: 800
Chief place: Megalokhorió

Regular service from and to Athens (Piraeus) twice weekly (25 hours). Local connections in Dodecanese: Rhodes – Sými – Tílos – Nísyros – Kos – Kálymnos – Léros – Lipsí – Pátmos – Arkí – Agathonísi – Sámos.

Boat services

Tílos (Italian Piscopi) is a bare and rugged island in the Dodecanese (Southern Sporades), lying half-way between Rhodes and Kos. The inhabitants make a modest living from farming, on terraces which have been laboriously built up over the centuries, and fishing. Throughout the island's history its fortunes were closely linked with those of Rhodes.

Situation and characteristics

Sights

The chief place on the island, Megalokhorió (pop. 350), lies above the Bay of Ayios Antónios on the north coast. It occupies the site of ancient Telos (some remains of walls). On the hill of Ayios Stéfanos, to the north of the village, is the medieval Kástro, built on ancient foundations, with a handsome church (16th c. frescoes).

Megalokhorió

South of Megalokhorió, on the road to Livádia, the island's port, are the ruins of the Venetian Castle of Mesariá. Near by is the Kharkadió Cave, in which the bones of prehistoric dwarf elephants were found.

Livádia

In the centre of the island is the deserted village of Mikrokhorió. At its north-western tip is the early 18th c. Monastery of Ayios Panteleímon. Tílos also has a number of ruined medieval castles and some 25 churches, chapels and monasteries of the 13th to 18th c. most of them in a dilapidated state.

Mikrokhorió
Ayios Panteleimon
Monastery

The rocky island of Tílos

1·5 km (1 mile) north-west of Tílos lies the islet of Gaidouronísi (lighthouse) and 3 km (2 miles) south-east the island of Antitílos.

Tinos/Tenos Τῆνος/Tínos   D4

Region: Aegean Islands
Island group: Cyclades
Nomos: Cyclades
Area: 195 sq. km (75 sq. miles)
Altitude: 0–713 m (0–2339 ft)
Population: 9000
Chief place: Tínos

Boat services

Regular service from and to Athens (Piraeus) several times daily (5 hours; cars carried); from and to Rafína twice daily (5 hours). Local connections with neighbouring Cycladic islands.

Situation and characteristics

Tínos is the south-eastern continuation of the mountain massif which extends from Euboea by way of Andos. Its highest peak is Mount Tsikniás (713 m (2339 ft)), at the east end of the island. The inhabitants live by farming (terraced fields). Characteristic features of the landscape are the Venetian-style tower-like dovecots, of which there are some 1300. There are also numerous windmills.

Panayía Evangelístria, Tínos ▶

Tinos

Dovecot

In ancient times, from the 3rd c. B.C. onwards, the Sanctuary of Poseidon and Amphitrite was a major religious centre and in our own day, since the early 19th c., the island has possessed a leading shrine of the Orthodox Church. Held from 1207 to 1712 by Venice, Tínos had the longest Frankish period of any part of Greece, and in consequence its population includes a considerable proportion of Roman Catholics. The Orthodox population began to increase from 1822, when – during the War of Liberation – a nun named Pelagia, guided by a vision, found a wonder-working icon of the Panayía, which soon became the object of annual pilgrimages on the feasts of the Annunciation (25 March) and Dormition (15 August), so that Tínos developed into a kind of Greek Lourdes. The island came into international prominence when on 15 August 1940, two months before Mussolini's declaration of war, an Italian submarine torpedoed the Greek cruiser "Elli", which was lying in Tínos harbour for the Feast of the Dormition.

Sights

Tínos town

The island's capital, Tínos (pop. 3000), a little town of whitewashed cub-shaped Cycladic houses, is a conspicuous sight above a wide open bay on the south coast. Originally a modest coastal village, it became the chief place on the island after the Turks destroyed the original capital on Mount Exómbourgo (below). From the harbour a broad processional avenue leads up (15 minutes) to the Orthodox Pilgrimage Church of Panayía Evangelístria, an imposing structure built between 1823 and 1830, using stone from the Sanctuary of Poseidon and the Temple of Delian Apollo. The interior is richly furnished, its principal treasure being the wonder-working image of the Panayía Megalokhóri. From the marble terrace there is a magnificent view.

˚ Panayía Evangelístria

˚ Archaeological Museum

Below the church is the Archaeological Museum, which contains finds from the Sanctuary of Poseidon and Amphitrite, including architectural elements (in the courtyard) and, on the upper floor, large pottery vessels, among them a pithos with relief decoration depicting the birth of Athena from the head of a winged Zeus (7th c. B.C.). The present town occupies the site of the island's ancient capital, Asty (5th c. B.C.).

At Kiónia, 4 km (2½ miles) west in Stávros Bay (remains of ancient harbour), are the remains of the Poseidonion, the Sanctuary of Poseidon and Amphitrite, the Hellenistic or later rebuilding of an earlier (5th c.) sanctuary, with a marble exedra at the east end and a sundial made by Andronikos.

Mount Exómbourgo

13 km (8 miles) north of Tínos town, on the southern and eastern slopes of Mount Exómbourgo, a steep-sided granite cone 553 m (1814 ft) high (ruined Venetian castle; panoramic views), are the surviving remains – three churches and a fountain-house – of the island's medieval capital, which was devastated by the Turks.

In the north-west of the island, south of Pánormos Bay (beach), are a number of marble quarries. The marble is widely used for building houses.

In Pánormos is the house once occupied by the noted sculptor Khalepas, now a museum. The neighbouring village of Pýrgos is noted for its marble-workers.

South Pýrgos, in Istérnia, stands a church with tiled domes.

Yiaros/Gyaros   Γυάρος/Yiáros   D4

Region: Aegean Islands
Island group: Cyclades
Nomos: Cyclades
Area: 37 sq. km (14 sq. miles)
Altitude: 0–489 m (0–1604 ft)
No inhabitants; closed area

No boat services.

Yiáros is an arid and desolate island in the Cyclades, north-west
of Syros. After the Second World War, particularly under the military dictatorship, it was a prison island and place of internment.

Zakynthos/Zante   Ζάκυνδος/Zákinthos   D2

Region: Ionian Islands
Island group: Ionian Islands
Nomos: Zákynthos
Area: 406 sq. km (157 sq. miles)
Altitude: 0–758 m (0–2487 ft)
Population: 30,000
Chief place: Zákynthos

Airport 6 km (3½ miles) from Zákynthos town. Daily flights from
Athens and Kefallinía.

Air services

Ferry Kyllíni–Zákynthos several times daily (1¼ hours).

Boat services

Zákynthos (Italian Zante), one of the Ionian Islands, lies in the
Ionian Sea only 16 km (10 miles) off the west coast of the
Peloponnese. The western half of the island is occupied by a
karstic plateau rising to 758 m (2487 ft), the eastern half by a
fertile and intensively cultivated alluvial plain with a luxuriant
growth of vegetation. With its beautiful scenery and excellent
bathing beaches, Zákynthos is a very popular holiday island.

Situation and
characteristics

Since the time of Homer the island has been known by the
name it still bears, said to be derived from the wild hyacinth
(*Hyacinthus orientalis* L.). Settled at an early period by
Achaeans and Arcadians, it soon developed into a centre of
trade and seafaring whose influence extended as far as the
Iberian Peninsula, where it founded the colony of Zakantha,
later known as Saguntum. In 455 B.C. the Athenian Admiral
Tolmides made the island a dependency of Athens. After the
Peloponnesian War it became a member of the Attic maritime
league. In 217 B.C. it was conquered by the Macedonians, in
191 B.C. by the Romans. After being devastated by the Vandals
it was captured by the Normans, and later was ruled by Frankish
dynasties. It was occupied by the Turks in 1479 but recovered
two years later by the Venetians, who held it until 1797.
Thereafter it shared the fortunes of the other Ionian Islands.
The island has preserved an Italian and Venetian stamp. It
was the birthplace of the Italian poet Ugo Foscolo (1778–
1827) and the Greek poets Dionysios Solomós (1798–1857),
author of the Greek National Anthem, and Andréas Kálvos
(1792–1869).

History

Zakynthos

Zákynthos town and harbour

As a result of the devastations suffered in the course of an eventful history and of severe earthquake damage (particularly in 1515 and 1953) the island has preserved few old buildings.

Sights

Zákynthos town

The chief town, Zákynthos (pop. 12,000), on the site of its ancient predecessor, extends in a wide arc round the gently sloping shores of a bay in the south-east of the island. Above the town are the ruins of a Venetian castle (view) which is believed to have collapsed in the 1515 earthquake.

°Museum

The only one of the town's magnificent Venetian mansions to have survived the 1953 earthquake is the residence of the Roma family, with the charming Chapel of Kyra ton Angelon. Other notable churches are Ayios Nikólaos, on the harbour, and Ayios Dionýsios, with the relics of the island's patron saint. The Municipal Museum has a fine collection of Byzantine wall-paintings, icons and iconostases. The Solomós Museum contains the tombs of Solomós and Kálvos and relics of the island's history and culture.

Pitch springs

14 km (8½ miles) south-west of Zákynthos, at the village of Kerí, are the famous pitch springs mentioned by Herodotus. The pitch has been used since ancient times for the caulking of ships. The springs are now much less productive.

Church of Ayía Mávra

11 km (7 miles) west of Zákynthos, in the village of Makhaiadron, stands the Church of Ayía Mávra, with a typical interior (much reconstructed) and a beautiful peal of bells.

Anafonítria Monastery

35 km (22 miles) north-west of Zákynthos is the 15th c. Anafonítria Monastery (15th c. icons, 17th c. frescoes), in which St Dionysios was a monk. At the northern tip of the island is the Blue Grotto (accessible only by boat).

Practical Information

The removal of any object – even a fragment of pottery or a stone – from an ancient site and the export of antiquities without a permit is strictly prohibited and subject to severe penalties.

Warning

Accommodation

See Hotels
See Camping
See Youth hostels

Airlines

Head office:
Leoforos Syngrou 96,
Athens;
tel (01) 92 92/111

Olympic Airways

In the United Kingdom:
2 Chalkhill Road,
London W6;
tel. (01) 846 9966 and 846 9080

In the United States:
647 Fifth Avenue,
New York NY 10022;
tel. (212) 838 3600
toll free (800) 223–1226

In Canada:
1200 McGill College Avenue,
Suite 12505
Montreal H3B 467;
tel. (514) 878 3891
80 Bloor Street West,
Toronto M55 2VI;
tel. (416) 920 2452

Olympic Airways – the Greek national airline – has desks at all commercial airports in Greece.

In Greece:
Odos Othonos 10,
Athens;
tel. (01) 3 25 06 01

British Airways

Greek Skies,
Odos Kapodistrias 20A,
Corfu;
tel. (0661) 3 37 95–96

Plotin of Crete SA,
Iráklion,
Crete;
tel. (081) 28 68 81

W. Morphy & Son,
Odos Votsi 2,
Pátras;
tel. (061) 42 07 00

Windsor Tours Ltd,
Platia Kyprou 1,
Rhodes;
tel. (0241) 2 77 56

Odos Nikis 13,
Salonica;
tel. (031) 23 83 26

In the United Kingdom:
Head Office, Speedbird House,
Heathrow Airport, PO Box 10
Hounslow TW6 2JA;
tel. (01) 897–4000

In the United States:
Ticket Office,
530 Fifth Avenue,
New York, NY 10017;
tel. (212) 687 1600

Pan Am

In Greece:
Odos Othonos 4 (2nd floor),
Athens;
tel. (01) 3 23 52 42–45

In the United Kingdom:
193 Piccadilly, London W1V 0AD
tel: (01) 750–9316, (01) 409–0688

In the United States:
Pan American Building
200 Park Avenue,
New York, NY10166;
tel. (212) 687–2600;
toll free (800) 221–1111

TWA

Odos Xenofondos 8,
Hilton Hotel,
Ellinikón Airport,
Athens;
tel. (01) 3 22 64 51

In the United States:
605 Third Avenue,
New York, NY 10158;
tel. (212) 290–2141;
toll free (800) 892–4141

Air services (domestic)

The most important commercial airport in Greece is Ellinikón (Hellenikon) International Airport, 12 km (7½ miles) from Athens city centre. There are also international flights to and from Salonica and other Greek airports, including Iráklion (Crete), Corfu, Rhodes and Santorin, particularly during the summer holiday season.

Greece has a dense network of domestic air services, and Athens has air connections with all the principal Aegean islands – Chíos, Corfu, Crete (Iráklion and Chaniá), Kárpathos, Kefallinía, Kos, Lemnos, Léros, Lésbos, Melos, Mýkonos, Páros, Rhodes, Sámos, Santoríni, Zákynthos. It should be noted, however, that Greek domestic air timetables cannot always be implicitly relied on: it is advisable, therefore, to check in advance that your particular flight is actually operating at the time shown in the published timetables.

Antiques and antiquities

The export of antiques and antiquities from Greece is strictly prohibited and subject to heavy penalties. There is, of course, no difficulty about taking out replicas of works of art, etc., such as can be bought in the National Archaeological Museum in Athens and the Archaeological Museum in Iráklion (Crete).

Banks (trápeza)

Banks are open Monday to Friday from 8 a.m. to 2 p.m.   Opening times

Banks at airports, the larger seaports and railway stations have longer opening hours. The exchange offices at frontier crossing points are usually open throughout the day.

Bathing beaches

Places which offer particularly attractive facilities for bathing are noted in the individual entries in the "A to Z" section of this guide.

Among islands with sandy beaches are Thásos, Lemnos, Lésbos, Kálymnos, Rhodes, Crete (north coast), Kefallinía and Corfu. There are shingle beaches on Thásos, Lésbos, Chíos, Sámos and Santoríni. Islands with rocky coasts, on which there are often attractive little coves for bathing, are the Cyclades, Santorín, Crete (south coast) and Corfu (north coast).

Camping

Although there are now large numbers of camp sites in mainland Greece, there are still relatively few on the islands. There are good sites on Ándros, Corfu, Crete, Folégandros, Íos, Kefallinía, Kos, Lefkás, Léros, Páros, Sýros, Thásos, Tínos and Zákynthos.

Camping outside officially recognised sites is prohibited in Greece.

Car ferries

If you want to take your car to Greece but are put off by the thought of the long drive through Yugoslavia the alternative is to use one of the numerous ferry services between Italy and Greece. There are regular ferries from Venice and Ancona to Athens (Piraeus), from which there are services to the Aegean islands. The ferries from Ancona, Bari and Brindisi usually also call at Corfu. The ferry services run by Med Sun Lines between Ancona and Piraeus continue to Iráklion (Crete) and Rhodes, sometimes putting in also at Santoríni.

Car ferries operating during the main holiday season
(Italy– Greece)

Ancona–Katakolon–Iráklion–Santoríni–Rhodes	weekly	Med Sun Lines
Ancona–Igoumenitsa–Pátras	several times weekly	Marlines
Ancona–Igoumenitsa–Pátras	twice weekly	Minoan Lines
Ancona–Corfu–Igoumenitsa–Patras	four times weekly	Strintzis Lines
Ancona–Pátras	four times weekly	Karageorgis
Bari–Corfu–Igoumenitsa–Pátras	several times weekly	Ventouris Ferries, Piraeus
Brindisi–Corfu–Igoumenitsa–Pátras	daily	Adriatica/Hellenic Mediterranean Lines
Brindisi–Corfu–Igoumenitsa–Kefallinía–Pátras	daily	Strintzis Lines
Brindisi–Corfu–Igoumenitsa–Pátras	daily	Fragline, Athens
Brindisi–Pátras	daily	Anco Ferries, Piraeus
Otranto–Corfu–Igoumenitsa	five times weekly	R Line
Venice–Piraeus–Iráklion	weekly	Adriatica
Venice–Piraeus	weekly	British Ferries

Caravans

Owners of trailer and motor caravans should check the maximum permissible dimensions before booking on a car ferry.

Island-hopping

Connections between individual islands (passenger and car ferry services) are noted in the entries in the "A to Z" section of this guide. For general information, see Inter-island travel.

Adriatica,
agents: Sealink UK Ltd,
P.O. Box 29,
Victoria Station,
London SW1V 1JX;
tel. (01) 834 8122

Anco Ferries,
agents: Amathus Holidays,
51 Tottenham Court Road,
London W1P 0HS;
tel. (01) 636 6158

Fragline,
agents: Peco Tours,
52 Heath Road,
Caterham, Surrey CR3 5RQ;
tel. (0883) 48511

Hellenic Mediterranean
Lines,
18 Hanover Street,
London W1R 9HG;
tel. (01) 499 0076

Karageorgis,
36 King Street,
London WC2E 8JS;
tel. (01) 240 2695 and 240
5461

Med Sun Lines Ferry Ltd,
Cosmopolitan Holidays Ltd,
91 York Street,
London W1H 1DU;
tel. (01) 402 4255

R Line,
c/o CIT,
10 Charles II Street,
London SW1;
tel. (01) 930 6722

Agents for Fragline, Marlines,
Strintzis Lines and
Ventouris:
Viamare Travel Ltd,
33 Mapesbury Road,
London NW2 4HT;
tel. (01) 452 8231

Information

Car rental

Corfu:
Leofóros Alexandras,
tel. (0661) 3 88 20
Corfu International Airport,
tel. (0661) 3 25 65
Corfu Hilton,
tel. (0661) 3 65 40–9
Apt 51, New Port,
Odos Xenofondos Strategou
46,
tel. (0661) 3 80 89

Crete:
Odos Tzanakaki 58,
Chaniá,
tel. (0821) 5 05 10
Chaniá Airport,
tel. (0821) 5 47 97
Leoforos Eleftheriou
Venizélou,
Khersonisos,
tel. (0897) 2 24 65
Odos Kothiri/
Odos Theotokopoulou,
Ierápetra,
tel. (0842) 2 37 67
Odos 25 Avgoustou 58,
Iráklion,
tel. (081) 22 54 21
Iráklion International Airport,
tel. (081) 22 54 22

Crete (*cont.*):
Leoforos Eleftheriou
Venizélou, Mália
(March–October only),
tel. (0897) 3 12 38
Odos Arkadiou 94,
Réthymnon,
tel. (0831) 2 31 46
Odos Akti Koundourou,
Ayios Nikólaos,
tel. (0841) 2 84 97

Kos:
Odos Panayi Tsaldari, Kos
(April–October only),
tel. (0242) 2 42 72

Rhodes:
Odos Gallias 9, Rhodes,
tel. (0241) 2 49 90
Rhodes Palace Hotel,
Rhodes
(April–October only),
tel. (0241) 2 36 61
Rhodes International Airport,
Rhodes,
tel. (0241) 9 28 97
Oceans Club,
Psalidi/Rhodes
(April–October only),
tel. (02420) 2 39 34

Avis

Practical Information

Budget/Sixt

Chíos:
Odos Petrokokinou,
Chíos,
tel. (0271) 2 75 82

Corfu:
Odos Xenoforou,
Corfu,
tel. (0661) 2 20 62

Crete:
Odos Akti Koundourou 36,
Ayios Nikólaos,
tel. (0841) 2 28 00 and
    2 88 45
Odos Karaiskaki 46,
Chaniá,
tel. (0821) 5 27 78
Odos 5 Avgoustou 34,
Iráklion,
tel. (081) 2 35 13–15
Iráklion International Airport,
tel. (081) 23 51 82
Odos Venizelou,
Mália,
tel. (0897) 3 13 39
Leoforos Koundourioti 83,
Réthymnon,
tel. (0831) 2 43 86
Odos Venizelou,
Khersonisos,
tel. (0897) 2 21 94

Kos:
Kos International Airport,
tel. (0242) 2 31 87
Platia Bessa 3, Kos,
tel. (0242) 2 24 55
Karavia Beach Hotel,
Kos,
tel. (0242) 2 31 87

Rhodes:
Rhodes Airport,
tel. (024) 2 25 08
Leoforos Allison & Rhodes,
tel. (024) 2 25 08

Samos:
Odos Themistokleous
    Soufouli,
tel. (0273) 2 71 46
Leoforos Lykourgou
    Logotheti,
Pythagórion,
tel. (0273) 6 11 16

Santorín:
Thera,
tel. (0286) 2 21 80

Thásos:
Odos Venizelou 28,
Thásos,
tel. (051) 22 87 85

europcar

Corfu:
Odos Kapodistriou 76,
Corfu,
tel. (0661) 3 84 97

Crete:
Odos Akti Koundourou,
Ayios Nikólaos,
tel. (0841) 2 20 20
Odos Tzanakaki 28,
Chaniá,
tel. (0281) 2 88 18
Odos 24 Avgoustou 28,
Iráklion,
tel. (081) 22 32 40

Rhodes:
Odos Ethelonton
    Dodekanision,
Rhodes,
tel. (0241) 2 28 16

Santoríni:
Thera,
tel. (0286) 2 22 21

Hertz

Corfu:
Odos Xenofondos Stratigou,
Corfu,
tel. (0661) 3 66 35
Corfu Airport,
tel. (0661) 3 35 47

Crete:
Platia Koundourou 17,
Ayios Nikólaos,
tel. (0841) 2 88 20

Crete (*cont.*):
Astir Palace Elounda,
Ayios Nikólaos,
tel. (0841) 4 15 80
Elounda Beach Hotel,
Ayios Nikólaos,
tel. (0841) 4 14 12
Capsis Hotel, Ayía Pelayía,
tel. (081) 23 33 95
Odos Tzanakaki, Chaniá,
tel. (0821) 2 90 19

Chaniá Airport,
tel. (0821) 6 33 85
Odos Venizelou 8,
Khersonisos,
tel. (0897) 2 20 09
Creta Maris Hotel,
Khersonisos,
tel. (0897) 2 21 55
Odos 25 Avgoustou 44,
Iráklion,
tel. (081) 22 98 02
Hotel Petra Mare,
Ierápetra,
tel. (0842) 2 86 73

Odos Khortatzi 1,
Réthymnon,
tel. (0831) 2 62 86
El Greco Hotel,
Réthymnon,
tel. (0831) 7 12 81
Réthymna Beach Hotel,
Réthymnon,
tel. (0831) 2 94 90

Hertz (*cont.*)

Corfu:
Odos Xenofondos
  Stratigou 34,
Corfu,
tel. (0661) 3 62 23 and
  3 68 98

Rhodes:
Odos 28 Oktovriou 18,
Rhodes,
tel. (0241) 2 19 58 and
  3 27 27
Rhodes Airport,
tel. (0241) 9 31 05

InterRent

Crete:
Odos Tzanakaki 62B,
Chaniá,
tel. (0821) 5 68 30
Leoforos 25 Avgoustou 76,
Iráklion,
tel. (081) 22 52 91 and
  24 17 66
Iráklion Airport,
tel. (081) 28 08 91
Leoforos Koundourioti 72,
Réthymnon.
tel. (0831) 2 92 04

Sámos:
Odos Lykourgou Logotheti
  65,
Pythagórion,
tel. (0273) 6 15 22 and
  6 12 59
Kokkari, Sámos,
tel. (0273) 2 25 09
Odos Themistokleous
  Sofouli 85,
Sámos,
tel. (0273) 2 88 33–34

Chemists

Chemists' shops (pharmacies) can be identified by a cross on a
round plate above the entrance and the word ΦΑΡΜΑΚΕΙΟΝ.

Monday, Wednesday and Saturday 8.30 a.m.–2.30 p.m.;
Tuesday, Thursday and Friday 8.30 a.m.–1.30 p.m. and
5–8 p.m.

Opening times

Consulates

See Embassies and consulates

Currency

The Greek unit of currency is the drachma (dr.), which is
divided into 100 lepta. There are banknotes for 50, 100, 500,
1000 and 5000 dr., and coins in denominations of 5, 10, 20 and
50 lepta and 1, 2, 5, 10, 20 and 50 dr.

Unit of currency

243

Practical Information

Exchange rates (March
1987) (subject to variation)

£1 sterling = 205 dr. 1000 dr. = £4.90
US $1   = 135 dr. 1000 dr. = $7.40

Import of currency

Visitors may take into Greece a maximum of 3000 dr. in Greek currency. There are no restrictions on the import of foreign currency either in cash or in travellers' cheques. Foreign currency amounting to more than US $500 per head should be declared on entry into Greece so that any unspent amount can be taken out again.

Export of currency

Visitors may take out a maximum of 3000 dr. in Greek currency. Foreign currency up to the value of US $500 may be taken out, or up to a higher amount if declared on entry.

It is advisable to take money in the form of travellers' cheques or to use Eurocheques. The principal credit cards are widely accepted in larger towns.

As is usual in countries with weak currencies, it is best to change money in Greece rather than outside it.

Customs regulations

Import

Visitors to Greece can import without payment of duty personal items as well as new articles for their own use or for gifts, up to a total value of 11,000 dr.

They may also take in, duty-free, 300 cigarettes (or 150 cigarillos or 75 cigars or 400 grams of tobacco), 4 litres of alcoholic drinks, 1·5 litres of spirits and 75 grams of perfume.

The following are accepted as items of personal use which are admitted without payment of duty: a camera with a reasonable number of films, a ciné-camera, a pair of binoculars, a portable radio, a portable record-player with up to 20 records, a tape-recorder, a portable typewriter, a bicycle, sports gear and camping equipment. These and other objects (e.g. a sporting gun) must be entered in the owner's passport.

The import of plants, and also of radio transmitters, is prohibited. A CB transmitter installed in a car may be taken in but may not be used in Greece.

Export

Visitors may take out provisions for the journey up to a value of US $50 and souvenirs up to a value of $150. The export of antiquities and works of art is prohibited except in rare cases with the authorisation of the State Archaeological Service in Athens. There is no difficulty about taking out replicas of antiquities or works of art.

Written-off cars

See Motoring: Customs regulations

Diving

See Sports

Drinks

See Food and drink

Electricity

With few exceptions electricity is 220 volts a.c.; on ships it is
frequently 110 volts a.c. Plugs have two round prongs, smaller
in diameter than those used in Britain. Adaptors for the flat-
prong North American-type plug should be brought along. An
adaptor also should be taken for an electric razor.

Embassies and consulates

United Kingdom

Embassy,
Odos Ploutarkhou 1,
Athens;
tel. (01) 7 23 62 11

Consulate,
Leoforos Alexandras 11,
Corfu;
tel. (0661) 3 00 55 and 3 79 95

Consulate,
Odos Papalexandrou 16,
Iráklion, Crete;
tel. (081) 22 40 12

Consulate,
Odos Votsi 2,
Pátras;
tel. (061) 27 73 29

Consulate,
Odos 23 Martiou 23,
Rhodes;
tel. (0241) 2 72 47 and 2 73 06

Consulate,
Odos Venizelou 8,
P.O. Box 10332,
Salonica;
tel. (031) 27 80 06 and 26 99 84

Consulate,
Odos Ayiou Theodorou,
Vathý, Sámos;
tel (0273) 2 73 14

United States

Embassy,
Leoforos Vasilissis Sofias 91,
Athens;
tel. (01) 7 21 29 51–59

Consulate,
Odos Vasileos Konstantinou,
Salonica;
tel. (031) 26 61 21

Canada

Embassy,
Odos Ioannou Yennadiou 4,
Athens;
tel. (01) 7 23 95 11–19

Emergencies

The most useful source of assistance for visitors is the Tourist Police (Astynomia allodapon), tel. 171 in Athens, check with operator elsewhere.

Events

January	New year's Day; St Basil's Day (1st in many places); Three Kings' Day (Epiphany; the Blessing of the Waters ceremony in many places); popular festivals (Ándros).
Carnival	Carnival celebrations (in many places).
Ash Wednesday	Celebrations, with picnics, kite-flying and Lenten dishes (in many places).
25 March	National Day (celebrated everywhere).
April	Feast of St Spyridon (patron saint of Corfu; on Corfu).
Greek Holy Week	Procession with lighted candles on Good Friday; Midnight Mass on Easter Saturday; feast, with lamb on the spit, on Easter Day (everywhere).
23 April	St George's Day (in many places).
May	Departure of the sponge-divers (Kálymnos); Labour Day (1st everywhere), with flower festival; anniversary of reunion with Greece (21st; Corfu); dance festival, commemorating the battle for Crete (end May; Chaniá, Crete).
May/June	St Paraskevi's Day (Bull Fair; Lésbos).
June	Midsummer bonfires (21st; Rhodes); Klydonas folk festival (end of month; Piskokéfalo and Krousta, Crete).
June/July	Navy Week (in many port towns).
July	Fair, with folk-dancing (beginning of month; Levkimi, Corfu); Wine festival (Réthymnon, Crete); Raisin Festival (Sitía, Crete).
August	Fair, with traditional celebrations (beginning of month; Anóyia, Crete); Festival of the Panayía (Mother of God; 15th; in many places); Cretan Wedding (Kritsá, Crete); Feast of St Dionysius, patron saint of Zákynthos (24th; Zákynthos).
September	Naval Festival, commemorating victory over the Turks (8th–9th; Spétsai); Chestnut Festival (end of month; Elos Kisamou, Crete).

National Day (28th; everywhere).	October
Feast of St Spyridon (4th; Corfu); commemoration of Arkadi Monastery (8th; Réthymnon, Crete); Feast of St Andrew, patron saint of Pátras (30th; Pátras).	November
Christmas Eve (everywhere; children go round singing carols); New Year's Eve (everywhere).	December

Ferries

See Car ferries

Filming

See Photogaphy and filming

Folk traditions

In recent years the old Greek traditional costumes have become rarer, but in some parts of the country they are still to be seen. Thus on the island of Crete, for example, men can still sometimes be encountered wearing the characteristic Cretan breeches (vraka) and black headscarf; and the old costumes are also sometimes worn on Kárpathos, in the southern part of Rhodes and on Corfu. The picturesque uniform of the Evzones (the former royal bodyguard), who still mount guard, for example, at the National Memorial in Athens, is derived from an old Albanian costume.

Many old traditional customs still find expression in the numerous Church festivals (particularly the Easter celebrations and patronal festivals) and in family celebrations in country areas.

Within recent years Greek folk-music, with its characteristic rhythms and its (to Western ears) unusual intervals, has become widely known in the rest of Europe, and it has also been a major influence on Greek light music. In addition to the popular *bouzouki*, a mandoline-like stringed instrument, the *santouri* and various woodwind instruments feature prominently in Greek folk-music.

The best-known folk-dance is the *sirtaki*, a kind of round dance centred on one leading dancer.

Food and drink

Greek hotels provide a mainly international cuisine, with some Greek dishes and garnishings added for a touch of colour. In restaurants (see entry) the national cuisine predominates, showing Eastern (mainly Turkish) influences and making much use of olive oil, garlic and herbs.
The Greek table will always be supplied with bread (*psomi*), salt (*alati*), pepper (*piper*) and sugar (*zakhari*).

Greek cuisine

An important role is played in the daily life of the Greeks by the coffee-house or café (*kafenion*), which is not merely for drinking coffee but, like the ancient Greek agora, performs a social function as a place for meeting friends, for conversation, for playing cards or other games and for doing business. Coffee is served with a glass of water (*neró*); *ouzo*, the aniseed-flavoured national aperitif, is accompanied by small pieces of cheese, olives, etc. (*mezes*).

In towns there is also the *zakharoplastion*, the Greek equivalent of a tea-shop, which serves pastries and sweets (usually *very* sweet) to the accompaniment of French coffee and other beverages.

Food

Hors d'œuvre (*orektiká*)

There is a wide choice of hors d'œuvre. In addition to the appetisers (*mezes*) served with the aperitif, the range includes prawns, seafood, vine-leaves stuffed with rice (*dolmádes*) and salads (*salátes*).

Soups

Greek soups are usually very substantial, and are often made with eggs and lemon juice. *Fasolada* is a popular thick bean soup; others include pepper soup (*pipéri soúpa*), made with vegetables and meat, clear bouillon (*somós kreátos*), and some excellent fish soups (*psárosoupes*).

Meat (*kréas*)

The favourite meats in Greece are lamb (*arnáki*) and mutton (*arní*), usually served roasted or grilled. Also very popular are *souvlaki*(meat grilled on the spit) and *yiros* (meat grilled on a vertical spit and cut off in thin slices). *Kokorétsi* are lamb entrails roasted on the spit.

Vegetables and salads

Typical Mediterranean vegetables are artichokes (*angináres*), aubergines – eggplant (*melitsánes*), courgettes – squash (*kolokithákia*) and peppers (*piperiés*), usually stuffed or cooked in oil. Salads include lettuce (*marulli*), tomato salad (*tomáto saláta*), asparagus salad (*sparánga saláta*) and Greek or "country" salad (*khoriatikí*), made of lettuce, tomatoes, olives and ewe's-milk cheese (*feta*).

Fish (*psári*)

Fish and seafood feature prominently on the Greek menu. The commonest species are sea-bream (*sinagrída, tsipoúra*), sole (*glóssa*), red mullet (*barboúni*) and tunny (*tónnos*), together with lobster (*astakós*), mussels (*mydia*), squid (*kalamári*) and octopus (*oktapódi*).

Desserts (*desér*)

The commonest desserts are an ice (*pagotó*) or fruit, of which there is a wide choice, varying according to season – watermelons (*karpoúsi*), musk-melons (*pepóni*), peaches (*rodákina*), pears (*akhládia*), apples (*míla*), oranges (*portokália*), grapes (*stafylia*) and figs (*syka*).

Cheese (*tyrí*)

Most Greek cheeses are made from ewe's milk or goat's milk, which is also used to produce yoghurt (*yaoúrti*).

Drinks

Wine (*krasí*)

The commonest Greek drink is wine, either red (*mávro krasí*) or white (*áspro krasí*); there are both dry and sweet wines. The everyday table wines are resinated to improve their keeping qualities (*krasí retsináto*), giving them a characteristic sharp

Freshly caught squid

taste which takes time to appreciate; they are, however, good for the digestion and stimulating to the appetite.

The ancient Greeks also had a preference for resinated wine, and traces of resin (*retsína*) have been found in the oldest amphoras. The resin is added during fermentation. There are also unresinated red and white wines which comply with EEC directives; they are identified by the letters VQPRD on the label. The Greek wines best known outside Greece are the white wine of Sámos and Mavrodaphne, a sweet red wine.

The brewing of beer in Greece dates from the reign of King Otto I, a native of Bavaria. The beers, almost all brewed to Bavarian recipes, are usually excellent. The consumption of beer in Greece has increased considerably in recent years.

Beer (*bíra*)

The commonest aperitif is *ouzo*, an aniseed-flavoured spirit usually drunk with the addition of water, which gives it a milky colouring. *Rakí* is similar, but stronger. *Mástikha* is a liqueur made from the bark of the mastic tree (*Pistacia lentiscus*). Greek brandy (*konyák*) is fruity and relatively light.

Spirits (*pnevmatódi potá*)

These include mineral water (*metallikó neró, sóda*), the very popular orangeade and lemonade (*portokaláda, lemonáda*), and freshly pressed fruit juices (*portokaláda fréska*).

Soft drinks

Coffee comes in different strengths and degrees of sweetness – e.g. *kafés glykis vrastos* (with plenty of sugar), *kafés varis glykos* (strong and sweet), *kafés elafros* (light), the popular *kafés metrios* (medium strength with little sugar), and *kafés sketos* (sugarless).

Coffee (*kafés, kafedáki*)

Practical Information

Tea (*tsai*)

In addition to *mávro tsai* ("black" tea) there are various herbal teas, including *tsai ménda* (peppermint tea) and *tsai tou vounnoú* (an infusion of mountain herbs).

Hotels (xenodochió)

Categories

Hotels are officially classified in six categories – L (luxury), A, B, C, D and E. As a rule visitors are likely to find suitable accommodation, according to price range, in the first four of these categories.
In the following list the luxury-class hotels are marked with an asterisk.
The following are a guide to the prices you could expect to pay for accommodation.

Category	Single room	Double room
L (luxury)	£27–£45 ($44–$74)	£41–£114 ($66–$184)
A	£14–£20 ($22–$33)	£23–£34 ($37–$55)
B	£9–£16 ($15–$26)	£14–£23 ($22–$37)
C	£7–£10 ($11–$16)	£11–£16 ($18–$26)
D	£4·50–£7 ($7–$11)	£7–£10 ($11–$16)
E	£3–£5·50 ($6–$9)	£6–£8 ($9·50–$12·50)

Hotels on Aegina

In Ayía Marína:
Apollo, B, 203 b.
Argo, B, 116 b.
Motel Aegli, C, 14 b.
Akti, C, 44 b.
Ammoudia, C, 26 b.
Aphaea, C, 32 b.
Blue Horizon, C, 28 b.
Galini, C, 67 b.
Hermes, C, 25 b.
Isidora, C, 33 b.
Kalliopi, C, 25 b.
Karras, C, 52 b.
Karyatides, C, 58 b.
Kyriakakis, C, 57 b.
Liberty, C, 40 b.
Magda, C, 40 b.
Marina, C, 55 b.
Nuremberg, C, 24 b.
Oasis, C, 35 b.
Panorama, C, 49 b.
Pantelaros, C, 106 b.
Possidon, C, 48 b.
Saronis, C, 20 b.
Sole, C, 24 b.
Ta Tria Adelfia, C, 32 b.

In Perdika:
Aegina Maris, B, 310 b.
Moondy Bay, B, 144 b.
Hippocampus, D, 28 b.

In Aíyina town:
Danaë, B, 100 beds
Nafsika, B, 66 b.
Areti, C, 39 b.
Avra, C, 57 b.
Brown, C, 48 b.
Faros, C, 72 b.
Klonos, C, 84 b.
Artemis, D, 44 b.
Marmarinos, D, 43 b.
Miranda, D, 37 b.

In Souvala:
Ephi, C, 59 b.
Galaxy, C, 28 b.
Saronikos, D, 33 b.

On Angístri:
Kekryfalia, C, 16 b.
Dina, D, 28 b.
Galini, D, 44 b.
Manaras, D, 48 b.
Mylos, D, 23 b.
Saronis, D, 34 b.

Alónnisos

In Alónnisos town:
Alkyon, B, 21 b.
Galaxy, C, 103 b.

Amorgós

Mike, C, 19 b.

In Ándros town:
Paradissos, B, 76 b.
Xenia, B, 44 b.
Aegli, C, 26 b.

Aegeon, D, 31 b.
Astynea, D, 39 b.
Paradissos, D, 46 b.

Near Syntagma Square:
*Amalia, Leoforos Amalias 10, L, 188 b.
*Athénée Palace, Odos Kolokotroni 1, L, 176 b.
*Athens Hilton, Leoforos Vasilissis Sofias, L, 960 b.
*Caravel, Leoforos Vasileos Alexandrou 2, L, 841 b.
*Grande Bretagne, Platia Syntagmatos, L, 662 b.
*King George, Platia Syntagmatos, L, 223 b.
*King's Palace, Odos Panepistimiou 4, L, 396 b.
*St George Lycabettus, Platia Dexaminis, L, 278 b.
Astor, Odos Karageorgi Servias 16, A, 234 b.
Attika Palace, Odos Karageorgi Servias 6, A, 147 b.
Electra, Odos Ermou 5, A, 180 b.
Electra Palace, Odos Nikodimou 18, A, 196 b.
Esperia Palace, Odos Stadiou 22, A, 338 b.
Olympic Palace, Odos Filellinon 16, A, 168 b.
Arethusa, Odos Mitropoleos 6–8, B, 158 b.
Athens Gate, Leoforos Syngrou 10, B, 202 b.
Athinas, Odos Vasilissis Sofias 99, B, 162 b.
Christina, Odos Kallirois 15, B, 173 b.
Galaxy, Odos Akadimias 22, B, 192 b.
Metropol, Odos Stadiou 55, B, 100 b.
Palladion, Odos Epistimiou 54, B, 115 b.
Plaka, Odos Kapnikareas 7, B, 123 b.
Titania, Odos Panepistimiou 52–54, B, 754 b.

Round Omnia Square:
Ambassadeurs, Odos Sokratous 67, A, 370 b.
King Minos, Odos Pireos 1, A, 287 b.
Academos, Odos Akadimias 58, B, 220 b.
Achillion, Odos Ayiou Konstantinou 32, B, 980 b.
Alfa, Odos Khalkokondyli 17, B, 167 b.
Arkadia, Odos Marni 46, B, 154 b.
Athens Center, Odos Sofokleous 26, B, 259 b.
Cairo City, Odos Marni 42, B, 140 b.
Candia, Odos Deliyanni 40, B, 252 b.
Dorian Inn, Odos Pireos 15–19, B, 287 b.
El Greco, Odos Athinas 65, B, 167 b.
Eretria, Odos Khalkondyli 12, B, 119 b.
Grand Hotel, Odos Veranzerou 10, B, 190 b.
Ilion, Odos Ayiou Konstantinou 7, B, 166 b.
Ionis, Odos Khalkokondyli 41, B, 174 b.
Marathon, Odos Karolou 23, B, 174 b.
Marmara, Odos Khalkokondyli 14, B, 252 b.

Near National Archaeological Museum:
*Acropole Palace, Odos 28 Oktovriou 51, L, 173 b.
*Park, Leoforos Alexandras 10, L, 279 b.
Divani-Zafolia, Leoforos Alexandras 87–89, A, 353 b.
Atlantic, Odos Solomou 60, B, 275 b.
Plaza, Odos Akharnon 73, B, 239 b.
Xenophon, Odos Akharnon 340, B, 310 b.

Chíos

In Chíos town:
Chíos Chandris, B, 294 b.
Perivoli, B 29 b.
Xenia, B, 50 b.

Aktaeon, C, 53 b.
Diana, C, 98 b.
Kyma, C, 82 b.
Pelineon, D, 36 b.

Corfu

In Ayios Gordios:
Agios Gordios, A, 388 b.
Alonakia, B, 30 b.
Chrysses Folies, C, 40 b.
Diethnes, D, 30 b.

In Ayios Ioánnis:
Marida, A, 26 b.
Sidari Beach, C, 52 b.
Vladimir, C, 40 b.

In Ayios Stéfanos:
Nafsika, C, 31 b.
Saint Stefanos, C, 16 b.

In Alykai:
Kerkyra Golf, A, 444 b.
Alykes Beach, C, 29 b.
Salina, C, 31 b.
Sunset, C, 101 b.

In Anakharavi:
Filorian, A, 40 b.
Ionian Princess, B, 171 b.
Flora, C, 33 b.
Anastasia Beach, C, 30 b.

In Anemomylos:
Arion, B, 199 b.
Marina, B, 192 b.

In Arillas:
Arilla Beach, C, 62 b.
Marina, C, 32 b.

In Assyrmatos Potamou:
Gefyraki, C, 54 b.

In Barbati:
Barbati, C, 54 b.

In Benítses:
Odyssey Apartments, A,
112 b.
San Stefano, A, 470 b.
Eugenia, B, 36 b.
Hesperides, B, 32 b.
Potamaki, B, 288 b.
Bella Vista, B, 42 b.
Corfu Maris, C, 48 b.
Loutrouvia, C, 44 b.
Avra, D, 37 b.
Benítses, D, 28 b.

In Cavos Lefkimis:
Cavos, C, 39, b.

In Corfu town:
Corfu Palace, L, 195 b.
Cavalieri, A, 91 b.
Anthis, B, 86 b.
Astron, B, 63 b.
King Alkinoos, B, 102 b.
Olympic, B, 90 b.
Arcadion, C, 95 b.
Archontiko, C, 46 b.
Atlantis, C, 112 b.
Bretagne, C, 75 b.
Calypso, C, 34 b.
Dalia, C, 32 b.
Hermes, C, 62 b.
Ionian, C, 150 b.
Splendid, C, 30 b.
Acropole, D, 37 b.
Constantinoupolis, D, 94 b.
Europa, D, 70 b.
Nea Yorki, D, 74 b.
San Rocco, D, 34 b.

In Dafnila:
Eva Palace, A, 323 b.
Robinson Club-Hotel
    Daphnila, A, 481 b.

In Dassia:
Corfu Chandris, A, 558 b.
Dassia Chandris, A, 467 b.
Elaea Beach, A, 366 b.
Ekaterini, B, 36 b.
Paloma Bianca, B, 64 b.
Amalia, C, 48 b.
Dassia, C, 102 b.
Jason, C, 67 b.
Tina, C, 35 b.
Scheria, D, 32 b.

In Ermones:
Ermones Beach, A, 504 b.

In Ghaena:
Achilleus, B, 138 b.

In Gastouri:
El Greco, B, 27 b.
Argo, C, 28 b.
Sissy, C, 21 b.

In Glyfada:
Grand Hotel Glyfada Beach,
    A, 465 b.
Glyfada Beach, B, 66 b.

In Gouviá:
Corcyra Beach, A, 487 b.
Radovas, A, 221 b.
Angela, B, 38 b.
Park, B, 237 b.
Artemis, C, 53 b.
Elizabeth, C, 39 b.
Galaxias, C, 67 b.
Gouviá, C, 40 b.
Iliada, C, 62 b.
Pheacion, C, 70 b.
Theodora, C, 93 b.
Sirena, D, 50 b.

In Kanóni:
*Corfu Hilton International,
L, 515 b.
Ariti, A, 312 b.
Corfu Divani Palace, A,
306 b.
Royal, C, 176 b.
Salvos, C, 176 b.

In Kassiópi:
Frossyni's Gardens, A, 38 b.

In Komeno:
*Astir Palace, Corfu, L, 590 b.
Kerkyra Club Marina, A, 46 b.
Komeno Villas, C, 42 b.

In Kontokali:
*Kontokali Palace, L, 467 b.
Intermezzo Apartments, A,
20 b.
Ledra, C, 36 b.
Telessila, C, 63 b.
Panorama, D, 38 b.
Pyrros, D, 49 b.

In Liapádes:
Elly Beach, B, 78 b.
Liapades Beach, C, 34 b.

In Messonghi:
Gemini, B, 75 b.
Maria House, C, 35 b.
Melissa Beach, C, 56 b.
Rossis, C, 57 b.
Roulis, C, 30 b.

In Moraitika:
*Miramare Beach, L, 285 b.
Delfina, A, 151 b.
Messonghi Beach, B, 1587 b.
Solonaki, B, 33 b.
Margarita, C, 47 b.
Sea Bird, C, 31 b.
Three Stars, C, 58 b.

In Nissaki:
Nissaki Beach, A, 443 b.
Asprochori, C, 72 b.

In Palaiokastrítsa:
Akrotiri Beach, A, 238 b.
Oceanis, B, 123 b.
Palaeokastritsa, B, 293 b.
Apollon, C, 46 b.
Odysseus C, 64 b.
Hermes, D, 38 b.

In Perama:
Alexandros, A, 138 b.
Aeolos Beach, B, 637 b.
Akti, B, 107 b.
Oasis, B, 124 b.
Aegli, C, 71 b.
Continental, C, 40 b.
Fryni, C, 34 b.
Pontikonissi, C, 84 b.
Spinoulas, C, 30 b.

In Potamos:
Elvira, B, 76 b.
Zorbas, D, 31 b.

In Pyryí:
Anna-Liza, A, 72 b.
Pyrgi, C, 106 b.
Ionia, D, 36 b.

In Roda:
Roda Beach, B, 685 b.
Aphroditi, C, 40 b.
Silver Beach, C, 63 b.
Village Roda Inn, C, 32 b.

In Sidari:
Afroditi Beach, C, 35 b.
Astoria, C, 36 b.
Mimoza, C, 67 b.
Three Brothers, C, 70 b.

In Sinarades:
Yaliskari Palace, A, 420 b.

In Tsaki:
Regency, A, 343 b.

In Ypsos:
Sunrise, B, 72 b.
Ypsos Beach, B, 114 b.
Doria, C, 39 b.
Mega, C, 61 b.
Platanos, C, 58 b.
Costas, D, 46 b.

Crete

In Amoudara:
Agapi Beach, A, 391 b.
Dolphin Bay, A, 354 b.
Agapi Village, B, 141 b.
Minoas, C, 67 b.
Tsangaraki, C, 83 b.

In Amoudares:
Virginia, B, 36 b.

In Ammoudi:
Polydoros, B, 11 b.

In Arkhánes:
Dias, B, 55 b.

In Ayía Galíni:
Stella, B, 19 b.
Acropolis, C, 34 b.
Adonis, C, 39 b.
Astoria, C, 42 b.
Galini Mare, C, Areti, D, 63 b.

In Ayía Marína:
Santa Marina, B, 120 b.
Amalthia, C, 76 b.

In Ayía Pelayía:
Capsis Beach, A, 1090 b.
Peninsula, A, 301 b.
Panorama, B, 97, b.
Perla, B, 49 b.

In Ayía Roumeli:
Aghias Roumeli, B, 13 b.

In Ayios Nikólaos:
*Minos Beach, L, 233 b.
*Minos Palace, L, 282 b.
*Mirabello Village, L, 251 b.
Archontikon, A, 20 b.
Cretan Village, A, 22 b.
Hera Village, A, 88 b.
Hermes, A, 379 b.
Mirabello, A, 332 b.
Triton, A, 22 b.
Amalthia, B, 38 b.
Ammos, B, 56 b.
Adriani Beach, B, 142 b.
Coral, B, 323 b.
Domenico, B, 46 b.
El Greco, B, 70 b.
Ikaros, B, 35 b.
Iris, B, 41 b.
Magda, B, 47 b.
Miramare, B, 86 b.
Olga, B, 45 b.
Rea, B, 220 b.
Sand Apartments, B, 56 b.
Sun Rise, B, 35 b.

In Ayios Nikólaos (*cont.*):
Acratos, C, 60 b.
Alcestis, C, 45 b.
Alfa, C, 61 b.
Almyros Beach, C, 73 b.
Apollon, C, 111 b.
Creta, C, 50 b.
Cronos, C, 68 b.
Du Lac, C, 75 b.
Europa, C, 64 b.
Greca, C, 40 b.
Helena, C, 77 b.
Kamara, C, 51 b.
Kouros, C, 45 b.
Lato, C, 48 b.
Lito, C, 69 b.
Myrsini, C, 60 b.
Panorama, C, 50 b.
Pergola, C, 46 b.
Sgouros, C, 48 b.
Zephyros, C, 48 b.

In Chaniá:
Contessa, A, 14 b.
Kydon, A, 191 b.
Doma, B, 56 b.
Lissos, B, 68 b.
Porto Veneziano, B, 120 b.
Samaria, B, 110 b.
Xenia, B, 88 b.
Aptera Beach, C, 92 b.
Astor, C, 68 b.
Canea, C, 94 b.
Diktynna, C, 66 b.
Kriti, C, 170 b.
Lucia, C, 72 b.
Omalos, C, 58 b.
Avra, D, 43 b.

In Eloúnda:
*Astir Palace Elounda, L, 551 b.
*Elounda Beach, L. 578 b.
*Elounda Mare, L, 150 b.
Elounda Marmin, A, 192 b.
Dririos Beach, B, 32 b.
Akto Olous, C, 96 b.
Aristea, C, 70 b.
Calypso, C, 30 b.
Selena Village, C, 64 b.
Maria, D, 20 b.

In Ferma:
Coriva Village, B, 69 b.

In Galatas:
Panorama, A, 309 b.
Creta Marina, C, 29 b.
Dolphin, C, 32 b.

In Gournes:
Evina, A, 50 b.
America, B, 126 b.

In Gouves:
Candia Beach, A, 403 b.
Marina, A, 462 b.
Aphrodite Beach, B, 446 b.
Calypso, C, 68 b.
Mon Repos, C, 70 b.
Sonia, C, 35 b.

In Ierápetra:
Ferma Beach, A, 314 b.
Koutsounari Traditional
   Cottages, A, 39 b.
Petra Mare, A, 422 b.
Ayanniotakis, B, 28 b.
Blue Sky, B, 45 b.
Atlantis, C, 134 b.
Camiros, C, 75 b.
Creta, C, 47 b.
Kyrva, C, 31 b.
Zakros, C, 88 b.

In Iráklion:
Astoria, A, 273 b.
Atlantis, A, 296 b.
Creta Beach, A, 249 b.
Galaxy, A, 264 b.
Xenia, A, 156 b.
Ares, B, 30 b.
Cosmopolit, B, 59 b.
Elaira, B, 32 b.
Esperia, B, 92 b.
Kastro, B, 63 b.
Mediterranean, B, 105 b.
Petra, B, 59 b.
Phaedra, B, 41 b.
Apollon, C, 96 b.
Arethousa, C, 47 b.
Asterion, C, 108 b.
Athinaikon, C, 77 b.
Blue Sky, C, 50 b.
Castello, C, 124 b.
Daedalos, C, 115 b.
Domenico, C, 73 b.
El Greco, C, 165 b.
Evans, C, 48 b.
Grabelles, C, 80 b.
Heracleion, C, 72 b.
Ivi, C, 33 b.
Knossos, C, 46 b.
Lato, C, 99 b.
Marin, C, 83 b.
Metropole, C, 75 b.
Mirabello, C, 42 b.
Olympic, C, 135 b.
Santa Elena, C, 60 b.
Selena, C, 52 b.

In Iráklion (*cont.*):
Egyptos, D, 48 b.
Florida, D, 34 b.
Hermes, D, 69 b.
Iraklios, D, 83 b.
Minos, D, 63 b.
Palladion, D, 45 b.
Phaestos, D, 41 b.
Porto, D, 32 b.
Rea, D, 37 b.

In Kalathas:
Tzanakaki Beach, C, 68 b.

In Kalo Khorio:
*Istron Bay, L, 199 b.
Elpida, C, 120 b.

In Karteros:
Minos Palace, A, 230 b.
Amnissos, B, 108 b.
Karteros, B, 104 b.
Motel Xenia, B, 48 b.

In Khani Kokkini:
Arina Sand, A, 452 b.
Knossos Beach, A, 207 b.
Themis Beach, A, 229 b.
Prima, B, 24 b.
Akti, C, 37 b.
Danae, C, 34 b.
Kamari, C, 62 b.

In Korakies:
Corakies Village, B, 38 b.

In Kounoupidiana:
Pyrgos, B, 33 b.

In Kourna:
Happy Days Beach, C, 69 b.

In Limin Khersonisou:
*Creta Maris, L, 1014 b.
Belvedere, A, 547 b.
Kastri Village, A, 44 b.
King Minos Palace, A, 253 b.
Lyttos, A, 601 b.
Dedalos Village, B, 46 b.
Glaros, B, 270 b.
Heronissos, B, 168 b.
Maragakis, B, 92 b.
Maria, B, 32 b.
Nora, B, 344 b.
Oceanis, B, 62 b.
Sergios, B, 143 b.
Villa Esperides, B, 54 b.
Zorbas, B, 40 b.
Albatros, C, 143 b.
Anna, C, 76 b.

In Limin Khersonisou (*cont.*):
Avra, C, 32 b.
Blue Sky, C, 38 b.
Diktina, C, 72 b.
Eva, C, 62 b.
Ilios, C, 132 b.
Iro, C, 79 b.
Melpo, C, 67 b.
Miramare, C, 67 b.
Nancy, C, 49 b.
Nefeli, C, 53 b.
Niki, C, 57 b.
Palmera Beach, C, 123 b.
Pela Maria, C, 168 b.
Thalia, C, 69 b.
Villa Margarita, C, 43 b.

In Linoperamata:
Apollonia Beach, A, 585 b.
Zeus Beach, A, 717 b.

In Máleme:
Crete Chandris, A, 767 b.

In Mália:
Ikaros Village, A, 326 b.
Kernos Beach, A, 519 b.
Mália Beach, A, 354 b.
Sirens Beach, A, 422 b.
Ariadne, B, 59 b.
Calypso, B, 78 b.
Costas, B, 64 b.
Grammatikaki, B, 91 b.
Phaedra Beach, B, 133 b.
Artemis, C, 45 b.
Elkomi, C, 55 b.
Florella, C, 56 b.
Mália Holidays, C, 150 b.
Sofokles Beach, C, 64 b.
Sun Beach, C, 42 b.
Armonia, D, 37 b.
Drossia, D, 34 b.

In Mátala:
Mátala Bay, C, 104 b.
Chez Xenophon, D, 43 b.
Zafiria, D, 34 b.

In Mokhlós:
Aldiana Club, B, 262 b.

In Mýrtos:
Esperides, C, 112 b.
Myrtos, C, 32 b.

In Palaíokastro (Rodia):
Rogdia, C, 42 b.

In Palaiokastro (Sitía):
Hellas, B, 24 b.
Marina Village, C, 54 b.

In Palaiokhóra:
Elman, B, 41 b.
Lamboussakis, B, 18 b.
Lissos, C, 21 b.
Livykon, d, 36 b.

In Pánormos:
Lavris, B, 56 b.
Pánormos Beach, C, 61 b.

In Perama:
Marelina, B, 377 b.

In Perivolia:
Kantaras, C, 128 b.
Minos, C, 145 b.

In Piskopiano:
Kalimera, B, 32 b.

In Plakias:
Calypso Cretan Village, A,
    204 b.
Lamon, B, 46 b.
Neos Aliantos, B, 102 b.
Aliantos, C, 35 b.
Sophia, C, 48 b.

In Platania:
Stethali, B, 44 b.
Tryfon, C, 48 b.

In Póros:
Dafne, B, 38 b.
Galini, C, 95 b.
Pasiphae, C, 32 b.
Poseidon, C, 49 b.
Prince, C, 50 b.
Vines, C, 40 b.

In Réthymnon:
El Greco, A, 573 b.
Rithymna Beach, A, 1082 b.
Adele Beach Bungalows, B,
    99 b.
Brascos, B, 151 b.
Eleonora, B, 62 b.
Elina Holidays, B, 40 b.
Hen, B, 62 b.
Idaeon, B, 133 b.
Jo-An, B, 93 b.
Kríti Beach, B, 100 b.
Olympic, B, 113 b.
Orion, B, 138 b.
Xenia, B, 50 b.
Astali, C, 63 b.
Bali Beach, C, 121 b.
Golden Beach, C, 139 b.
Ionia, C, 32 b.
Lefkoniko, C, 62 b.

Miramare Beach, C, 45 b.
Pavlos, C, 36 b.
Rina, C, 37 b.
Steris Beach, C, 55 b.
Valari, C, 55 b.
Minoa, D, 37 b.

In Sissi:
Porto Sissi, A, 30 b.

In Sitía:
Sitian Beach – Kappa Club,
   A, 310 b.
Sunwing, A, 180 b.
Maresol, B, 47 b.
Alice, C, 69 b.
Crystal, C, 75 b.
Helena, C, 42 b.
Itanos, C, 138 b.
Mariana, C, 47 b.
Vai, C, 84 b.

Xenia, B, 7 r.

Elaphonissos, B, 21 b.

In Loutrá Aidipsoú:
Aegli, A, 150 b.
Kekrops, B, 50 b.
Kentrikon, B, 56 b.
Star, B, 62 b.
Taenaron, B, 54 b.
Anessis, C, 97 b.
Antigone, C, 52 b.
Capri, C, 87 b.
Galini, C, 68 b.
Irene, C, 55 b.
Istiaea, C, 63 b.
Kapolos, C, 98 b.
Knossos, C, 71 b.
Leto, C, 60 b.
Metropole, C, 59 b.
Mitho, C, 69 b.
Nefeli, C, 71 b.
Thermae Sylla, C, 116 b.
Diethnes, D, 76 b.
Palladion, D, 53 b.

In Amárynthos:
Blue Beach, B, 399 b.
Stefania, B, 152 b.
Flisvos, C, 43 b.
Artemis, D, 41 b.

In Ayíos Nikólaos:
Agios Nikolaos, B, 28 b.
Chryssi Ammoudia, B, 30 b.
Glaros, B, 24 b.
Kastoria, B, 57 b.
Park, B, 36 b.

In Stalis:
Anthoussa Beach, A, 259 b.
Creta Solaris, A, 30 b.
Penelope, A, 28 b.
Alkyonides, B, 54 b.
Blue Sea, B, 371 b.
Cactus Beach, B, 74 b.
Hera, B, 35 b.
Palm Beach, B, 40 b.
Sunny Beach, B, 55 b.
Zephyros Beach, B, 75 b.
Arminda, C, 99 b.
Electra, C, 38 b.
Heliotrope, C, 140 b.
Stalis, D, 76 b.

In Yeoryioupolis:
Gorgona, C, 70 b.

In Ayíos Yeóryios:
Alexandros, B, 54 b.
Vachos, B, 36 b.

In Bouros:
Karystos Beach Club, B,
   163 b.
Amalia, C, 306 b.

In Erétria:
Chryssi Akti, B, 193 b.
Perighiali Eretrias, B, 71 b.
Delfis, C, 168 b.
Xenia, C, 180 b.

In Kárystos:
Apollon Resort, B, 150 b.
Als, C, 60 b.
Galaxy, C, 136 b.
Hironia, C, 48 b.
Karystion, C, 75 b.
Plaza, C, 68 b.

In Khalkís:
Lucy, A, 156 b.
John's, B, 98 b.
Paliria, B, 200 b.
Hara, C, 80 b.
Kentrikon, C, 35 b.
Manica, C, 48 b.
Morfeus, D, 45 b.

In Kými:
Beis, C, 58 b.

Crete (cont.)

Delos

Elafónisos

Euboea

Practical Information

Euboea *(cont.)*

In Lefkanti:
Lefkanti, C, 126 b.

In Limni:
Limni, C, 91 b.

In Magoula:
Holidays in Evia, B, 659 b.
Miramare, B, 64 b.

In Malakonda:
Eretria Beach, B, 453 b.
Malakonda Beach, B, 296 b.

In Marmári:
Delfini, C, 39 b.
Marmari Bay, C, 188 b.
Michel-Marie, C, 56 b.

In Néa Artáky:
Bel-Air, B, 82 b.
Angela, C, 112 b.
Telemachus, C, 48 b.

In Néa Styra:
Aegilion, C, 51 b.
Aktaeon, C, 79 b.
Delfini, C, 85 b.
Nektarios, C, 68 b.
Venus Beach, C, 154 b.

In Pefki:
Amaryllis, C, 40 b.
Galaxias, C, 49 b.
Galini, C, 57 b.
Myrtia, C, 42 b.
Akrotirion, D, 29, b.

In Politika:
Evoiki Akti, C, 92 b.

In Steni:
Dirphys, C, 35 b.
Steni, C, 70 b.

Folégandros

Fani Vevis, B, 49 b.

Hýdra

Miramare, A, 50 b.
Miranda, A, 26 b.
Amaryllis, B, 22 b.
Delfini, B, 20 b.

Hydroussa, B, 72 b.
Leto, C, 74 b.
Argo, D, 16 b.
Dina, D, 21 b.

Ikaría

In Evdilos:
Eudoxia, B, 12 b.

In Thermai:
George, B, 16 b.
Apollon, C, 59 b.
Ikarion, D, 52 b.
Thermae, D, 46 b.

In Therma Lefkados:
Adamos, B, 12 b.
Anyfantis, B, 26 b.
Akti, C, 27 b.

Íos

Chryssi Akti, B, 19 b.
Armadoros, C, 50 b.
Corali, C, 25 b.
Delfini, C, 33 b.
Elisvos, C, 25 b.

Fragakis, C, 27 b.
Homer's Inn, C, 34 b.
Mare Monte, C, 30 b.
Sea Breeze, C, 28 b.
Mylopotas, D, 44 b.

Ithaca

Mendor, B, 68 b.
Odysseus, B, 17 b.

Kálymnos

In Kálymnos town:
Drossos, C, 97 b.
Olympic, C, 81 b.
Thermae, C, 30 b.

In Massouri:
Armeos Beach, B, 61 b.
Oasis, B, 22 b.
Cally Beach, C, 31 b.
Ioanna, D, 29 b.

In Myrties:
Themis, B, 17 b.
Delfini, C, 34 b.
Zephyros, C, 54 b.

In Pothea:
Aris, B, 33 b.
Evanik, C, 39 b.

In Kárpathos town:
Romantica, B, 37 b.
Panorama, C, 45 b.
Porfyris, C, 41 b.
Karpathos, D, 28 b.

In Pygádia:
Atlantic, C, 73 b.

Anagenissis, C, 18 b.
Anessis, C, 14 b.

Xenon Dimou Meghistis, B,
32 b.

Ioulis, B, 21 b.
I Tzia Mas, B, 48 b.

Kea Beach, B, 150 b.
Carthea, C, 67 b.

In Argostóli:
Xenia, B, 44 b.
Aenos, C, 74 b.
Agios Gerassimos, C, 28 b.
Cephalonia Star, C, 73 b.
Mouikis, C, 70 b.
Phocas, C, 33 b.
Regina, C, 40 b.
Tourist, C, 38 b.
Allegro, D, 32 b.

In Ayía Effimia:
Pylaros, C, 17 b.
Logara, C, 43 b.

In Antimákhia:
Mastichari Beach, B, 21 b.

In Kardámena:
Norida Beach, A, 553 b.
Carda Beach, B, 127 b.
Panorama, C, 40 b.
Stelios, C, 24 b.
Valinakis Beach, C, 141 b.
Alma, D, 24 b.
Paralia, D, 21 b.

In Kefalos:
Carlos Village, A, 492 b.
Hellas, B, 33 b.
Sidney, D, 40 b.

In Kos town:
Caravia Beach, A, 563 b.
Continental Palace, A, 393 b.
Dimitra Beach, A, 261 b.
Agios Konstantinos, B,
232 b.
Alcyon, B, 42 b.
Alexandra, B, 150 b.
Alki, B, 37 b.
Amerikana, B, 26 b.
Anne, B, 34 b.
Arion, B, 32 b.
Artemis, B, 110 b.
Astron, B, 136 b.
Atlanta Beach, B, 80 b.
Constantia, B, 32 b.
Gallia, B, 39 b.

In Kos town (*cont.*):
Ippoton, B, 78 b.
Kos, b, 262 b.
Meropis, B, 36 b.
Olympia, B, 41 b.
Oscar Sevasti, B, 42 b.
Paritsa, B, 76 b.
Theodorou Beach, B, 103 b.
Theoxenia, B, 78 b.
Afroditi, C, 33 b.
Anastasia, C, 77 b.
Anneta, C, 42 b.
Aspa Holidays, C, 38 b.
Asterias, C, 39 b.
Bahames, C, 56 b.
Bristol, C, 71 b.
Captain's, C, 52 b.
Costel, C, 71 b.
Delfini, C, 34 b.
Diethnes, C, 121 b.
Ekaterini, C, 48 b.
Elisabeth, C, 32 b.
Elli, C, 150 b.
Elma, C, 92 b.
Galaxias, C, 42 b.
Galini, C, 60 b.
George, C, 59 b.
Imperial, C, 132 b.
Ippokratis, C, 48 b.
Kamelia, C, 42 b.
Karis, C, 54 b.
Koala, C, 48 b.
Kondia Beach, C, 101 b.
Koni, C, 37 b.

Practical Information

Kos *(cont.)*

In Kos town *(cont.)*:
Koulias, C, 51 b.
Marie, C, 39 b.
Maritina, C, 132 b.
Messoghios, C, 67 b.
Milva, C, 99 b.
Niriides Beach, C, 147 b.
Olga, C, 57 b.
Oscar, C, 108 b.
Paradissos, C, 100 b.
Pavlos, C, 121 b.
Phaeton, C, 48 b.
Possidon, C, 67 b.
Theonia, C, 89 b.
Titania, C, 109 b.
Veroniki, C, 36 b.
Virginia, C, 42 b.
Zephyros, C, 93 b.
Zikas, C, 93 b.
Dodekanessus, D, 33 b.
Hara, D, 33 b.
Helena, D, 35 b.

In Lambi:
Atlantis, A, 576 b.
Cosmopolitan, B, 148 b.
Alice Springs, C, 40 b.
Atlantis 2, C, 153 b.
Columbia Beach, C, 108 b.
Irene, C, 70 b.
Laura, C, 43 b.

In Mastikhari:
Andreas, B, 16 b.
Faenareti, D, 35 b.

In Mylos Lappa:
Albatros Beach, C, 117 b.

In Psalidi:
Oceanis, A, 651 b.
Ramira Beach, A, 500 b.
Sun Palace, A, 274 b.

In Tigaki:
Tigaki Toulas, B, 38 b.
Ilios, C, 92 b.
Meni Beach, C, 50 b.
Sunset, C, 100 b.
Villa Andreas, C, 36 b.

Kýthira

In Ayía Pelayía:
Kytheria, B, 15 b.

Kýthos

In Loutrá:
Xenia Anagenissis, C, 93 b.

In Mérikhas:
Possidonian, C, 158 b.

Lefkás

Lefkás, B, 186 b.
Niricos, B, 69 b.
Xenia, B, 128 b.

Lefkatas, C, 39 b.
Santa Mavra, C, 38 b.

Lemnos

In Mýrina:
*Akti Myrina, L, 250 b.
Kastro Beach, B, 140 b.
Lemnos, C, 58 b.
Sevdalis, C, 63 b.

Léros

In Lakkí:
Xenon Angelou, B, 16 b.
Artemis, C, 14 b.
Leros, C, 35 b.
Miramare, D, 22 b.

In Léros town:
Alinda, C, 41 b.
Athina, C, 27 b.
Helena, C, 33 b.
Maleas Beach, C, 85 b.
Panteli, C, 48 b.
Platanos, D, 14 b.

Lésbos

In Anyfanta:
Silver Bay, B, 150 b.

In Ayiásos:
Aghia Sion, B, 24 b.

In Kalloní:
Arisvi, C, 119 b.
Kalloni, C, 23 b.

In Kountouroudia:
Kountouroudia, B, 17 b.

In Kratigos:
Katia, B, 76 b.

In Mithymna-Molyvos:
Molyvos I, A, 56 b.
Delfina I, B, 129 b.
Molyvos II, B, 114 b.
Poseidon, B, 27 b.
Sea Horse, B, 27 b.

In Mystegna:
Petalidi, C, 37 b.

In Mytilíni:
Villa 1900, A, 19 b.
Argo, B, 60 b.
Blue Sea, B, 101 b.
Lesvion, B, 68 b.
Mytilana Village, B, 100 b.
Xenia, B, 148 b.
Sappho, C, 56 b.

In Neápolis:
Lesvos Beach, B, 78 b.
Neapolis Beach, C, 24 b.

In Pétra:
Petra, C, 34 b.

In Plomárion:
Oceanis, C, 78 b.

In Thermi:
Vostsala, B, 94 b.

Lésbos *(cont.)*

Kalypso, D, 28 b.

Lipsos

Adamas, B, 22 b.
Venus Village, B, 173 b.
Aphrodite of Milos, C, 34 b.
Chronis, C, 32 b.

Corali, C, 31 b.
Milos, C, 36 b.
Delfini, D, 42 b.

Melos

In Áno Merá:
Áno Merá, A, 124 b.

In Ayios Stéfanos:
Alkistis, B, 182 b.
Artemis, C, 39 b.
Panorama, C, 51 b.
Mino, D, 26 b.

In Kalafati:
Aphroditi, B, 180 b.

In Mýkonos town:
Leto, A, 48 b.
Cavo Tagou, B, 46 b.
Despotiko, B, 40 b.
Kouneni, B, 36 b.

In Ayios Yeóryios:
Anneza, B, 12 b.
Glaros, B, 14 b.
Acroyali, C, 27 b.
Anessi, C, 25 b.
Barbouni, C, 26 b.
Helmos, C, 21 b.
Iliovassilema, C, 39 b.
Kymata, C, 32 b.
Naxos Beach, C, 50 b.
Nissaki, C, 30 b.
Zeus, C, 29 b.
Galini, D, 26 b.
Panormos, D, 23 b.

Petassos, B, 31 b.
Poseidon, B, 40 b.
Rohari, B, 99 b.
Theoxenia, B, 93 b.
Aeolos, C, 48 b.
Korfos, C, 42 b.
Manoulas Beach, C, 57 b.
Marianna, C, 43 b.
Mykonos, C, 30 b.
Mykonos Beach, C, 50 b.
Pelecan, C, 44 b.
Thomas, C, 74 b.
Yannaki, C, 38 b.
Zannis, C, 36 b.
Apollon, D, 33 b.
Helena, D, 35 b.
Karbonaki, D, 39 b.

In Náxos town:
Aspra Spitia, A, 33 b.
Ariadne, B, 46 b.
Aegeon, C, 40 b.
Aeolis, C, 33 b.
Apollon, C, 34 b.
Coronis, C, 60 b.
Grotta, C, 35 b.
Hermes, C, 36 b.
Panorama, C, 33 b.
Sergis, C, 54 b.

Mýkonos

Náxos

Practical Information

Páros

In Alykí:
Afroditi, B, 40 b.
Angeliki, C, 26 b.

In Dryos:
Annezina, A, 26 b.
Julia, C, 23 b.
Ivi, C, 23 b.
Anoussakis, D, 21 b.
Dryos, D, 20 b.

In Marpissa:
Afentakis, C, 25 b.

In Náousa:
Hippocambus, B, 94 b.
Manto, B, 29 b.
Ambelas, C, 32 b.
Atlantis, C, 40 b.
Calypso, C, 46 b.
Minoa, C, 51 b.
Papadakis, C, 31 b.

In Páros town:
Aegeon, B, 45 b.
Apollon, B, 43 b.

In Páros town (*cont.*):
Arian, B, 16 b.
Dilion, B, 27 b.
Polos, B, 40 b.
Xenia, B, 44 b.
Alkyon, C, 46 b.
Argo, C, 83 b.
Asterias, C, 69 b.
Galinos, C, 65 b.
Georgy, C, 63 b.
Hermes, C, 36 b.
Nicolas, C, 83 b.
Oassis, C, 33 b.
Stella, C, 38 b.
Kontes, D, 53 b.
Livadia, D, 37 b.

In Pisso Livadi:
Andromachi, B, 23 b.
Marpissa, B, 21 b.
Leto, C, 28 b.
Pisso Livadi, C, 24 b.
Vicky, C, 28 b.

In Pounta Parikias:
Holiday Sun, A, 101 b.

Pátmos

In Grikos:
Grikos, B, 36 b.
Xenia, B, 62 b.
Ioanna, C, 22 b.
Panorama, C, 37 b.

In Skála:
Kastelli, B, 37 b.

In Skála (*cont.*):
Patmion, B, 42 b.
Skala, B, 90 b.
Chris, C, 48 b.
Iliovassilema, D, 37 b.
Kastro, D, 30 b.
Rex, D, 34 b.
Rodon, D, 36 b.

Paxí

Paxos Beach, B, 72 b.
Aghios Georgios, D, 30 b.

Piraeus

Cavo d'Oro, B, 134 b.
Diogenis, B, 146 b.
Homeridion, B, 112 b.
Estia Naftikon, B, 330 b.
Nufara, B, 84 b.
Park, B, 152 b.
Triton, B, 104 b.
Acropole, C, 42 b.
Anita, C, 47 b.
Argo, C, 47 b.
Arion, C, 69 b.
Atlantis, C, 93 b.
Capitol, C, 91 b.

Cavo, C, 89 b.
Delphini, C, 93 b.
Diana, C, 79 b.
Glaros, C, 80 b.
Ionion, C, 41 b.
Leriotis, C, 85 b.
Lilia, C, 21 b.
Louis, C, 32 b.
Niki, C, 32 b.
Phidias, C, 44 b.
Santorini, C, 63 b.
Skorpios, C, 44 b.
Seriphos, C, 59 b.

Póros

Epta Adelphia, B, 30 b.
Latsi, B, 54 b.
Neon Aegli, B, 132 b.
Pavlou, B, 66 b.
Poros, B, 173 b.
Saron, B, 46 b.

Sirene B, 228 b.
Theano, B, 49 b.
Aktaeon, C, 38 b.
Angyra, C, 87 b.
Chryssi Avgi, C, 145 b.
Manessi, C, 25 b.

Psará

Miramare, A, 50 b.

In Afándou:
Oasis Holidays, A, 70 b.
Xenia, B, 52 b.

In Arkhángelos:
Archangelos, D, 37 b.
Fivos, D, 26 b.

In Faliráki:
Apollo Beach, A, 539 b.
Blue Sea, A, 548 b.
Calypso, A, 479 b.
Colossos Beach, A, 962 b.
Esperides, A, 550 b.
Faliraki Beach, A, 550 b.
Rhodos Beach, A, 517 b.
Diamantis, B, 34 b.
Muses, B, 58 b.
Violetta, B, 26 b.
Dimitra, C, 72 b.
Edelweiss, C, 102 b.
Evi, C, 110 b.
Ideal, C, 44 b.
Lido, C, 38 b.
Sophia, C, 56 b.

In Ialysos:
Blue Horizon, A, 412 b.
Ialyssos Bay, A, 282 b.
Sun Beach, A, 176 b.
Lisa, B, 53 b.
Pachos, B, 44 b.
Green View, C, 62 b.

In Ixia:
*Miramare Beach, L, 330 b.
*Olympic Palace, L, 591 b.
*Rhodos Palace, L, 1220 b.
Apollonia, A, 34 b.
Avra Beach, A, 353 b.
Bel Air, A, 293 b.
Blue Bay, A, 442 b.
Caravel, A, 46 b.
Dionyssos, A, 523 b.
Elektra Palace, A, 400 b.
Elina, A, 277 b.
Elisabeth, A, 190 b.
Golden Beach, A, 431 b.
Metropolitan Capsis, A,
  1288 b.
Oceanis, A, 423 b.
Possidonia, A, 68 b.
Rhodos Bay, A, 611 b.
Leto, B, 184 b.
Solemar, B, 194 b.
Roma, C, 80 b.
Vellois, C, 92 b.

In Kremasti:
Blue Bay Kremasti, A,
  32 b.

In Kritika:
Sirene Beach, A, 156 b.
Poseidon, B, 63 b.

In Líndos:
Lindos Bay, A, 364 b.
Steps of Lindos, A, 310 b.

In Neokhorion:
Athina, B, 267 b.
Villa Rhodos, C, 53 b.

In Paradisi:
Doretta Beach, A, 546 b.

In Profítis Ilías:
Elafos-Elafina, A, 127 b.

In Reni:
Eden Rock, A, 720 b.
Paradise, A, 960 b.

In Rhodes town:
*Grand Hotel Astir Palace, L,
  700 b.
Belvedere, A, 394 b.
Blue Sky, A, 332 b.
Kairo Palace, A, 201 b.
Chevaliers Palace, A, 346 b.
Eva, A, 33 b.
Filerimos, A, 162 b.
Helios Palace, A, 64 b.
Ibiscus, A, 383 b.
Imperial, A, 151 b.
Issaias, A, 42 b.
Kamiros, A, 90 b.
Mediterranean, A, 292 b.
Monte Smith, A, 36 b.
Park, A, 153 b.
Regina, A, 116 b.
Riviera, A, 116 b.
Siravast, A, 170 b.
Sunwing, A, 738 b.
Verino, A, 24 b.
Acandia, B, 150 b.
Aglaia, B, 109 b.
Alexia, B, 257 b.
Amphitryon, B, 188 b.
Angela, B, 118 b.
Cactus, B, 336 b.
Constantinos, B, 246 b.
Continental, B, 218 b.
Corali, B, 217 b.
Delfini, B, 135 b.
Despo, B, 122 b.
Esperia, B, 362 b.
Europa, B, 190 b.
Manousos, B, 212 b.
Phoenix, B, 143 b.
Plaza, B, 244 b.

Practical Information

Rhodes (*cont.*)

In Rhodes town (*cont.*):
Spartalis, B, 141 b.
Thermae, B, 210 b.
Africa, C, 144 b.
Aphrodite, C, 101 b.
Carina, C, 108 b.
El Greco, C, 140 b.
Flora, C, 187 b.
Helena, C, 163 b.
Irene, C, 101 b.
Lydia, C, 111 b.

Majestic, C, 147 b.
Marie, C, 235 b.
Mimosa, C, 117 b.
Minos, C, 133 b.
Parthenon, C, 150 b.
Phaedra, C, 120 b.
Royal, C, 107 b.
Semiramis, C, 230 b.
Soleil, C, 154 b.
Rex, D, 51 b.
Rodini, D, 55 b.

Salamís

Gabriel, C, 40 b.
Akroyali, D, 17 b.

Votsalakia, D, 29 b.

Salonica (a selection)

*Makedonia Palace, L, 530 b.
Capitol, A, 353 b.
Electra Palace, A, 230 b.
Nepheli, A, 130 b.
Panorama, A, 85 b.
Astor, B, 159 b.
Capsis, B, 823 b.
City, B, 178 b.
El Greco, B, 162 b.
Metropolitan, B, 224 b.
Olympia, B, 208 b.
Olympic, B, 104 b.
Queen Olga, B, 261 b.

Rotonda, B, 142 b.
Viktoria, B, 127 b.
A.B.C., C, 208 b.
Aegeon, C, 112 b.
Amalia, C, 124 b.
Delta, C, 217 b.
Esperia, C, 132 b.
Mandarino, C, 136 b.
Park, C, 105 b.
Pella, C, 118 b.
Rex, C, 111 b.
Telioni, C, 120 b.
Vergina, C, 256 b.

Sámos

In Avlakia:
Avlakia, C, 28 b.

In Heraion:
Venetia, B, 26 b.
Adamantia, C, 60 b.
Faros, D, 27 b.

In Kalami:
Anthemis, A, 48 b.
Fenix, B, 26 b.
Kirki Beach, B, 36 b.
Myrini, B, 42 b.
Andromeda, C, 65 b.

In Karlóvasi:
Aegeon, B, 109 b.
Merope, B, 152 b.
Astir, D, 53 b.
Morpheus, D, 49 b.

In Kokkári:
Galini, B, 14 b.
Olympia Beach, B, 20 b.
Kokkari Beach, C, 84 b.
Venus, C, 88 b.

In Marathokambos:
Kerkis Bay, B, 48 b.

In Pefkakia:
Samos Bay, B, 70 b.
Iliokymata, C, 60 b.

In Potokaki:
El Coral, B, 16 b.
Hydrele, B, 29 b.
Potokaki, B, 22 b.

In Pythagórion:
Doryssa Bay, A, 334 b.
Fyllis, B, 34 b.
Phito, B, 142 b.
Villa Marie, B, 23 b.
Captain's House, C, 25 b.
Damo, C, 20 b.
Glicoriza Beach, C, 116 b.
Hera, C, 22 b.
Ilios, C, 62 b.
Labito, C, 34 b.
Polyxeni, C, 44 b.
Pythagoras, C, 55 b.

In Sámos town:
Galaxy, C, 61 b.
Toula, C, 16 b.
Acropolis, D, 23 b.
Artemis, D, 24 b.
Hera, D, 44 b.
Niki Ellina, D, 23 b.

In Vathý:
Aeolis, B, 97 b.
Eleana, B, 34 b.
Odysseas, B, 28 b.

Xenia, B, 14 b.
Niki Beach, C, 72 b.

In Soufli:
Orpheus, C, 34 b.
Egnatia, D, 14 b.

In Akrotíri:
Akrotiri, C, 30 b.

In Emborió:
Archaea Elefsina, D, 28 b.
Marianna, D, 20 b.

In Exo Gonia:
Nano, A, 18 b.

In Firá:
Atlantis, A, 47 b.
Kallisti Thira, C, 64 b.
Kavalari, C, 39 b.
Panorama, C, 34 b.
Pelican, C, 34 b.
Santorini, D, 48 b.

Perseus, B, 20 b.
Maistrali, C, 40 b.

In Apollónia:
Apollonia, B, 18 b.
Flora, B, 24 b.
Sofia, C, 22 b.

In Artemón:
Artemon, C, 54 b.

*Skíathos Palace, L, 385 b.
Esperides, A, 300 b.
Nostos, A, 208 b.
Alkyon, B, 160 b.
Mandraki, B, 55 b.
Xenia, B, 64 b.

In Glóssa:
Avra, C, 51 b.

In Skópelos town:
Archontiko, A, 22 b.
Amalia, B, 88 b.
Mon Repos, B, 30 b.
Panormos Beach, B, 57 b.
Prince Stafylos, B, 96 b.

Xenia, B, 38 b.

Xenia, B, 56 b.
Samos, C, 160 b.
Sibylla, C, 38 b.
Surf Side, C, 56 b.

In Xanthi:
Motel Natassa, B, 127 b.
Nestos, B, 142 b.
Xenia, B, 48 b.
Democritus, C, 69 b.
Xanthippion, C, 95 b.
El Greco, D, 65 b.

In Ia:
Perivolas, B, 127 b.
Laouda, B, 20 b.
Fregata, D, 40 b.

In Kamári:
Belonia Villas, A, 16 b.
Sunshine, B, 68 b.
Kamari, C, 104 b.
Orion, C, 40 b.
Blue Sea, R, 52 b.
Golden Sun, D, 30 b.

In Thíra town:
Antonia, C, 20 b.
Theoxenia, C, 20 b.
Palladion, C, 22 b.

Serifos Beach, C, 63 b.

In Kamáres:
Kamari, B, 35 b.
Stavros, C, 34 b.

In Platys Yalos:
Platys Yalos, B, 38 b.

Belvedere, C, 120 b.
Kanapitsa Beach, C, 45 b.
Villa Kika, C, 39 b.
Costis, D, 31 b.
Lalaria, D, 66 b.
San Remo, D, 59 b.

In Skópelos town (cont.):
Rigas, B, 80 b.
Aeolos, C, 79 b.
Angelikis, C, 34 b.
Captain, C, 33 b.
Denise, C, 41 b.
Sporades, C, 40 b.
America, D, 30 b.
Eleni, D, 64 b.

Samos (cont.)

Samothrace

Santorini

Sérifos

Sífnos

Skíathos

Skópelos

Skýros

Practical Information

Spétsai

Akroyali, A, 30 b.
Kasteli, A, 146 b.
Possidon, A, 83 b.
Spetses, A, 143 b.
Roumanis, B, 65 b.

Faros, C, 84 b.
Ilios, C, 51 b.
Myrtoon, C, 74 b.
Star, C, 68 b.

Symi

Aliki, A, 28 b.

Dorian, A, 20 b.

Sýros

In Ermoúpolis:
Vourlis, A, 17 b.
Ypatia, A, 21 b.
Athina, B, 14 b.
Hermes, B, 47 b.
Cycladikon, C, 29 b.
Europe, C, 51 b.
Nissaki, C, 78 b.

In Finix:
Olympia, C, 78 b.
Finikas, C, 25 b.

In Galissas:
Françoise, C, 46 b.

In Posidonía:
Delagrazia, B, 22 b.
Eleana, C, 51 b.
Poseidonion, C, 109 b.

In Vari:
Akrotiri, C, 41 b.
Alexandria, C, 58 b.
Domenica, C, 37 b.
Kamelo, C, 45 b.
Romantica, 58 b.

Thásos

In Glyfada:
Glyfada, C, 100 b.

In Limenariá:
Menel, C, 34 b.
Sgouridis, C, 27 b.
Ralitsas, D, 24 b.
Thalassies, D, 35 b.

In Makryammos:
Makryammos, A, 402 b.

In Pefkari:
Thassos, C, 67 b.

In Potamiá:
Kamelia, B, 24 b.
Blue Sea, B, 23 b.
Helen, D, 24 b.

In Prínos:
Elektra, B, 35 b.
Europa, B, 24 b.
Megalo Pefko, D, 27 b.

In Rakhóni:
Argyro, D, 56 b.

In Thásos town:
Roula, A, 12 b.
Possidon, B, 30 b.
Timoleon, B, 54 b.
Xenia, B, 50 b.
Angelika, C, 50 b.
Laios, C, 49 b.
Lido, C, 33 b.
Villa Meressi, C, 40 b.
Viky, D, 34 b.

Tínos

In Kionia:
Tinos Beach, A, 339 b.

In Tínos town:
Aeolos Bay, B, 131 b.
Alonia, B, 64 b.
Favie Souzane, B, 63 b.
Theoxenia, B, 59 b.
Tinion, B, 47 b.
Asteria, C, 96 b.

In Tínos town (*cont.*):
Delfina, C, 73 b.
Flisvos, C, 66 b.
Leto, C, 36 b.
Meltemi, C, 77 b.
Oassis, C, 43 b.
Oceanis, C, 91 b.
Poseidonion, C, 73 b.,
Vyzantion, C, 54 b.

Zákynthos

In Alykaí:
Asteria, C, 37 b.
Astoria, C, 60 b.
Montreal, C, 56 b.

In Argasion:
Chryssi Akti, B, 146 b.
Levante, B, 120 b.
Mimoza Beach, B, 84 b.

In Argasion (*cont.*):
Agassi Beach, C, 64 b.
Captain's, C, 69 b.
Castello, C, 48 b.

In Bokhali:
Akrotiri, B, 31 b.
Varres, B, 67 b.

In Kalamaki:
Kalamaki Beach, B, 55 b.
Crystal Beach, C, 94 b.

In Laganas:
Esperia, B, 62 b.
Galaxy, B, 152 b.
Megas Alexandros, B, 79 b.
Zante Beach, B, 494 b.
Alkyonis, C, 37 b.
Ionis, C, 91 b.
Margarita, C, 46 b.
Sirene, C, 54 b.

In Planos:
Orea Heleni, C, 44 b.
Tsilivi, C, 105 b.

In Zákynthos town:
Kryoneri, B, 29 b.
Lina, B, 88 b.
Strada Marina, B, 201 b.
Xenia, B, 78 b.
Bitzaro, C, 70 b.
Diana, c, 91 b.
Gardelino, C, 40 b.
Libro d'Oro, C, 66 b.
Phoenix, C, 70 b.
Ionion, D, 45 b.

Information

Greek National Tourist Organisation
(Ellinikos Organismos Tourismou, EOT)

Odos Amerikis 2,
Athens;
tel. (01) 3 22 31 11

Head office

195–197 Regent Street,
London W1R 8DL;
tel. (01) 734 5997

In United Kingdom

Olympic Tower,
645 Fifth Avenue,
New York NY 10022;
tel. (212) 421 5777

In United States

627 West Sixth Street,
Los Angeles CA 90017;
tel. (213) 626 6696

National Bank of Greece Building,
168 North Michigan Avenue,
Chicago IL 60601;
tel. (312) 782 1084

1233 rue de la Montagne,
Montreal, Quebec H3G 1Z2;
tel. (514) 871 1532

In Canada

2 Bloor Street West,
Cumberland Terrace, Upper Level,
Toronto M4W 3E2;
tel. (416) 968 2220

Practical Information

Offices of Greek National Tourist Organisation in Greece

Athens	Odos Karageorgi Servias 2; tel. (01) 3 22 25 45
	Ellinikon Airport; tel. (01) 9 79 95 00
Piraeus	Marina Zeas; tel. (01) 4 13 57 16 and 4 13 57 30
Corfu	Governor's House, Corfu town; tel. (0661) 3 03 60
Crete	Odos Akti Tombazi 6, Chaniá; tel. (0821) 2 64 26
	Odos Xanthoudidou 1, Iráklion; tel. (081) 22 82 03 and 22 82 25
Kefallinía	Information Bureau, Argostóli; tel. (0671) 2 28 47
Kos	Information Bureau, Akti Koundourioti; tel. (0242) 2 87 24
Rhodes	Odos Arkhiepiskopou Makariou 5 and Odos Papagou, Rhodes town; tel. (0241) 2 36 55 and 2 32 55
Salonica	Platia Aristotelous 8; tel. (031) 27 18 88 and 22 29 35
Sýros	Platia Laikis Kyriarkhias; tel. (0281) 2 23 75

In places without a tourist information bureau information can be obtained from the Tourist Police (Astynomia allodapon).

Inter-island travel

Passenger traffic to the Greek islands is mainly by boat, though a number of islands now have air services. The boat services to and between the islands, and the means of transport on the islands themselves, vary very widely: for details, see the descriptions of the individual islands in the "A to Z" section of this guide.

Boat services

The boat services to the Aegean islands mostly leave from Athens (Piraeus), though there are also some services from Salonica. The connections between islands are less direct, and if you are visiting a number of islands it may be necessary to return to Piraeus between visits.

An indispensable means of transport in the islands: the caique

The Ionian Islands have connections with the mainland ports of Pátras and Igoumenitsa.

Tickets must usually be bought at the port office of the shipping line. In view of the frequent changes in timetables and the heavy demand, particularly during the main holiday season, it is advisable to inquire well in advance of the date on which you propose to travel.

A helpful publication which gives timetables of boat services is the "Key Travel Guide" to Greece and the Middle East, published monthly.

There are boat services between nine of the larger islands and 24 smaller ones, most of which are subsidised to encourage visitors to visit the less-well-known islands. For information apply to the Greek National Tourist Organisation (see Information).

Island-hopping

Olympic Airways fly from Athens to Corfu, Zákynthos, Chaniá and Iráklion (Crete), Chíos, Kos, Léros, Lemnos, Mýkonos, Mytilíni (Lésbos), Rhodes, Sámos, Skíathos and Thera (Santoríni), and from Salonica to Rhodes, Iráklion (Crete) and Lemnos. (See entry on Airlines for further information.)

Air services

Language

In most parts of Greece visitors are likely to come across local people with some knowledge of English or another European language, but it is always helpful, particularly in country areas, to have at least a smattering of modern Greek.

The modern language is considerably different from ancient Greek, though it is surprising to find how many words are still spelled the same way as in the time of Homer. Even in such cases, however, the pronunciation is likely to be very different. This difference in pronunciation is found in both the main forms of modern Greek, *dimotiki* (demotic or popular Greek) and *katharevousa* (the "purer" official or literary language), which diverge considerably from one another in both grammar and vocabulary.

All official announcements, signs, timetables, etc., and the political articles in newspapers are written in katharevousa, which approximates to classical Greek and may be deciphered, with some effort perhaps, by those who have learned Greek at school.

The ordinary spoken language, however, is demotic. This form, the result of a long process of organic development, has now also established itself in modern Greek literature, and it is used in the lighter sections of newspapers.

The Greek Alphabet

Letter		Anc. Gk	Mod. Gk	Pronunciation
A	α	alpha	álfa	*a*, semi-long, as in "apple"
B	β	beta	víta	*v*
Γ	γ	gamma	gháma	*gh*; y before e or i
Δ	δ	delta	dhélta	*dh* as in "the"
E	ε	epsilon	épsilon	*e*, open, semi-long, as in "egg"
Z	ζ	zeta	zíta	*z*
H	η	eta	íta	*ee*, semi-long, as in "cheese"
Θ	θ	theta	thíta	*th* as in "thin"
I	ι	iota	ióta	*i*, semi-long, as in "cheese"
K	κ	kappa	kápa	*k, ky*
Λ	λ	lambda	lámdha	*l*
M	μ	mu	mi	*m*
N	ν	nu	ni	*n*
Ξ	ξ	xi	ksi	*ks*
O	ο	omicron	ómikron	*o*, open, semi-long
Π	π	pi	pi	*p*
P	ρ	rho	ro	*r*, lightly rolled
Σ	σ	sigma	síghma	*s*
T	τ	tau	taf	*t*
Y	υ	ypsilon	ípsilon	*i*, as in "egg"
Φ	φ	phi	fi	*f*
X	χ	chi	khi	*ch* as in Scottish "loch"; before e or i, somewhere between *ch* and *sh*
Ψ	ψ	psi	psi	*ps*
Ω	ω	omega	omégha	*o*, open, semi-long

[1] written ς at the end of a word

There is no recognised standard system for the transliteration of the Greek into the Latin alphabet, and many variant spellings are found.

The position of the stress in a word is very variable, but is always shown by an accent – formerly either by an acute, grave or circumflex accent but now, following a recent simplification, always by an acute.

The "breathings" over a vowel or diphthong at the beginning of a word, whether "rough" (') or "smooth" (') are not pronounced. The diaeresis (¨) over a vowel indicates that it is to be pronounced separately and not as part of a diphthong. Punctuation marks are the same as in English, except that the semicolon(;) is used in place of the question-mark (?) and a point above the line (·) in place of the semicolon.

Numbers

0	midén	31	triánda énas, miá, éna		Cardinal numbers
1	énas, miá, énas	40	saránda		
2	dío, dió	50	penínda		
3	tris, tría	60	eksínda		
4	tésseris, téssera	70	evdomínda		
5	pénde	80	ogdónda, ogdoínda		
6	éksi	90	enenínda		
7	eftá	100	ekató(n)		
8	okhtó	101	ekatón énas, miá, éna		
9	enneá	153	ekatón penínda tris,		
10	déka		tría		
11	éndeka	200	diakósi, diakósies,		
12	đodeka		diakósia		
13	dekatrís, dekatría	300	triakósi, -ies, -ia		
14	dekatésseris, dekatéssera	400	tetrakósi, -ies, -ia		
15	dekapénde	500	pendakósi, -ies, -ia		
16	dekaéksi, dekáksi	600	eksakósi, -ies, -ia		
17	dekaeftá, dekaeptá	700	eftakósi, -ies, -ia		
18	dekaokhtó, dekaoktó	800	okhtakósi, -ies, -ia		
19	dekaennea, dekaennéa	900	enneakósi, -ies, -ia		
20	íkosi	1000	khíli, khílies, khília		
21	íkosi énas, miá, éna	5000	pénde khiliádes		
22	íkosi dío, dió	1 M	éna ekatommírio		
30	triánda				

1st	prótos, próti, próto(n)	10th	dékatos, dekáti	Ordinal numbers
2nd	défteros, -i, -o(n)	11th	endékatos, endeḱati	
3rd	tritos, -i, -o(n)	20th	ikostós, -i, -ó(n)	
4th	tétartos, tetárti, tétarto(n)	30th	triakostós, -i, -ó(n)	
5th	pémptos	100th	ekatostós, -i, -ó(n)	
6th	éktos	101st	ekatostós prótos	
7th	évdomos, evdómi	124th	ekatostós ikostós	
8th	ógdoos		tétartos	
9th	énnatos, ennáti	1000th	khiliostós	

half	misós, -i, -ó(n); ímisis	Fractions
one-third	tríton	
one-quarter	tétarton	
one-tenth	dékaton	

Everyday expressions

Good morning, good day!	Kaliméra!
Good evening!	Kalispéra!
Good night!	Kalí níkhta!
Goodbye!	Kalín andámosi(n)!

Practical Information

Do you speak . . .	Omilíte . . .
English?	angliká?
French?	galliká?
German?	yermaniká?
I do not understand	Den katalamváno
Excuse me	Me sinkhoríte
Yes	Né, málista (*turning head to side*)
No	Okhi (*jerking head up*)
Please	Parakaló
Thank you	Efkharistó
Yesterday	Khthes
Today	Símera, símeron
Tomorrow	Avrio(n)
Help!	Voíthia!
Open	Aniktó
Closed	Klistó
When?	Potè?
Single room	Domátio mè éna kreváti
Double room	Domátio mè dío krevátia
with bath	mè loutró
What does it cost?	Póso káni?
Wake me at 6	Ksipníste me stis éksi
Where is . . .	Pou inè . . .
the lavatory?	to apokhoritírion?
a chemist's?	éna farmakíon?
a doctor?	énas yatrós?
a dentist?	énas odontoyatrós?
. . . Street?	i odós (+ *name in genitive*)?
. . . Square?	i platía (+ *name in genitive*)?

Travelling		
	Aircraft	Aeropláno(n)
	Airfield	Aerodromíon
	Airport	Aerolimín
	All aboard!	Is tas théses sas!
	Arrival	Erkhomós
	Bank	Trápeza
	Boat	Várka, káiki
	Bus	Leoforíon, búsi
	Departure (by air)	Apoyíosis
	(by boat)	Apóplous
	(by train)	Anakhórisis
	Exchange (money)	Saráfiko
	Ferry	Férri-bóut, porthmíon
	Flight	Ptísis
	Hotel	Ksenodokhíon
	Information	Pliroforía
	Lavatory	Apokhoritírion
	Luggage	Aposkevá
	Luggage check-in	Apódiksis ton aposkevón
	Non-smoking (compartment)	Dya mi kapnistás
	Porter	Akhthofóros
	Railway	Sidiródromos
	Restaurant car	Vagón-restorán
	Ship	Karávi, plíon
	Sleeping-car	Vagón-li, klinámaksa
	Smoking (compartment)	Dya kapnistás
	Station (railway)	Stathmós

Stop (bus)	Stásis	
Ticket	Bilyétto	
Ticket-collector	Ispráktor	
Ticket-window	Thíris	
Timetable	Dromolóyion	
Toilet	Apokhoritírion	
Train	Tréno	
Waiting-room	Ethousa anamonís	
Address	Diéfthinsis	At the post office
Air mail	Aeroporikós	
Express	Epígousa	
Letter	Epistolí	
Letter-box	Grammatokivótio(n)	
Package	Dematáki	
Parcel	Déma, pakétto	
Postcard	Takhidromikí kárta	
Poste restante	Post restánt	
Post office	Takhidromíon	
Registered	Sistiméni	
Stamp	Grammatósimo(n)	
Telegram	Tilegráfima	
Telephone	Tiléfono(n)	
Telex	Tilétipo(n)	
Sunday	Kiriakí	Days of the week
Monday	Deftéra	
Tuesday	Tríti	
Wednesday	Tetárti	
Thursday	Pémpti	
Friday	Paraskeví	
Saturday	Sávato(n)	
Week	Evdomáda	
Day	(I)méra	
Weekday	Katheriminí	
Holiday	Skholí	
New Year's Day	Protokhroniá	Holidays
Easter	Páskha, Lambrá(i)	
Whitsun	Pendikostí	
Christmas	Khristoúyenna	
January	Yanouários, Yennáris	Months
February	Fevrouários, Fleváris	
March	Mártios, Mártis	
April	Aprílios	
May	Máyos, Máis	
June	Yoúnios	
July	Yoúlios	
August	Avgoustos	
September	Septémvrios	
October	Októvrios, Októvris	
November	Noémvrios, Noémvris	
December	Dekémvrios	
Month	Min, mínas	

Manners and customs

The people of Greece are courteous to strangers and ever ready
to help them, without being over-officious. Belonging as they

273

do to an old seafaring nation, they show a lively interest in world events and international politics, but visitors will do well to observe discretion in discussing political matters, and above all to avoid thoughtless criticism of conditions in Greece.

It is pleasant to find a general absence of begging and guides, porters, etc., who do not pester visitors to employ them.

As in many southern countries, importance is attached to correct dress, though with the development of tourism there has been some relaxation in this respect.

Under a law passed in 1983 nude bathing is permitted on certain beaches, but regard should always be had to the feelings of local people.

Maps and plans

1:1,000,000	Bartholomew's Map of Greece and the Aegean
	Hallwag's Road Map of Greece
1:800,000	RV's Map of Greece
1:750,000	Baedeker's Map of Greece
1:700,000	Michelin's Map of Greece
1:650,000	Freytag & Berndt's Road Map of Greece
1:500,000	Kümmerly & Frey's Road Map of Greece
Various scales	AA Leisure Maps of Athens/Peloponnese/Cyclades, Corfu and Ionian Islands, Crete, Rhodes and Dodecanese
	Hallwag's maps of Corfu, Crete and Rhodes
	Freytag & Berndt's maps of Corfu, Crete, Cyclades, Kos/Sámos/Ikaría and Rhodes
	Clyde Leisure Maps of Athens/Peloponnese/Cyclades, Corfu and Ionian Islands, Crete, Rhodes and Dodecanese
	Efstathiadis' road maps of Corfu, Rhodes, Sporades, etc.
	Toubi's maps of Corfu, Rhodes and many other islands
Athens	Hallwag's plan of Athens, 1:8500
	Falk's Citymap of Athens
Sailing guides	H. M. Denham, "The Aegean – a Sea Guide", John Murray, London, 5th ed., 1983
	H. M. Denham, "The Ionian Islands to the Anatolian Coast – a Sea Guide", John Murray, London, 1982.

Motoring

Roads	The Greek road system has been considerably improved in recent years, and there are now asphalted roads everywhere in mainland Greece – though in the remoter areas they will often be narrow and winding. On the small islands there are still many unsurfaced roads. When driving at night it is necessary to keep a good look-out for animals and vehicles without lights.
Driving in Greece	Road signs and traffic regulations conform with international standards. Traffic travels on the right, with overtaking on the left. The use of the horn is prohibited in built-up areas. It is an offence to drive after taking *any* alcohol. Seat-belts must be worn. All vehicles must carry a warning triangle. In brightly lit built-up areas only sidelights are normally used. Some drivers switch their lights off altogether when meeting another vehicle.

The speed limit for passenger vehicles is 100 km p.h. (62 m.p.h.) on motorways and expressways, 80 km p.h. (50 m.p.h.) on ordinary roads and 50 km p.h. (31 m.p.h.) in built-up areas. Drivers exceeding the speed limit may have their driving licence confiscated and the car's licence plates removed. (The licence plates may also be removed in the case of a parking offence.) The maximum permitted dimensions of a car and trailer caravan (or boat trailer) are: height 3·50 m (11 ft 6 in), width 2·50 m (8 ft 2 in), length 15 m (49 ft).
Policemen with a knowledge of foreign languages bear an arm-band labelled "Tourist Police".

Speed limits

If a foreign car has an accident in Greece and becomes a write-off the customs authorities must be informed before the car can be scrapped.

Customs regulations

Opening times

See Banks

Banks

See Chemists

Chemists

Open throughout the year except on 1 January, 25 March, Good Friday (forenoon), Easter Day and 25 December.
All museums are closed on Tuesdays, except the National Archaeological Museum and the Byzantine Museum in Athens and the Archaeological Museum in Iráklion (Crete), which are closed on Mondays.

Museums and archaeological sites

See Postal and telephone services

Post offices

For the most part mid May to mid October shops are open Mon., Wed. and Sat. 8.30 a.m.–2.30 p.m., Tue., Thu. and Fri. 8.30 a.m.–1.30 p.m. and 5–8 p.m.; during the winter months hours may vary, and individual shops may keep special hours of their own.

Shops

Photography and filming

Visitors who want to take photographs or use a ciné-camera on an archaeological site must buy an additional ticket. Special permission is required for the use of a tripod, and a charge is payable, at different rates for amateur and professional photographers and varying according to the type and size of photographs. Application for a permit must be made and the appropriate fee paid in advance. Information is obtainable from the Greek National Tourist Organisation.
The photographing and filming of military installations is prohibited.

Postal services

Post offices (takhydromia) are usually open from 7.30 a.m. to 7.30 p.m.
Letter-boxes are painted yellow.

Post offices

Public holidays and feast days

Statutory public holidays

The following days are statutory public holidays:
New Year's Day (1 January); Epiphany (6 January); Independence Day (25 March); Okhi Day (28 October: "No" Day,
commemorating the Greek rejection of the Italian ultimatum in
1940); Christmas (25 and 26 December).

Religious feast days

In addition to the statutory holidays there are several religious
festivals, the most important of which are Easter (usually on a
different date from Easter in the Roman Catholic and Protestant
Churches), with a service which lasts through the night into the
early hours of Easter Day; Whitsun; the Feast of the
Annunciation (25 March); and the Feast of the Dormition
(Assumption; 15 August).
Shops and offices are closed on these days.

Radio

The Greek radio transmits news bulletins in English, French and
German every morning at 7.30 (Greek time).

Restaurants

The menu in a Greek restaurant is frequently presented in
English and/or other languages as well as in Greek. In the more
modest establishments it is usually only in Greek (and probably
hand-written at that). Except in the higher class restaurants, it
is quite normal, to go into the kitchen and choose for yourself.
The breakfast (próyevna) served in hotels is usually of the
normal continental type. Lunch (yévna) is normally served
between noon and 2 p.m., dinner (dípno) between 8 and 10 p.m.

Sailing

Entry

The passengers and crew of a yacht sailing in Greek waters are
officially classed as visitors in transit. On entering Greek water
the yacht must put in at a port with customs facilities for entry
and exit (see map). The port authorities will then issue it with
a transit log entitling it to free passage in Greek waters. During
their stay in Greece the passengers and crew must spend the
nights on board; any who propose to spend one or more nights
ashore or to leave Greece by some other means of transport
must have official entry and exit stamps entered in their
passports.
The transit log is valid for a single visit of up to a year. It must
be renewed annually or on re-entering Greek waters.

Small pleasure-craft

Small boats brought in by road are subject to broadly the same
customs regulations as private cars. They must be entered on
the owner's passport and can then be used for a period of up to
four months, which can be extended for a further eight months
by the customs authorities on deposit of security.

Chartering boats

Charter boats sailing in Greek waters must be officially
authorised and must fly the Greek flag. A copy of the charter

Greek Ports

Ports with customs facilities for entry and exit

1 Corfu town	10 Nafplion	19 Mytilíni (Lésbos)
2 Preveza	11 Piraeus (Zéa)	20 Chios
3 Argostóli	12 Vouliagmeni	21 Pythagórian (Sámos)
(Kefallinía)	13 Lavrion	22 Ermoúpolis (Sýros)
4 Pátras	14 Volos	23 Kos
5 Itea	15 Salonica	24 Santoríni
6 Zákynthos	16 Kavala	25 Rhodes
7 Pýrgos	17 Alexandroúpolis	26 Chaniá (Crete)
8 Pýlos	18 Myrina	27 Iráklion (Crete)
9 Kalamata	(Lemnos)	28 Ayios Nikólaos (Crete)

Other ports

29 Palaiokastrítsa (Corfu)	44 Póros	59 Ayios Nikólaos (Kéa)
30 Syvota	45 Palaiá Epidavros	60 Tinos
31 Parga	46 Aiyina (Aegina)	61 Mýkonos
32 Paxí	47 Glyfada	62 Skála (Pátmos)
33 Lefkás	48 Porto Rafti	63 Lakkí (Léros)
34 Vathý (Ithaca)	49 Kárystos (Euboea)	64 Kálymnos
35 Nafpaktos	50 Khalkís (Euboea)	65 Náxos
36 Corinth	51 Kamena Vourla	66 Parikía (Páros)
37 Methóni	52 Skiathos	67 Kamáres (Sifnos)
38 Limeni	53 Skópelos	68 Adámas (Melos)
39 Gythion	54 Ayía Kyriaki	69 Íos
40 Kapsáli (Kýthira)	55 Néa Roda	70 Katápola (Amorgós)
41 Monemvasia	56 Thásos	71 Kárpathos
42 Spétsai	57 Linariá (Skýros)	72 Sitía (Crete)
43 Hýdra	58 Ándros	73 Réthymnon (Crete)

contract and a list of the passengers and crew must be lodged with the port authorities at the port of departure, and the person in charge of the boat must carry copies of these documents.

A boat may be chartered only if the charterer and another member of the party can produce a sailing certificate or letter of recommendation from a recognised sailing club or can demonstrate their competence.

Information

A very helpful brochure published by the Greek National Tourist Organisation, "Sailing the Greek Seas", gives detailed information about entry and exit regulations, ports and supply stations, weather and navigation, boatyards, etc.

Information about chartering firms, types of boat and tariffs can be obtained from the Association of Boat and Yacht Rental Agents, P.O. Box 341, Piraeus, or from the Greek National Tourist Organisation.

Sailing schools

There are sailing schools in Athens and Salonica, on Corfu and Syros, and some other places. Information may be obtained from the Greek National Tourist Organisation.

Shipping

See Travel
See Car ferries
See Inter-island travel

Shopping and souvenirs

Greece offers visitors a wide choice of attractive souvenirs; but articles of this kind are now produced on a mass scale, and it may be necessary to look round a little to find items of good quality and taste.

Pottery is offered for sale in all price ranges, from poor imitations of ancient vases by way of good copies to the beautiful products of the island of Páros. Líndos, on the island of Rhodes, is famous for its plates and Arkhángelos, also on Rhodes, for its vases. Among other distinctive local products is the ware made on the island of Sífnos.

Fine hand-woven fabrics are produced on Skýros, Kárpathos and Rhodes. Articles with classical motifs (meander decoration, the Parthenon) are produced exclusively for tourist consumption. Flokati carpets, knotted woollen carpets which look rather like long-fleeced sheepskins, are another popular buy; they are made in natural wool or in a rich variety of colours. Also popular with visitors are Greek traditional costumes, embroidery, lace, leather goods (particularly handbags) and olive-wood carvings.

Those who have sufficient room in their luggage may be attracted by the elaborately carved child-sized furniture made on the island of Skyros.

Finally many visitors may be tempted by the rich assortment of sweets and other delicacies on offer – aromatic honey, fig-cake soaked in ouzo, chocolate, nougat, etc. – and the variety of nuts (walnuts, almonds, pistachios).

A very interesting exhibition of Greek handicrafts can be seen in the showrooms of the National Organisation of Greek Handicrafts in Athens (Odos Mitropoleos 9). The articles displayed are not for sale, but prospective purchasers can be put in direct touch with the craftsmen concerned. There is a similar exhibition on Corfu.

Also worth visiting is the Hellenic Artisan Trades Cooperative in Athens (Leoforos Amalias 56).

See Antiques and antiquities

Antiques, antiquities

Sports

There are public beaches and swimming-pools all over Greece, with a wide range of facilities (sports equipment, boat hire, children's playgrounds, restaurants, entertainments, etc.).

Water-sports

See entry

Bathing beaches

See entry

Sailing

Underwater diving with scuba equipment is permitted only in certain areas and subject to strict regulations; diving is permitted only between sunrise and sunset; divers who come upon submerged antiquities must not move them or photograph them, but must inform the nearest port authority, police station or inspectorate of antiquities; underwater fishing with breathing apparatus is prohibited; spear-guns may not be used by persons under 18 and they must not be used in harbours or off bathing beaches.

Diving

It is advisable in any event to inquire of the local port authority about regulations in the area.

There are decompression chambers at Athens (Greek Diving Club, Athens-Ellinikon), Salamís (Naval Hospital), Chaniá on Crete (naval base in Soúda Bay), Salonica (Milioglu School) and Palaiokastrítsa on Corfu (Barakouda School).

There are tennis courts at many hotels and bathing stations, and tennis clubs at Chaniá and Iráklion (Crete) and on Corfu and Rhodes.

Tennis

There are golf-courses at Athens and on Corfu and Rhodes.

Golf

Telephone services

Most of the Greek islands have direct dialling.

Telephone

From the United Kingdom to Greece: 010 30
From the United States or Canada to Greece: 011 30
From Greece to the United Kingdom: 00 44
From Greece to the United States or Canada: 00 1
The zero at the beginning of a local dialling code should be omitted.

International dialling codes

Tennis

See Sports

Time

Greece observes Eastern European Time, which is 2 hours ahead of Greenwich Mean Time. During the summer (April–September) Greek Summer Time, 3 hours ahead of GMT, is in force.

Tipping

Hotel tariffs normally include a service charge; if they do not, 15 per cent is appropriate (as it is in restaurants). In restaurants it is customary to round up the payment to the waiter and in addition to leave a small amount for his assistant.

Travel documents

Personal papers

Visitors from the United Kingdom, Commonwealth countries and the United States require only a valid passport for a stay up to three months. If they wish to stay longer than three months they must apply for an extension, at least 20 days before the end of the period, to the local police authorities.

Car papers

British driving licenses and registration documents and those of other EEC countries are accepted in Greece. Nationals of most other countries must have an international driving license. An international insurance certificate ("green card") valid for Greece is required. Although third party insurance has been compulsory in Greece since 1978, it is advisable to take out temporary insurance giving comprehensive coverage.
On entry into Greece details of the car, which must bear the usual oval nationality plate, will be entered on the owner's passport.

Health insurance

British visitors who need medical or dental care can obtain it under the Greek social insurance scheme on presentation of form E111 (obtained from the local Social Security Office before leaving Britain), but private treatment is likely to be quicker, and it is, therefore, advisable to take out a temporary insurance giving cover for health care.

Pleasure-craft

See Sailing

Travel to the Greek Islands

There are a variety of ways to reach Greece – by road or rail through Yugoslavia, by a direct flight to Athens, Salonica, Corfu, Iráklion (Crete) or Rhodes (or during the holiday season to certain other islands), or by road or rail to one of the Italian Adriatic ports and from there by ferry to Igoumenitsa, Pátras or Athens (Piraeus). For connections between the Greek mainland and the islands, and between different islands, see Inter-island travel.

By car

Taking your car on a visit to the Greek islands is advisable only if the size, road network and accessibility of the island in question justify the strenuous and time-consuming drive through Yugoslavia.

The shortest route from northern Europe is on the motorway (autoput) through Yugoslavia, from the Loibl Pass (frontier crossing Austria – Yugoslavia) via Belgrade, Skopje, Gevgelija/Evzoni (frontier crossing Yugoslavia – Greece) and Salonica to Athens (about 2500 km (1500 miles), tolls on some sections of Greek motorway).

The Yugoslav motorway is well built but is not a motorway in the full sense. There is no central divider between the roadways and there are numerous crossings. The traffic is heavy particularly during the holiday season, when many migrant workers as well as tourists are likely to be on the road and there is an increased danger of accidents. It is necessary, to drive with extreme care and to avoid driving at night.

Scenically more attractive, but still more time-consuming, is the Adriatic coastal road (Jadranska Magistrala), which turns inland at the south end, near the Albanian frontier, to join the motorway at Skopje.

An alternative possibility is to drive down through Italy and take one of the car ferries from Italian Adriatic ports (see Car ferries).

It is possible to travel to Greece by train, either on the Athens Express, which runs via Paris to Athens, or by connecting with the Hellas Express (Cologne to Athens) or the Acropolis Express (Munich to Athens); but the journey is long and tiring (it takes 3 days from London to Athens). This is not really to be recommended as a means of getting to Greece. By rail

This is the quickest and easiest way to get to Greece, though not the cheapest. There are direct flights from London to Athens (daily), Salonica and Corfu. There are also direct flights daily from New York to Athens. In addition there are numerous charter flights during the holiday season to Athens and many of the islands, usually carrying passengers who have booked one of the many package tours offered by travel-operators. By air

Water-sports

See Sports

Weather

See Facts and Figures, Climate
See When to go

When to go

In the Greek islands the year is divided into three main seasons rather than the usual four – the season of growing and flowering from March to June, the arid season from June to October and the rainy season from October to March.

The best times to visit the islands, for those who do not go solely for swimming and sunbathing, are from the second half of March to the end of May and during the months of

September and October, and sometimes also the beginning of November. The summer months, from mid June to the beginning of September, are usually very hot, and at this time of year insects, particularly mosquitoes, can be troublesome; suitable creams and repellants should therefore be taken.

In view of the meltemi, the sharp north wind which may blow up at any time during the year, and the roughness of some island roads and tracks, it is advisable to have some form of protective clothing and stout footwear.

From mid November to the end of March rain is frequent and fog not uncommon.

Wine

See Food and drink

Yachting

See Sailing

Youth hostels

There are youth hostels on Corfu, Crete (Ayios Nikólaos, Chaniá, Iráklion, Mália, Myrthios, Plakias, Réthymnon and Sitía) and Santorin.

Most hostels are open throughout the year. Advance booking is advisable and, during the main holiday season, essential. From 1 March to 30 September bookings must be accompanied by advance payment.

The stay at any one hostel is limited to 3 nights. Youth hostellers must produce a membership card issued by their national youth hostels association.

Information

Organosis Xenonon Neotitos Ellados, (Greek Youth Hostel Association)
Odos Dragatsaniou 4,
Athens 122;
tel. (01) 32 34/107 and 32 37/590

INDEX

The name Khóra ("'Village"'), by which the chief place on an island is frequently known, is not included in this index.

Index

Index

Index

The Principal Sights at a Glance (Continued from inside front cover)